EXTRA INNINGS

EXTRA INNINGS

FRANK ROBINSON
and Berry Stainback

McGRAW-HILL BOOK COMPANY

New York   St. Louis   San Francisco   Auckland
Bogotá   Hamburg   London   Madrid   Mexico   Milan
Montreal   New Delhi   Panama   Paris   São Paulo
Singapore   Sydney   Tokyo   Toronto

1 2 3 4 5 6 7 8 9 DOC DOC 8 9 2 1 0 9 8

ISBN 0-07-053183-8

LIBRARY OF CONGRESS CATALOGING- IN-PUBLICATION DATA

Robinson, Frank, 1935–
    Extra innings / Frank Robinson and Berry Stainback.
        p. cm.
    ISBN 0-07-053183-8
    1. Baseball—United States—History.   2. Afro-American baseball
players.   3. Discrimination in sports—United States.
I. Stainback, Berry. II. Title.
GV863.A1R582 1988
796.357'08996073—dc19   88-3032
                                                         CIP

Book design by Kathryn Parise

These words are dedicated to my loving wife, Barbara, my daughter, Nichelle, my son, Frank Kevin, and to the memory of my mother, Ruth Shaw, whose journey through life was far too short to share all of the accomplishments I enjoyed.

F. R.

This book is dedicated to Rita Hourigan Stainback and to the memory of Jackie Robinson.

B. S.

⑨ CONTENTS

⑨ *PREFACE*

EARLY in my career with the Cincinnati Reds, general manager Gabe Paul told me he had paid my dues that made me a member of the NAACP. "That's fine, Gabe," I said. "I like what the organization stands for and I'll acknowledge that I'm a member, but I'm not gonna be active in the NAACP. I just feel baseball and politics don't mix."

Later Jackie Robinson wrote me a letter saying that black players should speak out on civil rights issues. Jackie said it was particularly important that established players like myself speak out, but I didn't feel I could do so at that time. The truth was that I was afraid to sound off about the injustices to minorities that I saw every day in baseball. The minor protests that I had made in behalf of teammates in Cincinnati had led Bill DeWitt to label me a troublemaker. Blacks who spoke out were always called troublemakers; white players who sounded off were said to be "just letting off steam." I already had a desire to become a major league manager eventually, and what owner would hire a troublemaker as manager if he also happened to be black?

The only regret I have in my heart today is that I didn't speak out a whole lot more about baseball's injustices to blacks. If I and others had been hollering in the 1970s that blacks were being systematically excluded from positions of authority in the game, probably we would not have to holler so often now. The shame on baseball is that anyone has to holler in the first place—that is what this book is all about and why it was written.

The authors wish to thank Glenn Deutsch, Owen Kean, and Brian Silverman for their help in researching this book, along with Richard Lapchick, Director of the Study of Sport in Society at Northeastern University. And special thanks to Steve Bloom, who headed our research effort.

1

THE TRUTH IS OUT

*O*N April 6, 1987, Los Angeles Dodger general manager Al Campanis went on national television and revealed baseball's dirty big secret. Asked why there were no black managers or general managers in the major leagues, Campanis told *Nightline* host Ted Koppel it was because blacks "lack the necessities." In other words, blacks were not smart enough to manage in the big leagues, even though there had been a host of white managers over the years who were never confused with college professors, let alone brain surgeons.

What blacks themselves had known for decades had at last been acknowledged by a top baseball official, and Campanis's view of black capabilities was not isolated. It was so widespread that in the 40 years since Jackie Robinson integrated baseball, a grand total of three blacks had been permitted to manage in the major leagues. I managed the Cleveland Indians from 1975 through 57 games of the '77 season, and I managed the San Francisco Giants from 1981 through 106 games of the '84 season. Larry Doby managed the Chicago White Sox for all of 87 games in 1978, and Maury Wills managed the Seattle Mariners for 82 games in 1980 and 1981. In less than a season, no manager has much of a chance to succeed.

But the point is that in the past 40 years there have been hundreds of managerial changes in major league baseball, yet only three black men were judged worthy of hiring in that time. No big league club has hired a black general manager (GM), ever. And, through 1987, only one American-born black has been allowed to coach third base in the majors.

Bobby Tolan had the job with the Padres in 1980 but was removed the following year. Two Hispanics, who are regarded as black in this country though not in their native land, Ozzie Virgil with Seattle and Jose Martinez with Kansas City, coached third in 1987. They are the only other blacks I know of who have coached third in the majors.

That is because, until the introduction of the bench coach several years ago (and not all teams have one), the third base coach took over the team any time the manager was absent. The third base coach is traditionally next in line to become a manager if he wishes. That is where owners usually look first when they want to replace a fired manager: at third. So there haven't been more black third base coaches for the simple reason that they would have been in line to become managers. Obviously the powers that be did not want to have to deal with *that* situation.

The normal line of progression in baseball goes from bullpen coach to first base coach to third base coach (sometimes to bench coach), but blacks are almost never allowed in that line. They are not moved from the coaching box at first to third. For example, Manny Mota, a Hispanic black, has been first base coach for the Dodgers for more than ten years. The Dodgers have been imbued with a nonbigoted aura ever since they became the first major league team to sign a black player, Jackie Robinson, in 1947. But they have changed their third base coach many times in the years Manny Mota has coached at first, yet never was he offered a promotion that would put him in a position to possibly become a manager. Black coaches simply do not get the same opportunities to advance that white coaches are given.

I played for the Baltimore Orioles for six years and coached for them six more years, through the '87 season. They are my favorite organization in all of baseball, and the Orioles take pride in the fact that they promote from within. Earl Weaver, Cal Ripken, and Jimmy Williams all managed in the Orioles' minor league system for years before being moved up to coach with the big club. Ripken was the bullpen coach for a season plus, then served as the third base coach for almost ten years. When Weaver retired after the '86 season, Ripken was named manager and Williams moved from the first base coaching box to third.

Meanwhile, Elrod Hendricks, a Hispanic black, has been the Orioles' bullpen coach for 11 years without once being offered a promotion. In 1982, Hendricks told general manager Hank Peters that he wanted to come out of the pen and either work on the lines or become the pitching coach. He later repeated his desire to Peters and also told Weaver and

Ripken. The Orioles have changed pitching coaches three times in the past four years, but Ellie Hendricks wasn't even interviewed for the job.

"They keep telling me I'm more valuable to the ballclub in the bullpen," Hendricks says with a shrug. He lives with his family in Baltimore and hasn't thought about seeking a coaching job elsewhere, perhaps because there aren't that many openings for blacks. Out of 180 coaching jobs in the majors in 1987, only 21 were filled by blacks.

The ironic thing is that a number of Oriole pitchers *rely* on the advice of Elrod Hendricks because he has been around so long and knows them so well. The veterans Scott McGregor, Mike Boddiker, and Mike Flanagan, before he was traded, regularly went to Hendricks. But my team's long-standing tradition of promoting men who have served the organization with distinction did not apply to Elrod Hendricks, whose skin happens to be black.

The Orioles are not a racist organization, or I would not be working as a special assistant to team president Edward Bennett Williams in December 1987. I'm sure the Hendricks situation has been discussed in front office meetings, with someone saying, "What will Ellie think when he's passed over?" Then someone else undoubtedly would say something like: "I think he understands the ballclub needs him in the pen. He's happy enough. And if he's unhappy, what's he gonna do, quit? Where would he go?"

The answer to that is nowhere, because Hendricks wants to stay in Baltimore. So he remains stuck behind a screen in the outfield year after year.

John Roseboro was the best defensive catcher in baseball during most of his 13-year career in the majors. After he retired in 1970, he couldn't get a coaching job for two years. Then the California Angels hired him as bullpen coach in 1972, promoted him to first base coach the following season, and then pushed him back into the pen in 1974 for no known reason. Through the following four years Roseboro was the hitting instructor for his old ballclub, the Dodgers, who then fired him. For the next eight years, Roseboro kept trying to get back into baseball without success, saying, "I didn't go to college, but I have a Ph.D. in baseball and I can't use it."

After Al Campanis made his moronic television blunder, Roseboro said, "When I heard him, I felt this might be the biggest breakthrough for blacks in sports since Jackie Robinson broke into the majors. Campanis opened a door that will change the face of baseball again."

Roseboro did benefit. After knocking on doors that would not open for years, he finally got back into baseball as the Dodgers' minor league catching instructor. At season's end, Dodger president Peter O'Malley interviewed Roseboro for the job of farm director, but hired instead Charlie Blaney. His claim to fame was that he had been running Dodgertown, the club's spring training facility. Blaney was busy with baseball in the spring, but the rest of the year Dodgertown was a resort. How this experience made him a better candidate than Roseboro to head up the Dodgers' minor league organization is beyond me. Roseboro has since recovered from heart surgery and will remain with the Dodgers, so at least he has a job in baseball.

The vast majority of blacks who seek work in the game are not as fortunate. Jose Tartabull, a major league outfielder for nine years, managed in the Houston Astros' minor league system from 1982 through 1984. Since being fired, Tartabull has phoned or written to every ballclub in the majors seeking employment in their organizations. "Only two teams have written back, Kansas City and Seattle," Tartabull says. "But it's always the same. 'We're sorry.'"

Tartabull, a Hispanic black, got his one chance to manage. White managers in the major leagues and the minors bounce from team to team, but black managers must be successful almost instantly to get other opportunities to lead a ballclub.

George Scott has never even gotten one shot at managing in organized baseball in this country. After playing 14 years in the majors, Scott retired in 1979 and began applying, year after year, for a job as manager or roving instructor in the minor leagues. Nothing. So Scott left the country to get some experience managing, working six years in the Mexican League, where he said his teams won two pennants and finished second twice. Scott also managed winter league teams in Puerto Rico and Venezuela, but he still couldn't get a baseball job in this country. In the spring of 1987 Scott offered to work in the minor league system of the Red Sox, for whom he played over eight seasons, for as little as $12,000. Sorry, George.

"You don't have to be a genius to figure it out," Scott told writer Kevin Paul Dupont of the Boston *Globe*. "It's all alibis, what they [major league baseball organizations] give you. The bottom line is black and white and racism. Look at the managers. You telling me we don't have a black today who's qualified to manage in the major leagues? If that's true, then this country is in a world of trouble."

The only managing job Scott could land in 1987 was in the ultimate bush league, something called the Empire State League (ESL) on Long Island. Stocked by players who weren't drafted or who were cut in other leagues, the ESL teams played 50 games over a grueling seven-week schedule. The league's budget was so tight that players were paid only $700 for the season and the teams ended up with only four bats each.

"It's the only offer I've had," George Scott said at the start of the season. "They're paying me $350 a week. That's how much I want to manage. It's a chance for me to show that I'm a good baseball man."

The co-owners of the league, Jay Acton and Eric Margenau, appeared to be the ones who profited most from the ESL. They invested $150,000 to start the league and then sold one of the teams to a group of investors for $200,000 at season's end.

"Baseball has been a white game for a long time," Jay Acton said after he hired four blacks to manage his teams. "We didn't pick these people just because they were black. We picked them because of their baseball skills. They were the four best managers we could put out there."

Four who would work for $350 a week. It's hard to tell whether the blacks were given an opportunity to manage or an opportunity to be exploited.

But at least they got the chance to manage in this country. Joe Foy, who had played with four teams for over six years in his major league career, retired in 1971 and put together a résumé which he sent to numerous ballclubs in an attempt to land a managing job in the minors. "I would have gone anyplace to start," Foy says, "the A level or even rookie league. But it's like an unwritten law that blacks don't get hired, has been for a long time. I asked about jobs quite a bit when I first got out. It was always the same, 'Maybe next year.'"

And it's not just managing jobs that blacks are denied. John Wyatt pitched for five years in his nine-year major league career (Kansas City, Boston, Yankees, Detroit, Oakland), so he thought he had a lot of good contacts when he retired in 1969 and went looking for a scouting job. He wrote letters to ballclubs that never replied.

"I always thought that I would never stay in the big leagues if I was only as good as the white boys," Wyatt told the *Globe*. "You always had to be better. There's never been no such thing as black being equal. With these jobs now, the same white guys get in and just keep getting a chance over and over, instead of giving a black guy a chance. Heck, it can't just be the blacks. There must be some dumb white boys too."

Luis Tiant pitched for six ballclubs in his 19 years in the majors, and he figures he would make an excellent pitching coach. He worked for the Yankees for several years as a coach and scout, but since then, nothing. "I call teams, I talk to them," Tiant told the *Globe*. "They tell you, 'Well, there's no job for you now. We'll call you when we have an opening.' Then two weeks after, they sign a guy, make him another one of their coaches. It's a bunch of crap."

One of the biggest cop-outs ballclubs use when they refuse to hire a black as a major league manager is, "You don't have the experience." I don't know how many times I heard that refrain personally, even from a man I regarded as a friend. Gabe Paul, who had been my first general manager when I played for the Cincinnati Reds, was the Yankee GM when I met him in Puerto Rico one winter. I was managing the Santurce team, a job I'd held for a number of years at the time. Gabe said to me, "Frank, if you had just one year's minor league managing experience, I'd hire you to manage the Yankees."

"What about this, Gabe?" I said. "I've been down here a bunch of years getting experience."

"Oh, this doesn't count," Gabe said.

The Yankees later hired Dick Howser and Lou Piniella to run the big club even though they had no managing experience. They are both white, of course. But whites are not required to go to the minor leagues as managers before they are hired by major league clubs. Yogi Berra, Ted Williams, and Lou Boudreau didn't manage in the minors, and neither did Jerry Coleman, Pete Rose, or George Bamberger. Joe Torre, Jim Fregosi, and Harvey Kuene didn't manage in the minors before being judged capable of managing in the majors, and neither did Ray Miller, Roger Craig, or Bobby Valentine. The list goes on and on.

I have heard a number of baseball executives say that they feel Bob Gibson would make a heck of a major league manager if he would just get some experience in the minors. Gibson was a highly regarded pitching coach in the majors for five years and has been a broadcaster of St. Louis Cardinals' games in recent years. Before the '87 season the Cardinals had no manager at their Louisville farm club, and Gibson asked his former teammate, Dal Maxvill, the St. Louis GM, for the AAA ballclub's job. Sorry, Gibson was told. But why, with his credentials, should Bob Gibson have to manage in the minor leagues in the first place? Because he's black?

Bobby Tolan, who played the outfield for 14 years in the majors and one in Japan, has wanted to manage ever since he retired in 1979. Tolan finished up in San Diego, and the Padres hired their radio announcer,

Jerry Coleman, as manager in 1980. (Did he have any managing experience? No. Does this suggest there's hope for announcer Bob Gibson? No.) Coleman wanted to hire Tolan as a coach, but because of a misunderstanding with general manager Jack McKeon, Bobby didn't join the team until June.

"I joined the team in Houston, and Jerry told me to sit with him and watch for a few games because he was gonna have me coach third base," Tolan says. "I did, and then I coached third from June on. It was really fun, getting the signs from the manager and then being in total control, using my own judgment. Since I had ideas of wanting to manage someday, it was great coaching third. For a manager to put that kind of trust in you makes you feel good."

The Padres finished last, Coleman returned to the radio booth, and Frank Howard was brought in as manager in 1981. "Jack McKeon took me off third and made me the first base coach," Tolan says. "I was also the hitting coach, and McKeon said I'd be closer to the hitters, even though first was no closer than third to home plate. But for the next two years McKeon moved me into the dugout near new manager Dick Williams. It seemed like he was phasing me out, from third base to first base into the dugout."

After the '83 season McKeon fired Tolan but said, "We know you want to manage, and you can take the job with our Beaumont, Texas, AA team." Tolan took it because he had no other choice. "I didn't want to give up my major league job and be put down in the minors where you can't be seen," he says. "But as it turned out, I enjoyed managing, which came pretty easy to me. We finished first in '84 and second in '85 with a combined winning percentage close to .600."

That winter, with the Padres' AAA farm team job open, Tolan thought when he was summoned to the office of farm director Tom Romanesco that he would be offered the manager's position. Instead he was fired. "Romanesco didn't say why I was let go, just that the organization wanted to make some changes," Tolan says. "And they gave the AAA job that I thought should've been mine to Larry Bowa—who had no managing experience. It seems like every time I get a shot at something, I get knocked down. Then in 1987 they gave Larry Bowa the Padres' managing job. Whenever I see things like this happen, I ask myself, 'Why him and not me?' Are whites smarter? No. More experienced? No."

Bobby Tolan went back to the minors in 1986, as a roving hitting instructor for the Seattle Mariners; then Dick Williams brought him back as the Mariners hitting coach in 1987. "We set 13 offensive club records, and Dick was very pleased with my work," Tolan says. "But one day he called me in and said, 'They're trying to replace you, but I'm gonna fight it.' Dick went over some people's heads, but they let me go anyway.

"I asked GM Dick Balderson why, and he said it was a lack of communication between me and the players," Tolan says, "which I don't buy. One player was a bad apple, though I won't mention his name. But every time I offered him help with his hitting, he turned me down. Then he turned a couple of other players against me. He even told one player, 'It's either me or Bobby Tolan,' so I feel it was this guy who got me fired."

Donn Clendenon has been looking for a job in baseball ever since he retired as a player in 1972. Unable to find employment, Clendenon went back to college and earned a law degree in 1978 and has since worked for several corporations, in personnel and labor relations areas. He has also sent out scores of résumés to baseball teams applying for jobs. The answers are always the same: "There is nothing at this time."

Despite all the talk you hear from team owners and general managers that minorities need experience to manage in the major leagues, the fact is that very, very few members of minorities are even allowed to get experience managing in the minors. Many organizations simply have refused to hire minorities to manage in their farm systems. The Detroit Tigers, for example, had never hired a black to manage in their minor league organizations through the '87 season.

Going into that season there were 16 professional minor leagues in the United States, made up of 154 teams. Only 9 of those 154 teams were managed by blacks or Hispanics, none in AAA or AA ball. In fact, only three of the minority managers were handling full-season class A clubs. The other six minority managers ran teams in rookie leagues that are classified as A, though they play only partial seasons, from June to September. It was all too apparent that minority managers were not being given positions that would springboard them to the major leagues.

The situation is absolutely disgraceful. Twenty-five percent of the players in the majors are black or Hispanic, but only 5 percent of the managers in the game are black or Hispanic—all of them in the low minors. There are 9 blacks or Hispanics and 171 whites managing the 180 ballclubs, including those in the majors, that comprise professional baseball in this country. Yet many of baseball's powers that be insist there is no bigotry in the game known as "our national pastime."

But even in the hiring of players blacks face discrimination. In almost every case when a roster decision has to be made between two players of equal talent, one white, the other black, the white player will be kept and the black sent packing. The good-field, no-hit player is almost always white.

Richard Lapchick, the author of *Broken Promises: Racism in American Sport,* says, "If you are a black baseball player, in order to be valuable you must be better by far than whites." As director of the Center for the Study of Sport in Society at Northeastern University, Lapchick examined the performances of all the major league players in 1985. He found that 32 percent of the black players had batting averages of .280 or better, compared to 15 percent of the white players. Also, 40 percent of the black pitchers, but only 11 percent of the whites, had earned-run averages under .300. The percentages refer only to American-born blacks; if Hispanic blacks were included, the white percentages would decrease.

But fewer black players are signed by major league organizations every year because scouts are not looking at high school baseball the way they used to. In recent years the emphasis has been on scouting college players, and relatively few blacks play college baseball. Football and basketball are the sports of choice among blacks who attend college, much as they always have been.

In June 1987 baseball commissioner Peter Ueberroth announced that he would see that the ballclubs no longer overlooked blacks and other minorities in hiring employees. He put in an affirmative-action plan, hired outside consultants to check on it, and said, "Baseball's effort is in place. Each team has appointed an executive who is responsible for making sure that fair and equal opportunity exists."

It was about time. Benjamin Hooks, the executive director of the NAACP, had already gone public with the fact that there were 879 administrative positions in baseball, but only 17 of them were held by blacks and 13 by Hispanics and Asians. Of the 26 major league baseball teams, 15 had no minorities in management positions.

I was not at all surprised to read those facts in the newspapers. For years players and former players have been asking me how they should go about trying to get a job in baseball. I've told them to contact all the people they know who are in positions of authority and anyone else they can think of on a ballclub that might have an opening. Normally, the more people who know you are looking for work, the better your chances of being hired. Unless you happen to be black.

Veteran pitcher Ray Burris is black. After he was released by the St.

Louis Cardinals at the end of the '86 season, he contacted each of the other 25 major league clubs hoping to continue pitching. Although he was turned down as a player, Burris got lucky. Milwaukee general manager Harry Dalton gave him a job that had been offered to me in 1984, assisting Dalton and also doing some scouting and coaching in the minors.

But during spring training of 1987 and throughout the season, I began talking on the phone with Burris, with Braves' coach Willie Stargell, and with an old friend, Ben Moore, about putting together a list of blacks we knew who were out of baseball and wanted to find employment in the game they had devoted so much of their lives to. Then, as the season was about to open, Dodger general manager Al Campanis went on *Nightline* and told the nation exactly why so few blacks were employed in baseball after their playing careers were over.

People all across the country seemed to be shocked by Campanis's sentiments, and he was quickly fired. But I don't think he should be blamed for repeating an idea that he had heard expressed in closed meetings for many years. In fact, seven and one-half years before Campanis blurted out what *Nightline* host Ted Koppel called "garbage" on national television, Campanis had voiced the same kind of theories in the Philadelphia *Daily News*. Stan Hochman interviewed him as part of a series on the scarcity of black managers in baseball. In April 1987, Hochman wrote: "Campanis babbled then about blacks lacking buoyancy as a reason why you see so few black swimmers. It was suggested then that the lack of country clubs that accept blacks might have more to do with it than the lack of buoyancy. Campanis brushed that idea aside."

There was a twofold irony in the fact that Campanis lost his job. First, he was only on the program as a substitute for Don Newcombe, a black man. Second, Campanis was there to honor the memory of Jackie Robinson on the fortieth anniversary of his having integrated baseball.

As if to excuse Campanis for his views, some people pointed out that he had helped a lot of black players get to the major leagues. But why did the Dodgers sign black players in the first place? Because they could help the ballclub win pennants and make more money for the owners. The Dodgers weren't doing something for blacks, who quickly showed they had the talent to play the game. But after their careers were over, the blacks were judged to no longer have any ability.

What, for example, has the Dodger organization done for its black players after they retired? Lou Johnson, Roy Campanella, Don Newcombe, and Tommy Davis work in the community relations department.

John Roseboro and Von Joshua are minor league instructors. But where were the black administrators, the people in real decision-making positions for the Dodgers?

In November of 1987, Dodger president Peter O'Malley finally hired a high-ranking black, Tommy Hawkins, as vice president of communications, a new position that will place him in charge of three departments: publicity, community services, and ticket marketing and promotions. But Hawkins, a radio and television broadcaster, is a former basketball player. Why couldn't O'Malley find a former Dodger player who was qualified for the communications job?

The answer is that he apparently didn't try. Earl Robinson is an ex-Dodger player who would have loved to be offered that job, and he is well qualified to handle it. A former All-American shortstop at the University of Southern California and one of the game's first black bonus babies in the 1950s, Earl Robinson played four years in the majors and then returned to college and earned a Ph.D. He is a former administrative assistant to Oakland A's owner Roy Eisenhardt and director of special projects. Earl Robinson is now the chairman of the speech and communications department at Laney College in Oakland, where he also runs the campus television station. But O'Malley chose an ex-basketball player rather than a man with baseball background.

The people hired by Peter Ueberroth to oversee his affirmative-action plan, Harry Edwards and Clifford Alexander, had no baseball background either. Many blacks and others were not satisfied with these appointments, because Edwards and Alexander were not fully aware of the problems of minorities in baseball. Edwards, a sociology professor, initially seemed to offer some promise as he had a reputation for getting things done, and at least he was a black voice who, it appeared, would be speaking regularly to the commissioner. But then Ueberroth took the teeth out of the appointment by announcing, "Harry Edwards is just a part-time consultant to me. He is a full-time teacher."

Ueberroth said the consulting firm headed by Clifford Alexander would meet with every major league ballclub and help the owners set "appropriate goals of hiring women and minorities." Alexander is a former secretary of the Army, and his partner, Janet Hill, is the wife of former football player Calvin Hill.

Those of us who were looking for change in baseball's hiring practices were not optimistic after Edwards told the press: "If minorities don't have a lot of new jobs at the end of the season, I won't be discouraged. I expect to be able to look back after three to five years and see the extent of the initial commitment. I intend to be in this for the duration, no matter how long that is. What's three to five years to me?"

Edwards's lack of urgency is not shared by the qualified blacks who have been denied the opportunity to work in baseball. When a strong-voiced black man like Harry Edwards is given the baseball commissioner's ear, that man should help make things happen for minorities as soon as possible, not produce a five-year plan. Edwards was given a budget of $250,000 and an annual salary of $250,000, so he can afford to take his time. In addition, Edwards is paid $80,000 a year by the University of California at Berkeley, and he says he makes up to 100 speeches, at $5000 per appearance, each year. I know black ex-players who are willing to work in baseball for the equivalent of three of Edwards's speech fees, yet they can't find a job.

With all the talk that baseball should hire a black manager, it seems that team owners were reluctant to fire their present managers no matter how badly their ballclubs were playing in 1987. For the first time since 1976, by June 15, 1987, no manager had been fired, even though Larry Bowa's Padres were 30 games under .500.

But on June 18, the Phillies fired John Felske, and the next day club president Bill Giles hired third base coach Lee Elia and said, "I chose the man I felt was best for the job," which is what owners always say about the managers they hire. Are they going to say, "I hired an incompetent"?

Many people recalled that when Lee Elia managed the Cubs, one reason he had been fired was for calling Cubs' fans "degenerates" and inviting them to kiss his backside on Michigan Avenue in Chicago. Tommy Harper, who had been fired as a coach by the Red Sox in 1985 after charging the club with allowing racist practices near their spring training base, said, "If you were a black and said those things Elia did, do you think you'd ever get another job in baseball? They would do something to you on Michigan Avenue, but it would not be a kiss."

The Reverend Jesse Jackson criticized Bill Giles, saying, "My real concern is not that they hired Lee Elia, but that no blacks or Hispanics were considered for the job. You tell a tree by what it bears. Peter Ueberroth has said there would be a new attitude. What has happened in Philadelphia reaffirms Al Campanis's point of view."

Speculation had it that Bill Robinson was the number one black candidate for the Phillies' managing job. He had played for the club, had been a minor league hitting instructor for the organization, and had been the first base coach and hitting instructor for the Mets in recent years.

"I'm sure the color issue would bring my name to the forefront," Robinson told the press before Elia was hired. "I'd like the Phillies front office to look upon me as a man and go from there. But for the first time, it doesn't hurt being black."

Maybe not, but Bill Robinson didn't get the job.

One man I had been talking to about baseball's prejudicial hiring practices since 1981 is Ben Moore. A former Phillies' scout and assistant baseball coach at the University of San Francisco, Moore had been in television until he joined the Giants' community relations department in 1982 and also did some scouting. In 1983 Moore had been my eye-in-the-sky coach with the Giants. Ben would call me two or three times a week, and after I began talking to Willie Stargell and Ray Burris in 1987, I put Ben in touch with them. Ben has conference calling service on his phone, so we often had conference calls.

Ben Moore also knew Harry Edwards, and the day of his appointment by the commissioner, Ben called him at his home. He reached Edwards's answering machine and left a message: "Harry, these are the names of some people I know you're gonna want to talk to. Frank Robinson, Willie Stargell, and Joe Morgan." Ben left both our business and private numbers.

Ten days later, none of us had heard from Harry Edwards. So Ben Moore called him again and left the same message.

Two weeks later, on July 4, I still hadn't received a call from Harry Edwards when I was asked to tape a *Face the Nation* from Minnesota, where the Orioles were playing. Edwards would be taped on the same program from Washington, along with Yankee owner George Steinbrenner and Georgetown basketball coach John Thompson. Neither before nor after the program did Harry Edwards ask to speak to me.

I found his attitude very strange. If the roles of Harry Edwards and me were reversed and I were looking into a problem that he had experienced for 35 years, as I have, I would have sought his counsel. He had to know that I was the only black man to manage two major league teams and that I had insights he couldn't have. I began to wonder just how serious Edwards was about his consultantship to the commissioner.

Face the Nation moderator Lesley Stahl asked Edwards if he was convinced that in two years there would be black managers and blacks in the front office.

"I'm not saying that blacks are gonna take off like a pack of starving dogs after a meat wagon with the door swinging open, at every opening in professional baseball," said Edwards, using a line he had been issuing the media for weeks. "But we're gonna see discernible progress in front offices from the high-profile positions right on down to accounting and marketing and so forth. In fact, I guarantee it."

"Discernible progress" in baseball's minority hirings was what many of us were waiting to see. By this date, the vast majority of team hirings of minorities had been as superficial as the actions taken by the Cubs. They hired six black employees, two of them secretaries and two members of the ground crew. The two middle-management job titles were director of personnel administration and director of financial accounting. Any black who is hired by baseball is a welcome change. But my concern is that ballclubs are going to be saying down the road, "We've got 35 percent of our work force in minorities now," yet we'll still have few blacks in decision-making roles. Owners always seem to have excuses as to why blacks aren't in those roles.

On *Face the Nation*, Lesley Stahl said to George Steinbrenner, "You don't see blacks moving up the ladder from the field into the front office the way whites do."

"Some of these young men are earning such tremendous salaries," Steinbrenner said, "it's hard to convince them to come into the front office to take a position that may start at $50,000."

I responded by saying that the few blacks who had turned down jobs were superstars—the only people who are offered work after they retire because they are thought to have impact on fans and the media. "But there are players who have played in the major leagues and in the minor leagues who are just *dying* for jobs," I said. "They've sent in applications and résumés, and these are thrown aside because the players don't have 'the name' that attracts attention."

Lesley Stahl said, "Do you feel now, George, that the situation's got to change?"

"I feel very strongly that we've got to bring minorities into baseball," Steinbrenner said. "To be honest with you, Frank, if you can give me the names of three young men who you feel fit that nonstar category that would like to get active in the front office and work their way up, I guarantee you I'll be in touch with them Monday or Tuesday, because I would love to give 'em an opportunity."

I laughed right on television, to think that George Steinbrenner could not come up with some nonsuperstar black ex-players from his own team who would like to get back into baseball. I mentioned Don Buford and Ray Burris, and then I was so stunned by Steinbrenner's stratagem that I stopped talking.

But later on the program I asked Steinbrenner the key questions that the owners of every baseball franchise should be required to answer: "In your opinion, George, why do you think there have not been more blacks or other minorities as managers over the course of baseball? Why aren't there more black third base coaches? Why aren't blacks considered—I mean really considered—for jobs of decision making in the front offices right at this moment? Why?"

"I'm as intent, I think, as Dr. Edwards is in getting the answers to this problem—if it's a problem," Steinbrenner said.

"What do you mean," Lesley Stahl asked, "'if it's a problem,' Mr. Steinbrenner?"

"It's a problem, George, and it has been there for years," I said.

"I think in a lot of ways baseball is not unlike society as a whole," Steinbrenner said. "I think it's something we have to deal with. And I think we have to make sure everybody has an equal opportunity in this country."

Then George Steinbrenner presumably went off to keep his promise to offer Don Buford and Ray Burris an opportunity by Tuesday, July 7. But five months later, neither Buford nor Burris had heard from Steinbrenner or the Yankees.

At one point on *Face the Nation*, Lesley Stahl asked Steinbrenner if he was ready to pledge to hire minorities for his team as soon as possible. In his rambling answer, Steinbrenner said that he had made no effort "to exclude anybody," that he had a black captain, Willie Randolph, and that the "chief accountant in my finance department happens to be a young black boy." Stories in the next day's papers reported that Steinbrenner had referred to a young black man as a "boy."

But the press did not report Steinbrenner's implication that there were no qualified blacks in the game who could be hired for front office positions. "There are blacks in baseball right now who have been wanting jobs, soliciting jobs in the front office, but they've been shut out," I said. Any black man would be offended by being called "boy," but even more offensive is being consistently rejected by employers who say you are not qualified for work when your background declares you are.

◦   ◦   ◦

At the 1987 All-Star Game in Oakland, Peter Ueberroth and Harry Edwards held a surprise meeting with the black players, coaches, and former players who were there. I was not invited, nor was Willie Stargell or Hank Aaron, who is the Atlanta Braves' farm director and the highest-ranking black in baseball. That was insulting, but worse was the fact that Edwards and Ueberroth offered no information on affirmative-action progress at the meeting.

When he heard about the meeting, Ben Moore called Edwards and left a message, "Harry, please give me a call." Several days later, Edwards phoned Ben, who said, "Hey, man, how can you have a meeting of black baseball people and not have Frank Robinson, Willie Stargell, and Hank Aaron there?"

"I want to talk to those guys, Ben, because they've got to head up this effort eventually," Edwards said. "Tell me where I can reach them, and I will get to them no later than Wednesday."

Harry Edwards's word proved to have all the reliability of George Steinbrenner's. Edwards didn't call any of us.

Ben Moore set up a conference call with him, me, Stargell, and Ray Burris. Willie came on the line and said, "Enough of this crap, we've got to have our own meeting." We all agreed to begin putting together our own organization that would provide information and services for blacks. So we all began calling people and collecting names, addresses, and phone numbers that Ben Moore printed out on his computer. At the end of the season we had a mailing list of 200 people.

We called our organization the Baseball Network, and providing information to guys who were looking for jobs in the game became one of our major tasks. We felt Peter Ueberroth could be helpful there, but he was never available when we called him. We also had problems getting people in the commissioner's office to return our calls. When we did get through and asked an assistant to provide us with a team-by-team breakdown of the minority hirings in baseball since the '87 season began, we were told a few days would be needed to assemble this information.

But when we called back, we were told no information was available. The commissioner was probably embarrassed that baseball had done so little in the hiring of minorities since the Campanis hullabaloo. A total of five managers were replaced, none by a black. Eight new general managers or team presidents were hired, and none of them were black. So much for affirmative-action at the top.

The Cubs had an opportunity to hire their first black manager by promoting their first base and batting coach, Billy Williams. He reportedly did a good job managing one of the Cubs' teams in the instructional league, but not good enough to earn him a shot at managing the big club in 1988. The Cubs gave the job to Don Zimmer, who had previously managed in San Diego, Boston, and Texas without distinction. He did have experience, which Williams lacked. That is what owners and general managers always say when they reject a black manager candidate.

But if experience is really all that important, why hasn't Gene Mauch won a single pennant in the 26 years he has managed in the major leagues? There are four managers in the majors today who had no managing experience when they were originally hired to run ballclubs—Jim Fregosi, Whitey Herzog, Pete Rose, and Bobby Valentine. Of course, they are all white, as is Lou Piniella, who was fired in 1987. And if experienced personnel were a requirement of the Cubs, why did they hire as their new general manager Jim Frey when he had no front office experience?

George Steinbrenner brought Billy Martin back to manage the Yankees for a fifth time in 1988 and elevated Lou Piniella to the general manager's position, though he had no experience in the front office. Putting Piniella over Martin seemed to be a strange move even for Steinbrenner. Piniella had told a number of people during the '87 season, "Billy Martin backstabbed me with George." In addition, Steinbrenner has called Piniella "the worst judge of talent in the organization," and that is not a prime qualification for a GM.

If Lou Piniella were a black manager, you have to wonder if Steinbrenner would have kicked him upstairs. But then again, if Piniella were black, you have to doubt that he would have been hired as the Yankees' manager in the first place.

The Baseball Network scheduled a meeting in early November, and Harry Edwards heard about it and called Ben Moore. "I know about the meeting, Ben, and I insist on being there," Edwards said. Ben then set up a conference call and Edwards finally spoke to me, Willie Stargell, and Ray Burris. We agreed to meet with him in Irving, Texas, the day after the Baseball Network's three-day meeting there.

We invited 200 people to join us in Texas, and 50 showed up. Some people simply couldn't afford to make the trip, and others who were employed in the game stayed home because, as one man put it, "I'm afraid I'll get fired if I come."

At the meeting Ben Moore, who had been working on the project for months without pay, was named executive director. Stargell, Burris, Curt

Flood, Jim Grant, and I were named board members. Then everyone had a turn at the microphone and shared his experiences with bigotry in baseball, as we pledged that what was said would stay in the hotel conference room. We identified the good people in the game and those who could not be trusted.

One of the longest discussions focused on the stress individuals go through when they are forced to leave baseball. A number of players brought their wives, and it appears there is a very high divorce rate among ballplayers near the end of their careers or shortly thereafter. A lot of men, losing their big salaries and their identities as ballplayers, have trouble dealing with the stressful transition. I may have been the only man there who had been married to the same woman for over 25 years.

Then we got down to the business of making information available to those who need it. We set up a number of groups, each headed by a chairman, to provide financial services, marketing services, and drug-awareness information. Our primary goal is to try to get people back into baseball. As jobs open up, we plan to present a list of qualified candidates to organizations that are hiring, and we hope that some of our people will be hired. We don't want people at any level who are unqualified to be hired just because they are minorities. The Orioles hired a young black man in the marketing department last summer and had to fire him in a matter of weeks. That wasn't good for the man, for the ballclub, or for minorities in general.

We also want to educate people about pay scales in the major leagues and in the minor leagues. Some guys have overpriced themselves when a job opened up. If a job pays only $30,000 and the guy expects to make $50,000, he's got to settle for the starting salary—just as he did when he came into baseball—and earn increases as he goes along. If you want to work in any business, that's the way it is.

We expect to give former players another viewpoint on jobs in baseball. If the Baseball Network had been in place earlier, we may have convinced Hal McRae to take the interim job that was offered him as manager of the Royals in September 1987, or convinced Billy Williams to accept the job as manager of the Cubs' AAA farm team in Des Moines, Iowa.

Both men turned down these job offers, and every man—black or white—certainly has the right to say no. But there is an issue here that's larger than the individual, I feel. We need minorities to accept jobs when they are offered, because that opens the door a little farther to others.

Hal McRae does not see it that way. "You can't take a job based on the scarcity of black managers," McRae says. "If I'm gonna do something for my race, the best thing I can do is be successful. And I don't think I was offered a fair opportunity in Kansas City—being interim manager for 36 days. They weren't going to give me enough time to prove if I could manage or not. As a rule, interim managers don't get the job the following year. I didn't want to put myself in that situation. If I'm gonna manage, I want a full season to put my ideas in place. In 36 days you don't get experience—that's a tryout."

I understand that Hal McRae had to stick by his basic principles and that he also really wanted to go home to Bradenton, Florida, to be with his family after 20 years in the major leagues. To be with his family, Hal also turned down the Royals' offer to become a hitting coach in either the majors or the minors. At age 42 he hadn't been around to see his son Brian, 20, grow up to play shortstop in the Royals' system, and now he wanted to spend time with his two other children. He finally took a job as a minor league hitting instructor with the Pirates, based in Bradenton. If he decides to manage in the future, he should be a good one.

Billy Williams wants to manage right now, and he got upset when he wasn't offered the Cubs' job. I can understand his frustration. Williams has been a major league hitting instructor and first base coach for years. He is a member of the Baseball Hall of Fame, and he has a lot to offer the game. I feel some of us in the Baseball Network could have been successful in encouraging Billy to take the job in Des Moines. "If you want to manage in the major leagues, Billy, Triple A is an excellent place to start," I would have told him.

In November 1987 the Baseball Network board members met with Harry Edwards, Clifford Alexander, and his partner, Janet Hill, as well as with two representatives from the commissioner's office, Ed Durso and Roland Hemmond. We asked pointed questions about what the affirmative-action plan was accomplishing, but we agreed not to disclose everything that was said at the meeting. One fact that needs to be stated is that Harry Edwards and Clifford Alexander do not communicate or in any way coordinate their activities. Edwards is supposed to be involved in working to get minorities jobs on the field, and Alexander is supposed to be working to improve minority hirings in the front office. Yet they don't even talk to one another.

Clifford Alexander said he didn't care if the minorities that were hired by front offices were people without baseball backgrounds. He also said he counted women as minority hirings whether the women were members of a minority or not. I told him I would never put down women, but to equate the difficulties they have getting jobs or promotions with the problems that blacks and other minorities have is ludicrous.

I also said to Alexander, "There have been quite a few minority hirings since the Campanis statement. Do you know what organizations have hired minorities and what positions these people hold?"

"No, I don't know," Alexander said, "and I don't care. When teams hire employees, we don't question them as to who the people are and what positions they are filling. That's not what we're here for."

"Well, since this is a minority issue you're working on," I said, "wouldn't it be more meaningful if you said to an organization, 'I see where you just hired a new employee. What is his or her job title and what are his or her duties?"

"No, as I said, that's not what we're here for," he said.

None of us in the Baseball Network were pleased that Harry Edwards had hired Al Campanis as an assistant. If Edwards needed someone to assist him in his assigned mission to get blacks coaching and managing jobs, it would have been much more appropriate for him to hire a black rather than a white baseball person. Edwards told us that Campanis had gotten Tommy Harper a job with the Montreal Expos as a minor league base-running instructor. It is commendable that Harper is back in baseball. He had been blackballed from the game for two years. Harper had been fired as a Red Sox coach after he criticized the ballclub for allowing the Elks Club in Winter Haven, Florida, where the team trains each spring, to invite as guests only nonminority Red Sox personnel. Harper sued the Red Sox, who made a settlement with him rather than go to court, but then no team would hire him. Now he has to coach in the minor leagues in order to work in the game he loves.

At least Harper is back in baseball, which is where he wants to be. But Harry Edwards didn't give us any details about what Campanis did, so we don't know what caused the Expos to hire Harper. But I personally don't see what Campanis could have done to influence the Montreal organization in Harper's behalf.

I had to laugh when I returned home from this meeting and read a story on Harry Edwards that was sent to me from the November 8, 1987, Baltimore *Sun*. Mark Hyman interviewed Edwards and wrote, "Edwards said he speaks 'every single week' to a group of ex-players that includes Frank Robinson, Joe Morgan, and Willie Stargell. He also said he reports in writing to Stargell each month." That is simply untrue.

The Baseball Network can only hope that the day comes when Harry
Edwards begins putting as much force into his actions on behalf of minorities as he puts into his rhetoric on the subject.

The Baseball Network board finally got to meet with commissioner Peter
Ueberroth in December. He said that baseball had increased its hiring of
minorities by 400 percent between 1986 and 1987. I told him that numbers can be deceiving, that there were still all too few blacks in decision-
making positions. Willie Stargell had been promoted from first base coach
to third base coach of the Atlanta Braves, and the Padres had made the
same move with Sandy Alomar, a Hispanic black. And I had been promoted to a decision-making front office job.

Overall, we were disappointed that more progress hadn't been made
in this area. But the commissioner convinced us that he and his consultants were going to work to get more minorities into decision-making positions. I left this meeting somewhat more hopeful.

Probably the most significant thing to come out of the meeting was
the commissioner's guarantee that the Baseball Network would now have
an ongoing line of communication with his office, with the offices of the
American and National League presidents, with Harry Edwards, and with
Clifford Alexander's firm. We would no longer be kept in the dark as to
what was being done—or what was not being done—in the effort to find
jobs for more minorities in baseball. I think the commissioner realizes
that the Baseball Network is a positive body of people that are here to
help solve a serious problem.

And the problem remains. That was all too apparent when the commissioner opened the winter convention in Dallas. There were 78 men in
the room from baseball's 26 teams. Only one of those 78 men was black:
Frank Robinson.

Many people I talk to are not sure of Peter Ueberroth's total commitment to changing baseball's hiring practices. Many agree with Don
Baylor's impression of the commissioner. "I don't know how serious he is
about correcting the situation," Baylor has said. "He put himself on the
line and said he was going to change the game for minorities, especially
in the front office. But there has been no real change."

When Bowie Kuhn was baseball commissioner, he had a black special
assistant, Monte Irvin. On retiring in 1984, Irvin presented the new commissioner, Peter Ueberroth, with a list of candidates, both black and

white, to replace him. Yet the commissioner, who says he wants to see more blacks hired in front office positions, has refused to hire a black for a job in his own office. That does not set a good example for teams like the California Angels and the Minnesota Twins, who report they had no significant hirings or promotions among minorities in 1987.

You can be sure the Baseball Network will keep an eye on such situations. We will be working toward the day when no one will have to put the word "black" before the name of a new coach or manager or general manager in baseball. On that day, the old-boy network that has held back minorities for so long will be finished, and the Baseball Network will be history. That'll be the day.

2

⑤ *"HAVE A GOOD YEAR/AND GET OUT OF HERE"*

I didn't know anything about racism or bigotry until I went into professional baseball in 1953. People are often shocked hearing me say that, and I can understand. Racial bigotry was far more blatant and pervasive in this country during those years of my youth than it is today. But it is no less dehumanizing.

I was born in Beaumont, Texas, August 31, 1935, moved to Alameda, California, a few years later, and finally settled in West Oakland, where I grew up and learned to play baseball. I was the youngest of my mom's ten children, but my brother Johnny was the only other child still at home when I was growing up. Our neighborhood was a mixture of Negroes, Mexicans, and Orientals, all living in attached two-story frame tenements, all getting along, few getting ahead. We were poor but I didn't know it. I thought I had just about everything I needed or wanted. I always got attention and love from my mom and my brother, so I felt very fortunate.

And race never came up in our household. Nothing was ever said about the color of people's skin, about anyone being different, or anything like that. I knew my skin was different from that of others in the neighborhood or at school. But I never had any feelings or thoughts about that. We were all just people.

I had friends who were white, friends who were Mexican, friends who were Oriental, and friends who were black. My first fight was with a black kid. A few days later we were friends. At times, having to pass through another kid's turf to get to school, I had to fight a black guy or a white guy. I remember fighting one white kid to get to school, fighting him again to get home for lunch, then fighting him once more to get back to school after lunch. None of the fights were ongoing wars, just flash battles. There were a number of black kids in my neighborhood who might suddenly take a dislike to me on a given day and pop me. We'd exchange bunches of punches, and be right back playing ball together the following day.

Through all the fights, all the competition on ball fields, I never once heard any racial name-calling. A guy might be a bleephead, but he wasn't a black or white bleephead.

I held my own in the fights, and I more than held my own on the baseball field. From the age of 6 or so on, baseball was the most important thing in my life. Every free moment I had, from dawn until darkness, I played baseball. I'd come home so late my mother would complain, "Frank, you've got to get home at dinnertime so you can eat right."

"Just leave whatever you've had on the stove, Mom," I'd say. "I'll take care of myself when I get in. As long as there's light, I'm gonna play ball."

I was always playing ball with older boys, because from the beginning I could hit the ball a long way. When I was 11, Jackie Robinson became the first black to play major league baseball, and some of my older teammates got all excited about the news. I didn't know what it was all about. I really wasn't aware that baseball had not been integrated. I had always played baseball with and against white players.

When I was told what Jackie Robinson's signing with the Brooklyn Dodgers meant, I said to myself, "Well, I guess this gives me the opportunity if I'm good enough to play in the major leagues."

In the early fall of 1949, having just turned 14 and begun the ninth grade at Westlake Junior High, I met George Powles, a man who was to have an immeasurable influence on my life. Powles was the baseball and basketball coach at McClymonds High School. On the side he also coached four or five other ballclubs every weekend, teams ranging from 8- to 10-year-olds up to his American Legion team. Powles asked me to join his Doll Drug Company team of mostly 15- and 16-year-olds.

In my first game I didn't get in until the fifth inning when I was sent up to pinch-hit. I drove the first pitch over the centerfielder's head and circled the bases with a home run. I stayed in the game, and the next time up I lined a shot off the left-field fence for a triple. "Frank," Powles told me after the game, "you made the team."

That spring of 1950 George Powles stunned me by inviting me to join his Bill Erwin Post 237 ballclub, which had won the American Legion national championship the year before. Fourteen of that team's 25 players on the two-year roster ended up playing professional baseball. The star of the team was catcher, J. W. Porter, who signed a $65,000 bonus contract with the Chicago White Sox. To this day I don't understand why J. W. didn't become an outstanding major league player. Porter had the size, the arm, the catching ability, and he was a power hitter with a picture-perfect swing.

I was just another player on that Legion team, which again made it to the championship series in Omaha, Nebraska. We won it, and in one game just after my fifteenth birthday I remember hitting a triple off the 350-foot mark in right center.

That fall I entered McClymond's High School, and my guidance counselor asked me one day what I planned to do with my life, what kind of career interested me. "I'm gonna be a major league baseball player," I told her. "I'm gonna sign a $75,000 bonus contract and play in the major leagues."

George Powles instilled a lot of confidence in me. He was such a thorough and patient teacher that I still draw on the baseball fundamentals he taught to this day. Powles spent hour after hour with us. He was a good person for kids to be around, especially ones like me who didn't have a father. After practice or games we'd go over to his house, sit around, and just talk baseball.

The McClymond's student body was mostly black, and therefore the team was mostly black. On the other hand, I was one of only two blacks on the Legion team. Powles seemed to think at first that that was why I was so painfully shy. But it wasn't my skin color that made me uncomfortable with people, it was my inherent unease with people until I got to know them a bit. Again, I was never in a situation in the Oakland area where I felt being black made me feel different.

That feeling came dramatically after I signed with the Cincinnati Reds in 1953 and went off to play with their Class C club in Ogden, Utah. I received a $3500 bonus and a monthly salary of $400—well over twice what the average Class C player earned. Ogden was in a Mormon state, and though I didn't know it, at that time the Mormon religion insisted that Negroes were inferior beings. I got my first taste of racial bigotry in Ogden.

My white teammates all lived in private homes. I and the only other black on the club, Chico Terry, had to share a hotel room. Chico, who spoke Spanish but had no one who could understand him in Ogden, had one word of English: "Coffee." We couldn't even go to the movies because we were black. So we two outcasts spent most of our time lying around our hotel room. There was nothing to do except wait to play ball and then return to the room. Here I was, a 17-year-old kid who had never been away from home for an extended time, depressed and lonesome.

The only thing I could do was phone my mother regularly, which helped. But I didn't burden her with my problems. I never had done that and never would. As a kid I learned to keep problems to myself and work them out myself. I had heard about other guys from the neighborhood who had left home and then called home to express their lonesomeness. I didn't want my mother to be worried about me. Basically I kept telling myself, "This is the situation, and you just have to make the best of it if you want to play major league baseball."

Playing ball every day kept me going, and I let everything out on the field. Even then I felt the most important offensive statistic in baseball is RBIs. And I drove in 83 runs in 72 games for Ogden, while batting .348.

The Reds promoted me to their Class AA club in Tulsa the next spring and tried to turn me into a second baseman. Nice try. After eight games of ineptitude around the base, I was demoted to the Class A Columbia ballclub and returned to the outfield.

I wasn't too happy about going to a team in South Carolina which had never had a black player before. Columbia now had two, and we stayed together in a big white private house that was immaculate. We ate at a good restaurant right around the corner. Of course, everything in Columbia was "Negro Only." One of the three movies admitted Negroes to the balcony, and being a movie nut, I appreciated the opportunity to frequent the place every time the show changed. But overall, living in Columbia was much better than life in Ogden.

Going on the road was another matter in 1954. Georgia was the worst state to play in, and we traveled to Augusta, Macon, and Savannah. In those cities we were bombarded by "nigger" this and "nigger" that. The favorite cry was, "Nigger, go back to Africa!"

I tried to put aside all the abuse from the stands. I had always been pretty determined, and I wasn't going to let anything stop me from doing my best on the ball field. The little refrain that kept running through my head was, "Have a good year/and get out of here, Have a good year/and get out of here."

The only problem I had on the field occurred in a home game when I slid into the Savannah second baseman and broke up a double play. The second baseman thought I had gone out of the baseline to upend him and hollered, "You dirty nigger!" I got up and punched him, he swung back, and the fight was over, as others intervened.

Some of the road trips did make me very bitter, not because of the name-calling but because of the travel conditions. For example, the bus ride to Macon took all night. When the bus stopped at a restaurant, the white guys went in, stretched their legs, ordered and ate a meal, then hit the rest room. We blacks had to stay on the bus, unable even to use the john. We had to wait until teammates brought us a sandwich, hold the Coke, please.

When we reached our destination, the white players would go to an air-conditioned hotel. When lucky, my black teammate and I would go to a private home. When unlucky, we had to go to the local YMCA. We had to wait for Negro cabs to take us to the ballpark, and we had to find Negro restaurants to get anything to eat. On some of those road trips, I'd get so frustrated and angry inside that I felt like I might explode. But I never showed it, even to my black teammate. I just kept biting on the bullet and playing hardball as hard as I could.

Twice I knocked myself silly crashing into fences going for fly balls, but both times I stayed in the game. Another time I had to be hospitalized overnight after being knocked out by a fastball that cracked me over the left eye. I was back in the batter's box two days later. I had to show everyone how much I wanted to play this game.

After a season in which I batted .336 and drove in 110 runs, I was invited to train with the Reds the following spring. But I was not to make the majors in 1955. I damaged my right shoulder that March, ended up back at Columbia, and was in and out of hospitals for over three months with an injury that no one could seem to diagnose accurately. When I played, it was at first base because I couldn't throw a ball 10 feet, and my shoulder was so weak I couldn't swing the bat worth a nickel.

Even the home fans had begun to get on me. I didn't like it, but I could take it, even the racial slurs—until they got personal. One night, though, when my batting average had shrunk to about .190, three local fans kept getting drunker and more abusive as the game wore on and I continued to flounder. The temporary stands in Columbia were only about 25 feet from first base, and the drunks were getting real personal by the sixth inning, yelling things like, "You nigger bleep, you cain't hit a lick, you cain't throw, you cain't do sheeeit!"

By the ninth inning I was seething. I singled with two outs in this game we were losing big, and I couldn't wait for the last out. The moment it came, I ran to the dugout, grabbed a bat, and raced toward the three drunks. Just as I got inside the fence at the temporary stands, my roommate Marv Williams wrapped his arms around me from behind and pinned me there. "It isn't worth it," he said. I struggled briefly, until I cooled down enough to realize he was right.

Ernie White, our manager, came running over yelling, "What's wrong here?"

In my first season playing for Ernie, I initially thought he was a racist, because in meetings when we'd be going over opponents, he would say things like, "Now how we gonna pitch this big nigger tonight?" I soon came to realize that Ernie White didn't mean anything by his phraseology. He'd talked that way all his life, and he just simply still talked that way.

Now I told Ernie why I was so furious, exactly what the drunks had called me. "Goddamn it!" Ernie cried. "Show me who they are, and I'll go get them for you!" He was furious now.

After being given a description of the guys, Ernie ran into the parking lot. As the trio pulled away, Ernie noted their license plate number. He wrote the car's owner a letter that said in part: "If you ever doubt the courage of Frank Robinson, I will arrange a meeting between you and him." Those three men were never seen at the ballpark in Columbia again that season.

My painful shoulder and poor play, combined with the abuse I was hearing, pitched me into a deep depression. I'd sit in my room staring at the walls, saying nothing to the only other black on the club, Marv Williams, and everything looked hopeless.

After several nights of this depression, as the team was about to leave for Charlotte, North Carolina, 90 miles away, I said to Marv, "There's no point in my going with this shoulder. I'm going home."

"If you're not going to Charlotte, I'm not going," Marv said. It was tough enough being a black player on a southern team; being the *only* black was too much for my roommate.

I went to the general manager, Bill McCarthy, and said, "I'm through. I can't play with my shoulder like this. I'm going home."

McCarthy tried to talk me into staying, but I said no. When the team bus pulled out, Marv and I stayed behind. That night the game was rained out in Charlotte, which meant I hadn't officially jumped the club. I sat and thought about what I had done. I was giving up any chance of ever becoming a major league ballplayer. I was throwing away my whole life by running away. I had never run from anything before.

I turned to Marv, who was seated across the room and looking forlorn, knowing what he was giving up too. "I've changed my mind," I said. "Let's go back."

"Yeah!" Marv said, smiling and looking like a load had been lifted from his back.

We had a friend drive us to Charlotte, agreeing to pay for his gas, and arrived just in time for a doubleheader. I managed to get a couple of singles and immediately felt better. I could still hit, even if my arm did ache.

Several days later I decided not to throw a ball at all for two weeks, and I didn't. Then I threw easily on the sideline for a week or so and the pain subsided in my shoulder. My arm gradually got stronger. When a runner tried to score from second on a drive I caught on a bounce in left field, I cut loose with my throw and nailed him at the plate.

Also, in the last six weeks of the season I batted .390 and hit ten home runs as we won the pennant in the Sally League. And most important, after all I'd been through, I knew I could play this game, knew I'd never be tempted to quit again. This black man was a battler and a winner, and he was going to the major leagues.

3

SOME CALLED
ME VICIOUS

*I*N 1956, at age 20, I became the regular left fielder for the Cincinnati Reds, was the youngest starter in the All-Star Game, and, after hitting 38 home runs, was voted the National League Rookie of the Year. I have to admit it was a season of rare accomplishments for me. Looking back, though, I was never very happy that year, never really comfortable.

Once again my environment was a factor, as it was far from what I had known in Oakland. Cincinnati, Ohio, was not a segregated city the way Ogden, Utah, was or the way any city in the deep south was at that time. But blacks could not live any place they could afford. Many places frequented by whites did not welcome black clientele. People did not go out of their way to be unfriendly, and being a ballplayer who was gaining a reputation, it was easier for me than it was for other blacks. But you always knew where you stood with people around the city if you were black. You had your place, period.

All the black players on the Reds stayed at the Manse Hotel, which was for Negroes, a comfortable place with modest rates. That was appealing for a kid making $6000 a year. Still, knowing there were hotels where I couldn't stay and places I could not go made me feel kind of restricted, shut out.

And somehow I never really felt that I was part of the ballclub, that I truly belonged. In those days veterans didn't take to rookies the way they do today, particularly when the player's having a fine season. Of course, I personally wasn't at all outgoing, realizing that rookies were seen and not heard. I didn't get many invitations to join teammates for a meal or whatever after games, none from a white player. I was the only everyday black player on the club.

The other blacks were pitcher Brooks Lawrence, first baseman George Crowe, outfielder Bob Thurman, and relief pitcher Pat Scantlebury, who was Cuban. They were all at least ten years older than I was, but I occasionally tagged along with them after ballgames. They liked to go to clubs and drink beer or whiskey and sit around talking baseball. I'd sit there listening and drink Coke after Coke until I was bloated by 1 or 2 A.M. But I was enraptured by their stories. They had all seen or played against various Negro League teams in years past. Bob Thurman, who was 39, had even played in the Negro League, I believe. They talked about guys like Cool Papa Bell, Josh Gibson, Satchel Paige, and the legendary third baseman Ray Dandridge, who finally was inducted into the Baseball Hall of Fame in 1987. I used to sneak into Oakland Oaks' games and had seen Dandridge play for them. Even at the end of his career Dandridge could still "pick it" at third and swing the bat.

Some nights with those guys, I felt like I was sitting there with an oral encyclopedia of baseball, I accumulated so much knowledge of the game, so many insights. I loved to hear how pitchers worked on hitters like Thurman and Crowe, and what they did to beat the guys on the mound.

"I knew the guy would throw me a slider on the first pitch, and it would be a good one that I could hit," Bob Thurmond would say of a pitcher. "Sure enough, he did. Only I gave it a big swing and missed. Okay. I knew he'd come back with it if he got in trouble on the count. I worked him to 3-and-2, and sure enough, here comes the slider. *Whack!* Base hit!"

I not only learned a lot about baseball from those guys but I learned to appreciate my circumstances more. Those guys had it much tougher getting to the major leagues than I did. More years in the minors, more exhausting travel schedules, far worse living conditions, and much lower wages. When their seasons ended, they would go on tour and play two or three exhibition games every day, seven days a week. They'd travel by bus, eat on the bus, change clothes on the bus, practically live on the bus. When the winter leagues began, they'd fly off to play in Puerto Rico, Cuba, or Mexico. They often made more money per game playing winter ball than they did in the States. One point they made again and again: They weren't black players in winter ball; they were just players.

"In Mexico," someone would say, "some of those bus trips would take over 20 hours. You'd play in 100° heat, and you couldn't even take a drink of water. You did, and Montezuma's revenge would literally knock the crap out of you and put you on your back for days."

I liked to be with my teammates because I wanted to be part of the group, be one of them. But I didn't like the late hours. So I spent most of my time after games lying around in my hotel room. After a period of days or weeks of staring at hotel walls, I'd go out for another night with the guys and absorb insights from their tales while bloating up on Coke.

The days were no problem. I loved it when we played night games, either at home or on the road. The next morning I would rise early and have breakfast. Then I would hurry out to the first movie showing that day, usually at 9 A.M. And I'd race from that show to another at 10:30 or 11, and often from there to a third movie. I followed the pattern of my childhood; when I wasn't playing ball, eating, or sleeping, I was at the movies. And I continued this routine, at least when I was on the road, for the next ten years or more. I was essentially a loner, and I loved to escape into the fantasy of films. Movies filled my time pleasurably and relaxed me until I could engage in my overwhelming interest: playing baseball.

I never relaxed on a ball field. I have always believed in going all out all the time. The baseline belongs to the runner, and whenever I was running the bases, I always slid hard. If the second baseman or short-stop was in the way, coming across the base trying to turn a double play, I hit him hard. Sometimes he got spiked. I slid into third base and into home plate the same way I slid into second—hard. I wanted infielders to have that instant's hesitation about coming across the bag at second or about standing in there awaiting a throw to make a tag when Frank Robinson was throwing his 195 pounds of "I don't give a damn about my body" at them. There are only 27 outs in a ballgame, and it was my job to save one for my team every time I possibly could. I had learned to play the game this way under George Powles back in Oakland, and I believed everyone should play the way I did—which was simply to win any way you could within the rules.

Never once in my 21 years as a major league player did I ever intentionally try to hurt another player. A runner who runs out of the base path is automatically out, and I have seen runners leave the base path to go after an opponent. I never did that. Or at least I have never been called out for running out of the baseline.

In my rookie year I had heard grumblings from opponents about the way I slid into them. In my second year the grumblings grew louder after I took out Milwaukee Braves shortstop Johnny Logan... for six weeks. I was on first when the ball was hit to the second baseman, who flipped to Logan for the force on me as I came in after him. He was crossing the bag when my spikes caught him in the shin. It took about 20 stitches to close the wounds.

As the years went on, I became known as a guy who cut down infielders. One opponent said, "That Robinson's deliberately vicious." Another time I spiked Dodger shortstop Don Zimmer when he came across second base out of position. Between innings I passed Dodger center fielder Duke Snider, and he snarled at me, "What are *you* trying to prove?" I couldn't believe a hard slider like Snider would say that.

It was interesting when Don Zimmer and I became teammates on the Reds some years later. Don said, "I hated Frank Robinson's guts when I played against him. But now that I've seen him play every day for a while, there's nothing dirty or mean about his play. He just plays hard."

Another ex-Dodger who later joined us, pitcher Don Newcombe, had far less insightful things to say about me. "I can't take Frank Robinson," Newcombe said. "That guy is trying to maim people." I couldn't imagine anyone saying something like that about a teammate, one who was out there trying to win for him. I learned later that Don was a drinker then, and maybe it was the alcohol talking. I was shocked to learn that he was a heavy drinker. He always came to the ballpark on time and was a very hard worker, particularly in his pregame running. Maybe he was trying to run the alcohol out of his system. All I know is that I was very cool to Don Newcombe after he called me a maimer. Don, of course, is now a recovered alcoholic, doing substance abuse counseling for the Dodgers.

Another point about players who go into infielders the way I always did: We pay for our aggressiveness. For every cut I have inflicted on an opponent in a slide, I received wounds in return. My hands, arms, and legs are striped with scars inflicted by spikes. The infielders trying to turn a double play at second usually leap to make their throws and to avoid the sliding runner. Naturally, when they leap, they also come down. At times on the runner. Many times on this runner.

The worst scar I received from a play at second took 30 stitches to close. We were playing the Mets and I was on first. The ball was hit to the shortstop, who threw to second baseman Ron Hunt. He caught the ball at the base, pivoted, and went into the air. When he came down, his spikes punctured my left bicep. Doctors said I wouldn't play for a month, but I was back in ten days.

Plays at home plate were not always healthful for me either. I tried to steal home against Pittsburgh. Not only did catcher Danny Kravitz tag me out on a close play, but he stepped on my left forearm. The result is the 5-inch-long ridge of scar tissue on my arm. It was an accident, and my only argument was that I thought I was safe. Still do.

On another play at the plate I slid in headfirst and was safe when the throw got by the catcher. He turned to chase down the ball and stepped on my left hand. Another accident.

Every spiking incident I've ever witnessed in the major leagues was an accident. I've heard that in the old days there were players who intentionally tried to spike opponents on the bases. Ty Cobb had the worst reputation. But I once heard Wahoo Sam Crawford, who played with Cobb, say at a banquet: "They always talk about Cobb playing dirty, trying to spike guys. The baseline belongs to the runner. If the infielders get in the way, that's their lookout."

Some infielders don't see it that way, and I exchanged words with a number of them over the years after going into them hard. In a game against Milwaukee in 1960, I exchanged more than words. It was the first game of a doubleheader at home, and I hit a blooper down the right-field line that rolled into the bullpen. First baseman Joe Adcock was still trying to recover the ball when I reached second, and I kept going for third. Third baseman Eddie Mathews set himself in front of the base, and the throw arrived just before I hit him. I went into him hard, feet first, and crossed my arms in front of my face to protect myself when he swung his glove down for the tag. My crossed arms didn't help. Mathews smacked me in the nose, and it started to bleed.

I didn't care about that. What annoyed me was that I was out. I got up and started away when Mathews said, "Cut out that crap, you son of a bitch!" I turned to yell back at him when he hit me a shot on the cheekbone under the right eye. He jumped on me, and I fell backward to the ground, where I threw punches up at him and he popped me again in the mouth. I was not at all unhappy when the fight was broken up.

Mathews was thrown out of the game, and I certainly couldn't play anymore at that time. I went into the clubhouse and saw in a mirror that my right eye was beginning to swell closed, my nose was bleeding, my cheekbone was bruised, my lower lip was cut, and I had a jammed thumb. Between games manager Fred Hutchinson said he didn't expect me to play in the second game.

"I can play and I'm gonna play," I said. I had to play. I couldn't let a little beating keep me out of the lineup.

I had a pocket full of gauze swatches, and a couple of times while at bat, I had to call time and stuff one up my nose to stop the bleeding. The fact that the vision in my right eye was so blurry worried me most, but that proved to be no problem. I had a walk, was hit by a pitch, hit a single, a double, and a two-run home run. I also made a good catch on a drive that cleared the box seat railing down the left-field line. I leaped, caught the ball, and held it as I flipped backward into the seats. Eddie Mathews had hit that ball. Thank you very much. And we won the game, 4-0.

At one point in the game I reached third base, and Mathews said to me, "I'm sorry it happened."

"Forget it," I said. "I understand." But I still went into Mathews as hard as I could during the remaining five years I was in the National League. Actually, after what I did to Eddie Mathews and his team in that second game, I figured I'd won the fight that day.

I was as aggressive at the plate as I was on the base paths and in the outfield. I stood as close to the plate as I could and stuck my head out over it so that I could get the best possible view of the ball when it left the pitcher's hand and so that I could protect the outside corner. If pitchers jammed me, my wrists were quick enough to get around on the pitch. And I dove into the ball as I strode to start my swing, but my reflexes were so sharp and my wrists so strong that I could stop my stroke before I turned over my wrists for a called strike. Writers at the time said Stan Musial and Ted Williams were the only other hitters who could halt their swing like that in midstream. That was nice to hear.

But pitchers were not at all happy to see me come up to the plate with my head hanging over it in what was known as "concussion alley." Many liked to throw fastballs inside and drive me off the plate. George Powles had schooled me well in how to get out of the way of inside pitches. Tuck your head into your shoulder and spin left. Quickly. If the pitch was too far inside, you spun and fell hard away from it. So a pitcher would knock me down, and I'd get right back up and hang over the plate again. At times, of course, I couldn't get out of the way of 90-mph fastballs that were well inside. In my rookie year, I was hit by pitches 20 times, which easily led the league. I led the league in being hit by pitches in each of my ten National League seasons.

In my second season I had a little scare when Ruben Gomez of the New York Giants hit me in the head with a pitch that cracked my batting helmet and sent me to the hospital for X-rays. As I had tripled and doubled my first two times up and the pitch that hit me was thrown *behind* me, manager Birdie Tebbetts was furious. He maintained that Gomez had deliberately thrown at my head. I hadn't even been able to fall back away from the pitch; if I had, it would have struck me in the face.

"They throw at Frank because he's colored, because they figure he can't fight back," Birdie told the press afterward. "Sure he's a good hitter, and good hitters get thrown at. But Gus Bell and Ted Kluzewski [of the Reds] don't go down. They're good hitters. I'm just tired of seeing this kid on the ground all the time. This is the eighth time he's been hit this year and it's only July—and the third time he's been hit in the head."

Tebbetts went on to say that over the years the top black hitters such as Jackie Robinson, Roy Campanella, Larry Doby, Luke Easter, Minnie Minosa, and Willie Mays had been thrown at more frequently than other equally dangerous hitters. That was probably true. Yet I still couldn't believe that I was being thrown at because I was black. I felt that pitchers were just trying to test me, to intimidate me into backing off the plate so they could work me outside, away from my power.

I played the day after the Gomez beaning and went on to have another good year. But in 1958 I was hit in the head under the helmet by Camilo Pascual of the Washington Senators during an exhibition game as we played our way north. It was the hardest I was ever hit. I woke up in the hospital in Portsmouth, Ohio, where we had been playing. Then they put me in an ambulance and drove me to Cincinnati. It was 120 miles away on a bumpy road, and my head felt every bump. I had a cerebral concussion, but there was no fracture.

When the season opened, I played even though I had constant headaches. And every time I stepped up to hit, I was scared to death. I could no longer bring myself to stride into fastballs. And on curveballs I would flinch and roll back on my heels and then have to reach for the pitch. There's no way you can hit with your rear end in the dugout. I received all kinds of advice and tried all kinds of new things in batting practice, but I just couldn't stop pulling out, which is what it's called when you draw away from the pitch and try to swing. The fear in my subconscious was just excruciating.

At the All-Star break, the midway point in the season, I was batting .240 and had hit exactly eight home runs. How I hit those, the way I was bailing out at the plate, remains a mystery. But the three days off while the All-Star Game was being played gave me time to sit down and think about my situation. Fear was going to drive me out of the game. I either had to conquer my fear or find another line of work. The only skills I had were in baseball, and I wasn't using them.

The night before the season resumed, we played an exhibition game in Seattle against our top minor league club. I swore that I would force myself to hang in there on every pitch. To do so, I would hit every pitch to right field, as you have to stay in there longer going to right than if you tried to pull the ball. I went to bat four times that night and got two hits, neither of them Hall of Fame variety. Both singles were hit off my thumbs and dinked into right field. But the fact that I had stood in there against a pretty fair fastball pitcher who had worked me inside restored my confidence.

Our next regular-season game was in San Francisco. In my first at-bat against Al Worthington, he threw me a slow curve that would have broken over the black on the outside corner of the plate, except I didn't rock back on my heels. I strode into the pitch and yanked it over the left-field fence. My next time up I had to face the man who had fractured my helmet the year before, Ruben Gomez. He tried to back me off the plate with an inside fastball, and I lined it to left. Then I felt my confidence was all the way back.

For the next eight years, I never again had a problem with fear of striding into pitches.

The only other problem I had in that third year in the majors was when manager Birdie Tebbetts was fired. Birdie was like a father to me. Early in my rookie season he sat me down against several of the best pitchers in the league, including Robin Roberts and Don Newcombe, and told me why. "I want you to look at this guy the first time around, Frank," Birdie said. "Watch the way he works on hitters."

Then he sat me down next to him and explained things to me, such as why infielders and outfielders were playing a certain hitter in such a way against the pitcher who was on the mound. And when we were at bat, Birdie liked to keep me and the other younger players near him because he was always teaching. He also liked to hit us with questions to make sure we were in the game. "What's the count?" he'd suddenly ask. "How many outs?" "If you were up, what would you do in this situation?"

Birdie taught me to study the opposition and to think ahead, to anticipate what the other manager, the other players could be expected to do in various situations. That very first year, when I was only 20, he made me see how important it was to stay on top of things, to never allow yourself to be surprised by an opponent.

He was a patient, gentle man. When I made a mistake, he would take me aside and explain what I had done wrong. I was shocked and very upset when Birdie was fired.

The man hired to replace Tebbetts was Jimmy Dykes—a man who had been managing for some 40 years! When I read that, I was excited. Dykes had managed the Philadelphia Athletics from 1918 until 1932, when team owner Connie Mack ran the club from the bench. But Dykes was back managing the A's from 1933 through 1939. Next he managed the Chicago White Sox from 1940 through 1946. After 28 years of steady employment, Dykes was out of business for five years. But the Athletics hired him once again in 1951, and he lasted until 1953. When he was fired, the former St. Louis Browns, who became the Baltimore Orioles, hired him for the '54 season. Dykes had been at his leisure until the Reds called. But I figured that after all those years of managing, Dykes had to have one of the most astute baseball minds in the world, that he had to be just bursting with knowledge to pass along to us.

I figured wrong. Jimmy Dykes told us the same thing every day. He'd clap his hands and say, "Just go up there and take your swings, fellas!" And he'd clap his hands and say, "If you don't get 'em today, fellas, you'll get 'em tomorrow!" And he'd clap his hands and say, "And if you don't get 'em tomorrow, you'll get 'em the next day!"

Jimmy Dykes was a very good clapper who liked to have a good time. He was the most happy-go-lucky, fun-loving manager I've ever known. Dykes liked to win ballgames, but he enjoyed himself whether he won or lost. We went 24-17 under Dykes, but he was fired at season's end. He wasn't out of work long. The Detroit Tigers hired him the next year, and he didn't get fired again until 1960. Then he moved to the Cleveland Indians. In 1961 the string finally ran out for Jimmy Dykes. But you had to say he had a helluva run, and I know he always enjoyed himself.

Our manager in 1959 was Mayo Smith, who had managed the Philadelphia Athletics in 1945 and the Philadelphia Phillies from 1955 until 1958. I guess Mayo felt it was time to change cities. Mayo Smith was among the most uninspiring leaders I've ever met, another nice guy who seemed to get managing jobs regularly in the major leagues for no discernible reason. Certainly with the Reds he had nothing to contribute. He just made out the lineup and sat on the bench. He sat on the bench very well.

Early on we had a pregame meeting in the clubhouse and catcher Ed Bailey asked, "Mayo, how are we gonna pitch Hank Aaron today?"

"Ed, you know him better than I do," Mayo said.

"I... I just thought with you managing the Phillies and facing Aaron," Bailey said.

"Well if you get down to it and there's any real question, hook 'em," Mayo said.

Throughout the meeting, on every question as to how we would pitch a guy, Mayo Smith said, "Well, hook 'em."

We stopped asking Mayo how to pitch opponents. On July 8 when we were in seventh place with a 35-45 record, Smith was fired. Of course, from 1967 into 1970 Mayo Smith managed the Detroit Tigers. Don't ask me why.

It was apparent in the first few years of my career that some managers were hired not necessarily for their special skills but simply because they had been managers before. That made as much sense to me as hiring a plumber because he had been in business for ten years, even though he had yet to discover how to install a washer in a leaky faucet.

4
⑤ BRUSHBACKS AND BEANBALLS

F_{RED} Hutchinson, who had managed the Tigers and the Cardinals, as well as our Seattle ballclub in the Pacific Coast League, replaced Smith as manager of the Reds in 1959. He was the most intense individual I've ever come across. People said that when Hutch got mad he didn't just throw furniture, he threw entire *rooms*. He was called "the Bear," and he had a fierce temper.

One night in Milwaukee he proved it after a tough loss. Wire cages covered the light bulbs on the ceiling in the runway leading from the visiting dugout to the clubhouse. As Hutch, his face clenched in anger and steam seeping from his ears, walked toward the clubhouse, he stopped at the first light and stared at it briefly. Then he reached up and, with his bare hands, tore the wire cage off the fixture and shattered the light bulb. As strong as a bear, Hutch proceeded to stop at every light fixture, tear off the wire screen, and smash the bulb, until he reached the clubhouse.

Another scene occurred at Forbes Field in Pittsburgh. We had a 6-0 lead over the Pirates with two outs in the ninth and nobody on base. When the smoke cleared, the Pirates had beaten us, 7-6. I went through a door in right field and hustled under the stands to the clubhouse to catch the Fred Hutchinson show. Hutch must have paused in the dugout because all the players were at their lockers when he stormed into the clubhouse. Hutch stopped, grabbed each side of his uniform shirt, and yanked—tearing the buttons off. He spotted a wooden folding chair, picked it up over his head, and slammed it to the floor. It bounced, but nothing broke.

Hutch growled, picked up the chair, swung it over his head, and slammed it to the concrete floor even harder. Not a splinter. He hefted the chair a third time and—sweat flying off his brow, spittle flecking off his scowl—slammed it down a third time. Nothing.

Hutch jammed his fists into his hips and glared at the chair. Then he picked it up, opened it, gently placed the chair on the floor, and sat on it. "I think," he said, "I've finally met my match."

All of us had been sitting there in silence, heads ducked, sneaking glances at the Hutch show, and then everyone broke out laughing.

But there were times when, knowing Hutch was going to explode, none of us wanted to be around him. In 1961 we won the pennant playing .604 baseball, and in 1962 we were just as good, playing .605 ball, but we finished third, 3½ games behind the Giants. And if we had won a few more games from the New York Mets that year, we might have returned to the World Series. An expansion team in 1962, the Mets were surely one of the worst ballclubs in the history of baseball, winning only 40 of 160 games for a percentage of .250.

We always beat the Mets in Cincinnati. For some reason, though, we had trouble with them in New York, playing in that weird, old stadium called the Polo Grounds. One Sunday we lost a doubleheader there. Immediately afterward we all hurried to the clubhouse in center field. As I trotted out there, I looked over my shoulder to see what Hutch was doing. He was just sitting in the dugout, hunched forward, staring at the ground.

"Wow," I thought, "we're in for some explosion."

When I reached the clubhouse, the guys were mostly dawdling or just sitting around their lockers, as players often do after losing when they know they should've won. But I peeled off my uniform and went right to the shower. Just as I returned to my locker and was toweling off, the phone rang. The clubhouse man answered it, listened, and hung up. "That was Hutch," he said. "He'll be here in 15 minutes. And he said if any player's still here—he'll tear 'em apart!"

I have never seen 25 ballplayers get out of their uniforms, showered, and into their clothes so fast. Some guys weren't even finished drying themselves. You looked around that room, and guys were throwing on clothes so rapidly that it was like you were looking at a speeded-up silent movie. In five minutes that clubhouse was *cleared*.

Hutch could really tear up a clubhouse, a bathroom, even his own office. In the old stadium in Cincinnati, Crosley Field, the manager's office was built up above the third base side, and under it was a walkway for fans to enter and exit on. The manager's office featured a huge glass window that looked out onto the field. After one of our tough losses at home, Hutch climbed up to his office, slammed the door, grabbed his desk chair, and flung it into that window. Fans who were trailing out of the ballpark on that walkway below the window were rained on by shards of glass. Luckily the chair itself didn't pass through the window.

I had respect for Hutch as a manager, but I never could warm up to the man. He was just too tense to be in any way open or friendly. You could have a great ballgame, go 4-for-5 with a couple of extrabase hits and a few RBIs, and Hutch might pass you after the game and say, "Nice going." Then again he might not say anything at all. But you could count on him saying something if you made a mistake.

I had bounced back from my bad start after the beaning in 1958 to finish with 31 home runs, even though my batting average was only .269. But the next year, my first under Hutch, I batted .311, hit 36 home runs, and had 125 RBIs. So Fred Hutchinson knew that I could hit and knew that I was an all-out ballplayer. But in the spring of 1960, I had trouble with my right shoulder, as I had had trouble with it every spring since the problem first cropped up when I was in the minors.

This was Hutch's first spring training with us, and maybe he didn't realize that I had to take it easy throwing for a few weeks. He certainly didn't come to ask me about the fact that I wasn't throwing to the cutoff man with the other outfielders in practice. Then one day I tried to throw before I should have, and my right arm was very sore up in the socket area. I went in and told the trainer I would play in the exhibition game that afternoon, but I couldn't throw.

Hutch scratched me from the lineup, and later blasted me to a columnist for a Cincinnati paper. The story quoted Hutch as saying that I'd had that shoulder injury long enough, that I shouldn't have thrown from the outfield before I was ready. He also said that if I wasn't ready to play by opening day, I would be fined for every game I missed.

That pissed me off.

I was ready by opening day, but a series of minor injuries to my leg, ankle, and thumb muted my hitting during the first half of the season, when I batted only .259. All of a sudden I found my name was no longer in the starting lineup unless a left-handed pitcher was going against us.

In a two-week period, I played exactly three games, against lefties. Hutch told the writers that I couldn't hit right-handed pitchers. He didn't tell me anything.

When the writers asked my reaction to Hutch's statement, I said, "If I couldn't hit right-handed pitching I wouldn't be here, because I hit right-handed pitching better than left-handed pitching. But from where I'm sitting on the bench, I can't hit anybody."

Later my arm was bothering me again, and I had to sit out a couple of games as I was unable to throw. We were trailing in one of those games in the late innings when we loaded the bases with one out. Hutch rose and walked down the dugout looking for a pinch hitter. He stopped by me, paused, and moved on. The pinch hitter he sent up popped out, and we didn't score. After the game the writers asked me if I could have pinch-hit.

"I can't throw, but I can swing the bat," I said.

"Why didn't you tell Hutch?" I was asked.

"He didn't ask me," I said.

When the writers took that to Hutch, he said, "Frank should have told me he could hit."

I thought it was up to the manager to ask his players if they were physically able to do something. Birdie Tebbetts would have asked, as would every other manager I'd played for. Even "hook 'em" Mayo Smith.

The coach I was closest to on the Reds, Reggio Otero, took me aside after the incident hit the papers. Otero had been with the club since I joined it. A fine-fielding first baseman in his playing days, Reggie had worked with me there when I had been used at first in 1959. I was not a natural first baseman and did not like playing there, but we had no one other than rookie Gordy Coleman to play the position. So I also played 78 games at first in 1960.

But what Reggie Otero talked to me about then was Hutch. "He's not a bad guy, Frank. He's just stubborn like you. You know Hutch doesn't talk much. He's not like Birdie. I know you loved Birdie, but Hutch just has a different nature, and we all have to work with him. He wants to win as much as you do. Try to see things from his point of view. If you can't communicate with him because he doesn't communicate, come to me and tell me how you are."

That talk helped me a lot, and after that I never had a real problem with Fred Hutchinson again. He even praised my performance once or twice.

○　　　　○　　　　○

The baseball played in those days was a lot tougher than it is today for one simple reason—the brushback pitch. Every team had a pitcher or two who moved guys off the plate and occasionally hit batters in the ribs, in the buttocks, in the elbow, or in the head. No team had more pitchers who threw dusters than the Dodgers, both in Brooklyn and in Los Angeles. Don Drysdale annually led the league in batters hit by pitches. He threw hard and he threw tight. Drysdale hit me more than any other pitcher in my ten years in the National League. But the Dodgers had other pitchers who liked to knock you down—Roger Craig, Stan Williams, Larry Sherry, and Clem Labine among them.

Any time you hit a home run off any of them, you knew the next batter was going down on the first pitch, and maybe on the second, and you knew you would hit the deck in your next plate appearance. It was all part of the game, but sometimes it got out of hand.

We were always at war with the Dodgers because they were usually picked to win the pennant, and they were the team everyone measured himself against. Their pitchers refused to let you dig in at the plate; in one 1960 game Roger Craig hit me in the head with a fastball, but the batting helmet saved me, and I stayed in the game. Later that season my teammate Vada Pinson broke Craig's collarbone accidently, though some of the Dodgers held him responsible. The accident occurred in a rundown between third and home. Jim Gilliam threw the ball late to Craig at the plate, and Vada was too close to him to slide. So Vada ran into the bigger man and scored.

The next night Stan Williams, who liked to throw at batters, dusted off Pinson twice in the seventh inning. I hollered from the on-deck circle: "If you can't get a guy out with natural stuff, you don't belong in the big leagues."

Williams yelled, "Come and get it!" and motioned me to meet him on the mound.

I dropped my bat and charged him, but the umpires got in between us.

Williams threw the next pitch way inside and hit Pinson on the arm. Vada stole second and moved to third on my fly ball to left. Then Williams foolishly threw another duster that was so far over Gus Bell's head that he didn't have to duck, and the catcher had to chase the ball to the backstop. Pinson scored the winning run on that play.

The Dodgers weren't the only team with whom we battled. In one game against the Phillies our pitcher, Raul Sanchez, couldn't control his fastball. He wasn't throwing at anyone, but his pitches managed to hit three Phillies in succession. The last was 6-foot-8 pitcher Gene Conley, and that enraged manager Gene Mauch. He came running out of the dugout for Sanchez. Our second baseman, Billy Martin, intercepted Mauch and held him fast as the dugouts emptied. It was a rare peace-keeping effort that Martin attempted. But it ended when Conley stepped over and punched Billy. He let go of Mauch and started firing punches at Conley, of whom he later said in the clubhouse: "Fighting him is like fighting a two-story building."

A couple of Phillies grabbed me and wrestled me to the ground; then pitcher Robin Roberts called me a nigger. I broke free and went after Roberts, landing two quick punches before order was restored. Roberts apologized to me later, and I accepted it. I always accept apologies, because I think it takes courage to apologize. But that doesn't always change the way I feel about an individual. What had come out of Roberts's mouth during the scuffle, I felt, had come from his heart. An apology doesn't change what's in a man's heart.

We didn't have many pitchers who regularly dusted opponents, and that bothered me when my teammates and I were being knocked down. If opposing pitchers were going to try to intimidate me to keep me from doing my job, I thought it was up to the pitchers on my club to help me and help themselves by retaliating with dusters. Most pitchers that you knocked down a couple of times got the message. They didn't go to bat often enough to get used to biting the dust. But I never asked any of our pitchers to low-bridge an opponent to protect me.

I would speak to our pitcher when one of my teammates had been knocked down or hit by a pitch. "See what he just did to your teammate?" I'd say. "You got to protect your teammates." I didn't want anyone thrown at, just moved back off the plate.

We always knew when we were being thrown at. When a pitcher with good control started throwing *behind* hitters, that was a clue. And when one of my teammates was hit by such a pitcher, I'd tell ours, "Hey, let's stop this thing before it gets out of hand. He hit one of our guys; let's hit one of theirs and end it."

The umpires usually controlled the beanball battles pretty well. Typical was a game against Don Drysdale. The first pitch he threw to second baseman Don Blasingame was behind his head. After getting Blazer out,

Drysdale threw three pitches in a row at Pinson's ankles, making him skip. Then Drysdale jammed Vada, but he dinked the pitch off his thumbs over third and ran it into a double. Drysdale was so furious that his face was flushed when I stepped in. His first pitch was at my head, the second at my ribs. While I spat out some dust, home plate umpire Dusty Boggess stepped toward Drysdale and said, "That's enough of that. You do it one more time; you're out of there."

The next pitch smacked me in the forearm. Drysdale was ejected from the game, fined $50, and suspended for three days. Of course, suspending a starting pitcher for three days was meaningless, because he only started every four days anyway.

I finally made a close friend in baseball when Vada Pinson joined the Reds in 1959. Vada was also from Oakland and had played ball at McClymonds High right after I graduated. I first met him the year before in spring training in Tampa, Florida. He had checked into a Negro hotel, but I moved him into the boarding house where I and the other blacks stayed. The next year when he made the club, we became roommates on the road and we rented apartments near one another in Cincinnati. It was nice, and we had a good time palling around. Vada didn't share my fondness for movies (I wonder if anyone else would care to watch two or three movies a day) as he was more of a TV addict.

Vada Pinson was a very fastidious dresser, and I liked his style. I started spending a lot more money on clothes to try to keep up with him. Prior to that, most of my money had been spent on dating, on friends, and, mainly, on cars. I'd buy a new car, see another one I liked better a few months later, and trade in on it. I once traded a car that had less than 1000 miles on it. I set a record in 1957 when I owned five different cars. For a guy who had never had any money growing up, I really enjoyed myself.

My legs were so skinny that my nickname was "Pencils," and when I joined the Reds in 1956, we still wore those old baggy flannel pants. I was just happy to have a uniform, even though my legs made those pants look like balloons. But in 1959 our uniforms were a lighter flannel, tailors measured us in the spring, and we could order our uniforms to fit as we wished. Vada said he was ordering a tailored look with tapered pants, and I followed suit, or uniform. We wore our outer socks pulled up high, showing a lot of the white sanitary hose underneath, and we wouldn't go out on the field until we were dressed perfectly, shirtfront aligned with fly and not a wrinkle anywhere.

Vada also liked to spit-shine his baseball shoes. Before games and then after taking practice, he'd be in the clubhouse shining his shoes until they gleamed. We could tip the clubhouse man to shine our shoes, but Vada wouldn't let anyone touch his. I began doing up my shoes like his for a while. I even got him to put a spit shine on mine a few times so that they looked like patent leather. But after a few months of this shining routine, I gave up. I found that when I slid, I would turn my foot to the side and I'd scuff the outside of my heel: The leather there would never shine up again. I began tipping the clubhouse man once more.

We were always together, Vada and I. We roomed together, lockered and dressed side by side, sat together on team buses and plane trips, and threw the ball around before games to one another in warmups. We usually ate breakfast and dinner together; if not in a restaurant, then we'd order from room service and watch TV. Just about everywhere you saw Frank Robinson, you saw Vada Pinson. I had never been very close to anyone before, and it felt good.

5 ⊚
⊚ *"THAT GUY'S GOT A GUN"*

*T*HE Cincinnati Reds were not among the better-paying teams in base-ball, but I always felt that general manager Gabe Paul treated me fairly. My salary had increased from $6000 in 1956 to $30,000 a year in 1960. That seems like a pittance today when the minimum major league salary is over $60,000 per year and when some players earn over $2 million each season. But 30 grand in 1960 wasn't a bad wage when you could buy a fine car for one-tenth of that, and I expected a little raise for 1961.

Gabe Paul had left the club, and Bill DeWitt came in at season's end as the new GM. I had always negotiated my next contract and then gone to California to spend the winter with my family before heading for spring training. So I went to the Reds' office to see DeWitt. The secretary picked up the phone and told DeWitt I was there; then she told me I had to wait. With Gabe Paul you could drop by his office at any time. But Bill DeWitt had me sit there and wait for almost an hour. If this was how he treated his best hitter, I thought, I wondered how he handled utility players.

When I finally got in to see him, the first words out of DeWitt's mouth were not, "Hello, how are you?" He said, "You've got to take a pay cut."

"What?" I said.

"You had an off year," he said. "You batted .311 in '59, you drove in 125 runs, and you hit 37 home runs. Last year you batted .297, you had only 83 RBIs, and you hit only 31 home runs. You've got to take a pay cut."

"Wait a second," I said. "I know my stats were down a little, but I still led the club in batting average, RBIs, and home runs. That doesn't call for a cut. I've given this ballclub five good years, and in fact I think I deserve a little raise."

Then Bill DeWitt really stunned me. "I hear you don't always hustle," he said.

I was momentarily speechless. "Where did you hear that?" I asked.

"I have sources."

"Well your sources are wrong, Mr. DeWitt. Nobody on this ballclub plays the game harder than I do. Nobody in the league, either."

We went back and forth for over two hours. I didn't get a raise. I finally signed a contract calling for the same salary I'd earned in 1960. "Just wait until next year," I said. "I'll go out and have a good year, and when I come back here again—*I'll* be in the driver's seat." I left thinking, "And you'll pay through the nose, Bill CheapWitt."

Before I could take care of that, DeWitt messed with my mind some more. It was my own stupid fault. I had bought a little handgun in Florida early in 1960, and I carried it around loaded in my pocket because I always had between $250 and $2500 in cash on me. The gun just made me feel secure, and I didn't know I had to have a permit for it. The gun, a .25 Beretta, fitted in the palm of my hand and looked like a toy. I regularly shot the Beretta at the police firing range in Cincinnati, and the cops loved to make fun of it. "Did you buy that gun from a circus midget?" they said to me. It's a shame none of the cops ever asked if I had a gun permit. It's unfortunate that I bought the handgun in the first place. But I was just an immature 25-year-old, and in February 1961 the gun got me in trouble with the law.

The evening began innocently enough with me playing in a pickup basketball game in Cincinnati. Afterward I and two friends stopped at a little drive-in restaurant to eat. We sat at a horseshoe-shaped counter and ordered hamburgers. While I was chatting to one friend, the other suddenly got into an argument with three white men seated across from us. One of the men made a racial remark, and I stood up with my friends and said, "If you guys want trouble, come on."

Someone summoned the two policemen who were parked just outside the window. One of them said to us, not to the white men, "All right, boys."

I had a bad temper then, and I always reacted when anyone called me "boy" because when I played down south that was another way of saying "nigger." I said to the police, "We're not boys, we're men, and that's the way you should address us."

I said this calmly, but my friends got angry, and they got loud about being called boys. One of them refused to quiet down, and he was finally arrested for disturbing the peace. I drove to the station house and paid the $100 bail fee; then we went back to the drive-in to pick up our hamburgers.

The three white guys were now gone, so we sat down and started eating. But I looked into the kitchen, and the chef was standing there glaring at me. Then he raised an index finger to his throat and made a slicing motion, threatening me.

Furious, I stood up and said, "Well, come on."

He started toward me, and there was a carving knife in his right hand.

I reached into my jacket pocket with my left hand and brought out the Beretta. Holding it in my palm so he could see it, I shouted, "If you think you're a big man, come on."

The chef stopped dead in his tracks and yelled, "That guy's got a gun!"

The same two policemen were back outside the restaurant, and they hurried in and found the gun. I was taken to the station house and charged with carrying a concealed weapon. The cops must have tipped off Cincinnati sportswriter Earl Lawson, because he walked in minutes later. Lawson phoned Bill DeWitt to see if he would send a lawyer or someone down to bail me out. DeWitt said he'd see to me in the morning. Thanks, Bill, I thought.

If Gabe Paul had still been general manager, he would have come right down to the station house himself. That is exactly what he had done, in fact, when I ran into some trouble in Tampa during spring training in 1958. Blacks didn't have much they could do for entertainment during the off-hours in Tampa then. No movie houses or bowling alleys would accept us. We couldn't go to the jai alai fronton. We could buy tickets at the dog track, but we had to go downstairs, and you were so far from the track that you could hardly see the dogs running. What we did mainly was hang around Central Avenue in the Negro district where we could shoot some pool or stop in one of the little clubs there.

One night George Crowe, Jesse Gonder, and I were standing on a corner in the area about 11 P.M., just talking. I leaned on a metal street signpost that was loose, so I spontaneously shook it. At that moment two black policemen came by, and one said, "Get your hands off that!"

Some of the people in the Negro district disliked the black ballplayers because some players dated girls for six weeks during spring training, then dropped them. Obviously this cop knew we were players, and he wanted to hassle us. I should have kept my mouth shut, but I have a hard time doing that when I know I'm right.

"Are you kidding?" I said to the cop. "I'm not harming anything." I was still holding the signpost though I had stopped shaking it.

"I told you to get your hands off the sign," the cop said.

"Why?" I said. "I'm not hurting a thing."

Then the two cops grabbed me, and one started searching me. "What are you looking for?" I asked.

"Shut up," one said.

"Let's teach him a lesson," the other said, and they took me down to the station house.

But Jesse Gonder phoned Gabe Paul at the hotel, and in minutes he and Birdie Tebbets were there. I wasn't booked, and in a few minutes more I was free. That was what Gabe Paul thought of his players. To Bill DeWitt, players were just chattel.

Still, DeWitt may have done me a great service by forcing me to spend a night in jail. I sat up most of the night thinking about how stupid I'd been to ever buy a handgun. I wondered what the kids who idolized baseball players were going to think of Frank Robinson now. Baseball had given me everything I had, and I had just left a scar on its image by acting like a dumb kid. I realized it was time for me to grow up and start acting like a responsible adult.

In the morning I was released on a $1000 bail bond. Three weeks later I flew up to Cincinnati from spring training and, in testimony before a grand jury, pleaded guilty to carrying a concealed weapon. I was fined $250.

The only thing Fred Hutchinson said to me was, "That was a stupid thing to do."

"It was," I told him. "But sometimes a man learns from his stupidities."

Of course, I was reminded of the gun incident all season. When I returned to spring training I found a water pistol in my locker, left there by our catcher, Ed Bailey. I gave the pistol back to him and said, "Thanks, Eddie, but I can't use this. I'm on parole."

When we went to Bradenton to play the Braves, Henry Aaron and Felix Mantilla greeted me with a song sung at the top of their lungs: "Lay that pistol down, babe, lay that pistol down." Then pitcher Lew Burdette walked over and frisked me. "It's all right, Eddie," he called to Eddie Mathews, "he's clean."

Mathews laughed and said, "Hey, Robby, I'm not fooling around with you this year."

Fans were on me early that season, calling out things like "Frankie, get your gun!" and "Who do you think you are, Wyatt Earp?" Whenever I had an argument with an umpire, the cry was, "Pull your gun on him!"

But all the ribbing and bench jockeying I took served a purpose—it all goaded me to keep driving hard to have a great year. The fans and Bill CheapWitt combined to remind me never to let up.

I also became more of a leader on the ballclub in 1961. Hutch said, "Frank's the kind of leader Joe DiMaggio was," meaning the way I played set an example for my teammates. I also spoke out more in the meetings that the players convened without the coaches or manager present. I remember one meeting that was held, in May; as we were vying for first place, but we had abruptly gone into a slump. I stood up and said, "Let's stop making excuses for one another. We're playing lousy ball, and we've got to start correcting our mistakes. I know I've been swinging at too many bad pitches instead of waiting for my pitch and moving the runner over. A lot of you guys are swinging at too many first pitches and letting the pitcher get ahead of you. Particularly when we've got men in scoring position. We've got to start picking them up."

Other guys got up and admitted their mistakes, on the mound, on defense, on the bases, whatever. I think it helped. We won 10 of our next 12 games and moved into first place in June. The Reds had been picked to finish in the second division, but we battled hard all season and won the pennant, the first for Cincinnati in 21 years. Unfortunately, we lost the World Series to the Yankees in five games.

I didn't get too upset, perhaps because we'd tried our best and been beaten by a better ballclub. Also, I had marriage on my mind. I had met Barbara Ann Cole at the Coliseum in Los Angeles in August, and it had been love at first sight. I spoke to her on the phone just about every day thereafter, and we were married on October 28, 1961, in Los Angeles.

Then we flew to Cincinnati and began looking for a house to buy. A builder showed us a house we loved in a nice area. Barbara wanted to buy it immediately. But the agent said, "I'm sorry, I can't sell you this house here. But I can build you the exact same house in a black neighborhood."

We ended up renting an apartment in a racially mixed neighborhood, right around the corner from where Vada Pinson and his wife Jackie lived.

Barbara and Jackie became fast friends, and our neighbors, black and white, were all friendly. But none of the wives of my white teammates were very friendly to Barbara or the other black wives, until Pete Rose made the team a couple of years later. His irrepressible wife at that time, Karolyn, was friendly with everyone.

I remember coming home one night and finding Barbara very upset. "Jim Maloney's wife Carolyn told me that the wives of the Cincinnati players were not ready to invite the black wives to any of the baby showers coming up," Barbara said. "I thought I'd show her how small-minded they were by saying I'd send a gift anyway. But she said I couldn't even do that! Karolyn Rose heard about this and called to tell me she thought it was terrible."

Bigotry—I wondered if it would ever fade away. People kept writing that baseball had made things so much better for blacks, but it still had a long way to go as far as I was concerned.

Early in November it was announced that I had been voted the Most Valuable Player in the National League, which was quite an honor. I had expected that Orlando Cepeda of the Giants might win it after hitting 46 home runs and driving in 142 RBIs. But I'd had a good year, batting .323, hitting 37 home runs, and accumulating 124 RBIs, and my team had won the pennant.

I figured when I went in to negotiate my new contract with Bill DeWitt that I had the ammunition to justify a $20,000 raise. I sat down in DeWitt's office, and he said, "I'll give you a $2500 raise."

"That's an insult to offer me that figure," I said.

"Well, if I jump you up ten or fifteen thousand now, you'll come back next year and want twice as much. You go out and have another year like this one, and you can come back and get that kind of money."

"You know I'm not gonna sign for a paltry $2500 raise. I had a good year, helped the ballclub win a pennant, was named MVP, and I feel I deserve a $20,000 raise."

"Twenty thousand!"

You would have thought I had lifted his wallet. It took me five strenuous, demeaning negotiating sessions with Bill CheapWitt before I managed to get him up to a raise of $12,500.

I was a much better hitter in 1962, more patient, more consistent. I had 208 hits, more than I'd had in any other season, 39 of them home runs, and I drove in 136 runs. I also scored 134 runs and led the league in doubles with 51. But I was disappointed when we dropped out of the pennant race in September, and I suddenly found myself drained and tired of baseball. I was tired of being hit by pitches all the time, tired of the nagging injuries that kept cropping up. I disliked being away from Barbara and our young son, Frank Kevin. And one day I told writer Earl Lawson that I was going to retire at the end of the season. I was dead serious.

Phillies manager Gene Mauch said, "I know 91 pitchers and 9 managers in the league who will chip in $500 apiece if Robinson will go through with his plans to retire. That's $50,000 for him."

Before our last game of the season, Fred Hutchinson called a clubhouse meeting and said, "I see where this is the last game for one of us, and I think we should say an appropriate farewell to Robby."

Each of my teammates came over and solemnly shook my hand. The final player was shortstop Eddie Kasko, bearing a package. "We just want you to know how much we're going to miss you. And as a token of our esteem, we have a gift we're sure you'll be able to use on your new job." He tore the wrapping off the package and handed me a dented, scratched-up old lunchbox.

I thought I was still serious about retiring, but when I stopped by Hutch's office to say good-bye, I guess my subconscious was working because I said, "See you in the spring." And Hutch released one of his very rare smiles.

As usual, DeWitt opened contract negotiations with me by offering a raise of $2500. But he couldn't deny that I'd had the greatest year of my career. After four more sessions with him I finally got a good raise—$22,500—which brought me up to $65,000. Then I went out and had the worst year of my career.

There was not one game all season when I was physically 100 percent. One injury after another struck me—in the shoulder, elbow, thumb, legs—and I got a 30-stitch spike wound in an arm. I batted all of .259 with 21 home runs as the club finished fifth.

As if I didn't have enough trouble that season, some writers were reporting that Vada Pinson and I had formed a "Negro clique" on the ballclub. One wrote, "They say the two have formed a clique that is gnawing at the morale of the club...and that's why the Reds are not fighting for the flag."

What nonsense. Certainly Vada and I had been virtually inseparable for five years, but other duos or trios on the team palled around together, and they weren't called clique members. Neither Vada nor I had ever done anything to hurt the morale of our teammates. Jim Brosnan, our relief pitcher who wrote in his spare time, said in his book on the 1960 season that I was a hard man to get to know and that I'm "not the type of person you go out for a beer with."

How would Brosnan know? He never invited me to go out with him for anything. No white player on the Cincinnati Reds had ever asked me to join him for a meal or a drink. I have to admit that I didn't invite any white player to go out with me after a game either. Not until the spring of 1963.

That was when Pete Rose was a rookie who wasn't expected to have much chance of making the Reds at second base. Don Blasingame was a smooth pivot man, and he was coming off his best year at the plate. Pete Rose was by no means a good fielder that spring. He had hard hands on ground balls, particularly on balls hit to his right, and he couldn't make the double play with major league consistency. Add to these strikes against him the fact that most of the Reds' players didn't like Rose.

He was a cocky little dude who moved chest out like a bantam rooster and ran everyplace he went on a ball field, even to first when he drew a walk. That ticked off a lot of guys who regarded Pete as sort of a hot dog and called him "Charlie Hustle." They resented him, and the resentment got worse when Rose won the second base job from the popular Blasingame.

But I admired Pete Rose, the way he carried himself and the way he played hard every minute he was on the field. He reminded me of someone I knew. Playing hard had not contributed to my popularity. So when I saw that Pete Rose was being ostracized by most of my teammates— guys hardly talking to him, never inviting him out with them—I asked Pete one night if he would like to join Vada and me for dinner.

"Damn right, Frank," he said. "I'll be honored."

No other players warmed to Rose all season, so Vada and I became his friends and showed him the ropes around the league. We'd warm up together throwing a ball around before games. After games if Vada and I were going out for a bite to eat, we always tried to bring Pete along. He loved to talk baseball as much as I did. Being black and having gone through some hard times with aloneness myself, I felt for Pete, and he said he appreciated my thinking of him.

Pete Rose, hard hands and all, hustled his way to Rookie of the Year that season, batting .273. But nobody—I mean nobody—had any idea then what Pete would end up doing with his bat, acquiring over 4200 base hits in his career, more than any other player ever. He did it all on determination and hard work.

A couple of years later Karolyn Rose told Barbara that Pete's father had told him not to hang around with the black guys. Pete came to me and said the same thing. He loved and respected his father, but he totally ignored that advice about who he shouldn't hang out with.

Bill DeWitt gleefully cut my salary $5000 for the '64 season, though player salaries were not revealed in those days. I told the writers I'd taken a bad cut and said, "I'm going over to the Reds' office and have the stitches taken out."

DeWitt had labeled me a troublemaker for some years. Once I had assumed more of a leader's role in 1961, I began to speak out for myself and my teammates when I felt management was not doing right by us. As I became the oldest player in point of service on the team, other players would bring problems to me. I would speak to the manager as if they were *my* problems, and we'd work them out or he'd send me to the front office.

I remember one spring when the team was split into two squads, one to play a series in Mexico, the other to remain in Tampa. Those who were going to Mexico were told to vacate their rooms and store their belongings so the club could save some money at the Causeway Inn. Players staying in Tampa would double up. Vada was staying and I was to make the trip, but I said I didn't want to store my clothes for three days as they'd all have to be cleaned and pressed on my return.

I was told I could leave my stuff in the room with Vada, but the other players would have to store their belongings and double up. I protested, saying that wasn't fair to the other players, and finally I was able to persuade the powers that be to give everyone the same deal I had. For that and a number of similar incidents, I was called a troublemaker by DeWitt. I heard this so much I finally said, "So be it. But I am always going to speak out when I think I'm right."

Early in the '64 season Fred Hutchinson grew seriously ill. When word got out that he was taking cobalt treatments, we knew he had cancer. Coach Dick Sisler took over as manager, but Hutch came to the ballpark and sat on the bench every day. And every day he looked worse, weight steadily falling off him until he was so bent at the waist that he couldn't straighten up. He was obviously in great pain, his features set in a gaunt grimace. Every day we watched Hutch die a little more.

It was so trying, so tough on everybody on the ballclub, seeing Hutch wasting away, and everyone was trying so hard to win the pennant for him. I think many of us tried too hard, played too tight in an effort to win for Hutch. It was as if, in the back of all our minds, we had the feeling that every mistake we made on the field would intensify his pain. And I honestly believe that if it hadn't been for Hutch's physical presence on the bench, we would have won the pennant that year. We lost by only one game to the Cardinals.

But Hutch wanted to be with us. He knew he was dying, and he wanted to be around the team and the game he loved as long as he could. That was understandable.

By September Hutch was no longer up to coming to the ballpark. He made one final appearance in the last week of the season, now bent over like a very old man. He was helped to a chair in the middle of the clubhouse, and the room grew silent as he summoned the energy to speak. Then he said in a hoarse whisper, "I don't want you to win it for me; I want you to win it for yourselves."

We tried, but we just missed. Hutch died in November.

I felt I had a good enough year—a .306 average, 29 home runs, and 96 RBIs—to get my pay cut restored for 1965. Bill CheapWitt, naturally, didn't feel that way. We debated the point for months and I didn't sign my contract until a week before spring training. I got back only half my $5000 cut.

It didn't matter, because 1965 was my last year in Cincinnati. I'd had enough of Bill DeWitt, and I had little respect for his assistant, Phil Seghi, who traveled a lot with the ballclub and served as a spy for his boss. Seghi was a former minor league manager, and he loved to second-guess Dick Sisler. Dick was a very good manager, and he would have been better if the front office had just left him alone. But DeWitt and Seghi didn't really want to hire him in the first place. With Hutch ill but still present, though, DeWitt couldn't bring in an outsider. Then when we finished only a game out of first place, Sisler had to be rehired. Of course, they dumped him the first chance they got, the next year when we finished fourth.

But on December 9, 1965, my life in Cincinnati was history. I had been traded to the Baltimore Orioles in the American League, a club that had won 94 games and was looking to improve in 1966. I would see what I could do about that.

First, though, I had to sign an Oriole contract. But when I began negotiations with general manager Harry Dalton, I thought maybe I was still in Cincinnati. I had made $62,500 in 1965, and that was exactly what Dalton offered me.

"Look," I said, "it's traditional when you go out and trade for a top player that you give him a raise. Even if it's only a token raise, you want to welcome him. And after all, I'm coming off a pretty good year, Harry. I was third in the league in home runs with 33, second in RBIs with 113, and I batted .296."

"Those are pretty good stats, Frank," Dalton said, "but you didn't produce them for us."

"Wait a minute," I said. "I didn't trade for me. *You* did. I can't go ask Cincinnati for a raise."

We went back and forth for weeks. Dalton finally offered a $2500 raise, but I wanted $3500 more. That was where we stood when spring training opened in February and the rest of the players reported to the base in Miami. A week later Dalton convinced me to drive down there, and in a short meeting with him, I signed for the figure I wanted, $68,500. A $6000 raise was probably three times as much as I would have gotten in Cincinnati. I was happy.

6

CAMARADERIE IN BALTIMORE

B_{ARBARA} had given birth to our daughter Nichelle in August 1965, and now that our family was complete, we started looking for a house to buy in Los Angeles. We looked at a number of homes, and after I was traded, we began looking even harder. We finally found the house we wanted in a neighborhood we liked. But the agent, who was selling the house for a builder who had constructed several in the area, lived next door to the one we were after. He refused to sell us the house, saying the people across the street objected to a black family moving in.

I told an attorney friend about the situation. He simply bought the house himself and quick-deeded it over to Barbara and me. One of the first things Barbara did was walk across the street and ask the people who lived there if they objected to having black neighbors. "Not at all," she was told, and those people turned out to be our best neighbors. But the builder's agent who lived next door to us did not speak to us throughout the six years we owned that house. When we bought our current house in 1971, we had no problem.

While I was in spring training with the Orioles, Barbara flew to Baltimore to find us a house to rent there. She phoned me, very upset, a couple of days later. "Frank, I heard about this professor from Johns Hopkins University who had a nice house for rent this summer. I called him and said, 'I'm Barbara Robinson. My husband plays for the Orioles, and I understand you have a house for rent.' He said he did and invited me to come see the place. But when I showed up and he saw I was black, he decided he didn't want to rent the house after all. He must have thought I was Mrs. *Brooks* Robinson."

When Barbara had similar problems the next day, I was furious. I went to see Jerry Hoffberger, who owned the Orioles, and told him what was going on. "If my family can't find a place to live in Baltimore, there's no sense in my trying to play with this ballclub. I'll just have to take my wife and kids back to California."

"We won't have any problem with that, Frank," he said, and he phoned someone.

The next evening Barbara called and said she had rented a house. "I didn't have any real selection, and everything I saw was in a black neighborhood," she said. "The place I took is filthy, with dog mess all over it. But I'll have it cleaned and fumigated, and it'll be all right." Welcome to Baltimore, I thought.

The only other blacks on the Orioles, Paul Blair and Sam Bowens, also lived in black neighborhoods. But I didn't mind. The house wasn't bad and the neighbors were nice, though Barbara kept wanting to move to a better neighborhood in subsequent years. It only took her five years to find the place she wanted, which was in a white neighborhood. Then she found the neighbors there didn't like us. Black stars were cheered only on the field in Baltimore then.

And we gave the home fans plenty to cheer about in 1966. We were in and out of first in April and May, then moved in front for good in mid-June, and finished with a .606 winning percentage, nine games ahead of the Minnesota Twins. I personally had what is known as a "career year." I became the first man to win the Triple Crown since Mickey Mantle ten years before. I led the league in batting (.316), in home runs (49), and in runs batted in (122). I also became the only man ever to be named Most Valuable Player in both major leagues. To top off this fabled season, we swept the Dodgers in four World Series games and I was named MVP and awarded a new Corvette by the editor of *Sport* magazine, Al Silverman.

I'd definitely had something to prove after Bill DeWitt told the press he had traded me because I was "an old thirty." And I took a new approach, having been labeled a troublemaker and called hostile. I was tired of hearing those things said about me and decided I was going to make an effort to be just the opposite of what people thought I was. I wasn't going to stop knocking the shortstop on his butt when sliding into second. But I made an effort to be more outgoing, to be more relaxed, and to smile more.

It was easy with the Orioles, a great bunch of guys who liked to have fun. Boog Powell, our 240-pound first baseman, took one look at my skinny legs and started calling me "Pencils." So I started calling Boog "Crisco." Curt Blefary, our left fielder, was called "Cuckoo" because, well, because he was a little crazy. When Earl Weaver, who had managed Curt in the minors, joined us as a coach in 1968, Blefary went into a slump and was benched by manager Hank Bauer. Curt walked down to where Earl was seated in the dugout, grabbed the front of his shirt, and said, "Listen, you little bleep. If you ever become manager of this ballclub and don't play me, I'll kill you." Earl removed Curt's hand and told him to settle down, which he did, but you never knew what Cuckoo might do.

Relief pitcher Eddie Watts was called "Squatty Body" because he was kind of short and plenty wide. Our stopper in the bullpen, Dick Hall, was known as "Turkey" because his head was mounted on a long, skinny neck. Dave Johnson, our young second baseman, was known as "Dumb Dumb" because no matter how well he was playing, he was always thinking of ways to try and do better. Eventually he'd think himself right into a slump.

"You gotta be dumb to do that, Davey," we'd tell him. "When things are going all right, you've got to learn to leave 'em alone."

Relief pitcher Moe Drabowsky was the biggest prankster on the club, a guy who kept everyone loose. You had to stay loose around Moe and be ready to move instantly, or the next thing you knew you'd find your shoe burning. He loved to give hotfoots. On every road trip, as guys leaned back and kind of dozed on the buses and airplanes, inevitably someone would come flying out of his seat with a "Yowllll!" and start stomping his foot. We knew "The Footer" had struck again. In the clubhouse Moe liked to slip the heads of a couple of matches between the sole and the uppers of a guy's shoe, then run a trail of lighter fluid from it to his locker and light it. We'd watch the flame race across the room until the sole of the unsuspecting soul ignited. Moe not only got every player on the team, he even hotfooted owner Jerry Hoffberger one day.

Jerry was a good guy, and he liked to come down to the clubhouse occasionally and schmooze with the players. He always kidded me about the shine on my shoes; they didn't resemble Vada Pinson's, but they were kept glossy. One day he kidded me when his own shoes were all scuffed up. I flipped him a quarter and said, "Here you go, Jerry, get yourself a shine." He laughed and kept the quarter.

When Moe wasn't firing someone's foot, he was scaring the skivvies off our shortstop, Luis Aparicio. Luis was afraid of any animal, but snakes were his greatest fear. So Moe would roll up a towel, slip up behind Luis, loop the towel around Luis's neck, and cry, "Snake!" Luis would scream, drop whatever was in his hand, and run out of the clubhouse. Next, Moe went into a gag shop and bought a bunch of rubber snakes. He'd wait until Luis was seated and drop a snake over his shoulder, it would slide down Luis's chest, and he'd feel like it was crawling. Luis would jump sky-high.

We went to Anaheim for a series, and Luis was seated at the clubhouse table writing the names of people he was leaving tickets for. Moe sat down next to him with a snake around his neck that looked so real you expected it to move. Luis glanced at Moe and resumed writing, saying, "You not gonna get me with no rubber snake today, Moe."

"That right, Luis?" Moe said. He slid his chair closer to Luis, as if he were waiting for the ticket list, until the snake's head was sticking out over Luis's shoulder. Luis turned his head, and his eyes were about 2 inches from that snake that looked so real its tongue actually seemed to flick out and in. Then the snake started to slither onto Luis's shoulder. Luis jumped up, flipped the table over, ran out of the clubhouse, out of the dugout, and all the way into center field.

A bunch of us ran out to him, and Luis, trembling, said, "I not goin' back in there till that snake's gone! That goddamn Drabowsky, he's nuts!"

Moe had gone to a pet shop and bought a live snake. Next he bought six little goldfish and put them in the glass water cooler in the bullpen. Moe Drabowsky had previously pitched for the A's in Kansas City (the same A's, incidentally, that had originated in Philadelphia and now play in Oakland), and when we visited there, Moe put goldfish in his former team's bullpen watercooler. The next day he bought spray cans of paint in orange and black, the Oriole colors, and used them to spray the Kansas City pitching rubbers and home plates.

But Moe topped all his pranks during the game when he used our bullpen phone to call the Kansas City pen and, having pitched for manager Alvin Dark, imitated his voice in ordering ace reliever Jack Aker to warm up. Aker got up and started throwing earlier than he normally would. A few minutes later Dark noticed that Aker was throwing. He grabbed the bullpen phone and angrily said, "What's Jack doing warming up?"

Moe watched the confusion in the Kansas City bullpen while laughing as hard as he could. We joined him after the game when we learned what he'd done. As I said, big Moe kept us loose.

A couple of Baltimore writers suggested that Brooks Robinson, who was in his eleventh year as an Oriole, and I would have problems. But Brooks was a great person, and we got along very well from the beginning. In fact, we had lockers next to one another for six years and never had a cross word.

I suspect Brooks was a key reason why, for the first time in my 14 years in professional baseball, black players and white players had drinks together and meals together when we were on the road. Not every single night but two or three times on most road trips. None of the players ever really invited me, Paul Blair, and Sam Bowens to join them. But Brooks might ask me where I was going after a game, and not knowing the restaurants in most American League cities, I might say I wasn't sure. Then Brooks would say something like, "Well Boog, Jerry [Adair], Curt [Blefary] and I are going over to this restaurant."

"Maybe I'll see you there later," I'd say.

We always knew where the group was going, and we'd end up there when we wanted to sit around over a meal or a few drinks and talk baseball. We all wanted to be together on the Orioles because we enjoyed one another's company and had a lot of respect for each individual as a person and as a player. Even when the food wasn't all that good, the talk and the camaraderie made for a lot of fun.

The shame of it was that this kind of mingling of the races had never happened before and it never happened to me again after my six years in Baltimore. I guess my only real disappointment during that time was that the black players and the white players never got together socially when we were playing at home. Not once did we have a meal together in a Baltimore restaurant or get together at a player's home. The black players and the white players were close on the Orioles, but not *that* close.

Some people said I immediately established myself as one of the leaders of the Orioles, bringing a more aggressive style of play to the club. I think the other players saw a veteran player like me playing hard hardball and they said, "If he can take out an infielder with a slide, if he can dive for the ball in the outfield, if he can make an important steal by diving into a base headfirst, if he can run into a fence to make a catch—then, hey, why not us?" In the very first month of the season Luis Aparicio, the smallest player on the team, slid into the opposing shortstop, who was coming across second to make a throw for a double play. He threw the ball into the ground because Luis flipped him onto his back. Instead of having two men out and nobody on base, we had a runner on first who later scored in the inning. And other Orioles began playing hard hardball.

So I was a leader of the Orioles on the field and in the clubhouse. I'd hear somebody griping about not getting enough playing time, and I'd say, "Settle down, don't rock the boat, you'll get your at-bats." Sometimes I'd even go to manager Hank Bauer and tell him that so-and-so was unhappy and that maybe he should speak to the guy.

But the point is that people may wonder why I, as a team leader, did not make an effort to initiate some socializing in Baltimore among the white players and the three blacks on the club. Looking back, maybe I should have suggested that a bunch of us go out to dinner some night with our wives, or even have Barbara put together a dinner or a cookout for a group of the guys and their wives at our house. But I had never been one to invite teammates to my house. In Cincinnati Barbara was very friendly with the wives of Vada Pinson and Leo Cardenas, our shortstop, and on occasion she would arrange for the six of us to have a meal at our place or go out together to a restaurant. But I was always essentially a loner.

There was another reason why I couldn't arrange black and white socializing in Baltimore even if it had been my nature to do that kind of thing. I would have been afraid to. If I had invited teammates over to my house and one of the white players or his wife did not show up, it might have affected the Orioles as a ballclub. I was always a team man above all else. From the beginning of my career, baseball was my life.

I remember that early in the '62 season in Cincinnati—my first season as a married man—Barbara would complain about various racial slights when I came home from games. "Barbara, to survive and to achieve what I am out to achieve," I said, "I have to be the best ballplayer that I can possibly be, and I cannot be coming home and discussing racial issues in baseball and in society every night. Those issues are going to be there every day no matter what I say or do. You just have to accept the fact that this is the society we live in and go forward and do the best you can. That's what I'm trying to do."

This was during my tenth year out in the world playing baseball, but Barbara was not what I would call a worldly person. She had been sheltered and protected while growing up, first in Oklahoma and then in Los Angeles. I was just trying to educate her as to what was happening in the world at large and what you had to do in order to live with the racial slights or whatever and still make your own place.

Barbara said I didn't see as many of the black slights as she did, that I looked right through many things because I didn't want to see them. It wasn't that I didn't see things; it was just that I didn't acknowledge the minor slurs or incidents. How else would I ever have been able to get through those years in the minor leagues if I had let every little swipe at my black skin bug me and impinge on my performance on the ball field? Just like every other black player from Jackie Robinson on through the first decade of integration in the formerly white-only game, I did what I had to do to survive.

I told Barbara about an incident that happened to Vada Pinson and me in 1961 after we clinched the pennant in Chicago and flew home to Cincinnati. "When we landed, the whole city was out celebrating our victory," I said, "and we were all heroes. It was like New Year's eve, and people were dancing in the streets and cheering the Reds. Well, we were told there would be a party for the team at a little club downtown. So Vada and I hopped into a cab and went down there. But as we started walking into the club, the owner stopped us.

"'You can't come in here,' he said, 'no Negroes allowed.'

"There was a crowd outside the club, and a woman stepped over to the owner and said, 'That's Frank Robinson and Vada Pinson.'

"'Oh, well you guys are all right,' the owner said, 'go right in.'

"Barbara, I walked past that guy, Vada right beside me, marched into the place, through the bar, and out the back door. I never looked back. I wanted to be at that celebration with my teammates, but I couldn't be. And there was nothing I could have done about it except make a scene and mess up things for everyone. It just wasn't worth it. Vada and I went to a club where we knew we were welcome, ordered a drink, and toasted ourselves."

The only time all the Orioles' players got together socially in Baltimore in 1966 was at the invitation of a big fan who had a big house and a bit swimming pool. It started out as a good time for me on an off day, but ended up in near disaster. I was just lounging by the pool with Barbara and some of the other players who weren't swimming when Curt Blefary came over threatening to throw everyone in the pool. A couple of the guys grabbed me and said, "You're going in, Frank."

"I don't swim," I said.

"You're going in anyway," I was told.

"Okay, let go of me," I said, figuring I'd jump into the shallow end and they'd leave me alone. Anything for team unity.

The problem was that when I jumped into the shallow end, I slid down on the slippery tile into deeper water. When I came up, I was in over my head and too far from the side to grab on. I started slapping my arms but went under again. When I emerged a second time, panicked and gasping for air, I yelled, "Help, help me!" and went under again. I hit bottom and couldn't get to the surface again. I thought, "Here we all get together at a home outing, and I'm going to drown!"

Finally catcher Andy Etchebarren dove in, pushed me to the surface and over to the poolside, where two other guys lifted me out, and I could breathe once more. I was never so scared in my life.

I hadn't thought about that incident for years until Al Campanis said on *Nightline* that blacks did not have the "necessities" to be given managerial positions in baseball and then said there were other things that blacks could not do, like become swimmers because "they lacked buoyancy." Well, Al, here's one who can't swim a stroke.

The only other problem I had in 1966 occurred in June when I singled in a game and, while rounding first, heard my right knee pop. I'd torn cartilage in it. The knee kept taking on fluid that had to be drained. It was sore, but I had it taped and played anyway. Surgery was performed after the World Series, and I was walking around in a few days.

I wanted to be ambulatory as soon as possible because an agent had told me I could expect to make at least $20,000 in endorsements of products and commercial fees in the off-season. "After the year you've had, Frank, you can't miss," the man said.

As it turned out, I made one TV appearance and two $500 speaking engagements that winter. I asked the agent what happened. "Look," he said, "they don't want you, and there's nothing I can do about it." They didn't want me because I was black. At that time blacks weren't getting many commercial offers, but I thought this was a little ridiculous.

After the 1967 season, in which Carl Yastrzemski of the Red Sox won the Triple Crown and was named MVP of the league, he was signed up for commercial deals that would pay him $200,000 over the following three years. Yastrzemski is white.

At least I didn't have any trouble getting the salary I wanted for 1967. When I went in to see Harry Dalton, he handed me a sheet of paper and told me to write down the figure I wanted and he would write down the Oriole offer on another sheet of paper. I wrote "$125,000" and handed the paper to Harry.

"Geez!" he said.

I looked at his figure, "$100,000," and said, "Geez!"

We both laughed. Then Harry said. "We can't give you that figure, Frank."

"That's okay, Harry," I said, "because I can play for $100,000." That was the magic figure in those days, as only Ted Williams, Mickey Mantle, Willie Mays, and Sandy Koufax had earned as much in a season for playing baseball.

After I signed the contract, there was a press conference. Ballplayers were always at a disadvantage because teams did not release salary figures and players, myself included, foolishly did not exchange information about what their peers were earning to use in contract negotiations. But when a player reached the $100,000 mark, the ballclub announced it. A writer asked me, "You've got your 100 grand now, Frank, so where do you go from here?"

"What's wrong with $200,000?" I said.

"There's no way any player's ever going to make that kind of money," the writer said.

Now some players make close to $200,000 a *week*.

In 1967 I got off to an even better start than I had in my Triple Crown year, and by late June I was leading the league in batting average and RBIs and was second in home runs. But the team was playing terrible baseball. We were picked to repeat as pennant winners, and we weren't even playing .500 ball. Too many of the guys were just sitting back waiting for the breaks instead of going out and making things happen. I had spoken to a couple of the guys about this but had met only resentment from them.

Writers always tend to think that dissension's involved when a good team's suddenly going badly for a couple of months. After a 9-2 loss to the A's, a writer asked me if there was dissension on the Orioles. I thought a long moment before answering. Dissension wasn't the right word, but the one I uttered wasn't right either.

"It's jealousy," I said.

"What are they jealous of?" the writer asked.

"They're jealous of me, I think."

The moment I said it, I was sorry, but what I had said was all over the newspapers the next day. I know what I was trying to do, which was shake up the team, get guys mad enough to go out and play hard and win some ballgames. But we continued to play uninspired baseball.

About a week later we lost a game in the ninth inning that really ticked me off. We were leading by a run when the White Sox loaded the bases with one out. The next batter hit a ball to Boog Powell at first. He threw home for the force at the plate, and catcher Andy Etchebarren started to fire the ball back to first for an inning-ending double play. He had stepped off the plate and out on the cut of the infield grass. But the White Sox runner from third, Tommy McCraw, slid out of the baseline and knocked Andy down. Photos the next day showed clearly that the batter should have been called out. But the umpire did not call McCraw's interference and we lost.

So I was still angry the next night when I singled leading off the fourth inning. Brooks Robinson hit a hard grounder to third, and I went into second base a little harder than usual trying to stir things up by making sure I leveled the second baseman coming across for the throw. I was going to hit Al Weis with my legs, my body, or, as a last resort, my arms, but I was determined to take him out of the play. I did, but Weis's knee hit me just above the left eye and knocked me unconscious for about five minutes. Al Weis ended up requiring knee surgery, and I ended up with double vision for the next year and a half. I knew I was seeing double the next morning in the hospital. When a nurse asked me how many fingers she was holding up, I said, "Two"; then she told me she had only her index finger raised.

I sat out for a month at home in Baltimore, wondering if my vision would ever return to normal or if my career was over. That was the first time I thought seriously about managing. To stay in the game, I might have to quit playing and seek a manager's job in the minors. Gene Baker, a black ex-player, had broken that barrier by landing a job managing in the Cubs' farm system. Then I decided, double vision or not, I had to go back to the Orioles and see if I could hit.

I could, after a fashion and after changing my style of hitting. I couldn't pick up pitches quick enough to continue diving into the ball as I had, so I began rocking back on my heels. I guess I wasn't smart enough to back off the plate a bit, but I didn't want anyone to know I couldn't see well.

My double vision was up and down, not sideways. I found that as long as I tucked my chin into my shoulder I was okay, but once there was any movement, I had trouble. When I started my swing, I saw double. I knew I couldn't pick up the ball soon enough to get out of the way of it quickly. But somehow during this time I wasn't afraid at the plate. It wasn't until later, when the vision cleared up late in the next season and I thought about hitting in this condition, that I found it scary. Then I decided that in playing as I had with a serious vision disability, I must have been crazy.

What the injury did was short-circuit what I call my communication system at the plate. Soon after the ball leaves the pitcher's hand, I'd see the rotation on the ball, which told me whether it was a fastball or a breaking ball. Then I'd start my swing, and if it wasn't a pitch I wanted to hit, I would stop my bat; if it was my pitch, I would swing away. But with the double vision I couldn't check my swing because I couldn't read the pitch quickly enough and decide if it was a strike. By having to commit to a swing early, I no longer could take the close pitches.

I had been hitting .337 when I was injured, and somehow I finished at .311 with 30 home runs (only 9 in the last two months) and 94 RBIs. I thought I deserved a $30,000 raise. Harry Dalton disagreed, saying the Orioles had finished in sixth place, 15½ games out of first, and had drawn well under a million fans in 1967. I said neither of those circumstances was my fault and held out eight days into spring training before I finally settled for a salary of $115,000, placing me behind only Sandy Koufax ($135,000) and Willie Mays ($125,000) in pay for play in 1968.

I thought I would have a big season, but it turned out to be my worst. First I went out and played without conditioning my right arm properly, and I tore muscles in it on a throw back to the infield after a hit. I worked the arm into halfway decent shape by opening day, but late in April I was sidelined for 2½ weeks by, yes, fans, that traditional baseball injury— the mumps. But my worst problem continued to be the double vision that plagued me at bat. I ended up hitting .268 with a paltry 15 home runs and 52 RBIs. I just couldn't see the ball.

And for the first time, the fans in Baltimore booed me, not only because I wasn't hitting. Baltimore is a working man's town, and the fans were obviously annoyed that I had held out so long in the spring. After I would strike out at Memorial Stadium, some fan would bellow from the stands: "You're down to $90,000 now, Robinson!"

Every time I made an out, it seemed the fans got on me, and it hurt. Any time you hear a player say he doesn't hear the booing, that he shuts it out, he's lying. No one likes to be booed, particularly at home, and it really bothered me that these same people who had regularly cheered me now let me know they thought I was horse spit.

But the thing that bothered me most of all was my inability to perform at the plate and help the ballclub. With a number of my teammates also not playing up to their usual capabilities, the Orioles continued to flounder. And we were the ones who cost manager Hank Bauer his job. During the All-Star Game break, first-year coach Earl Weaver was named manager. In the fall Harry Dalton had fired three of Bauer's coaches, keeping only Billy Hunter at third base. Dalton had hired Earl Weaver, a long-time manager in the Orioles' farm system, and two other veteran coaches in the organization, pitching coach George Bamberger and bullpen coach Vern Hoscheit.

I had a lot of respect for Hank Bauer, who was a good manager to play for if you were a veteran. He was a little rough on some younger players and jumped on them for their mistakes. He wasn't much of a strategist: He used few bunts or hit-and-run plays; he just let us hit and play for the big inning. It was kind of a shame that he was fired because of our performance.

Still, I recalled when Bauer called a meeting after one of our bad series and rightfully chewed out a number of players for lackadaisical play. But then he snapped, "I'll be here when a lot of you guys are gone." Some of us just looked at one another. We knew a team doesn't fire its players; it fires the manager.

I hadn't passed more than a few words with Earl Weaver—which was a few more than Hank Bauer had passed with the coach who had been foisted upon him and whom he regarded as a threat to his job. But Earl immediately made a couple of moves that really helped our offense. He began platooning left-handed-hitting catcher Elrod Hendricks with Andy Etchebarren, who had trouble getting his bat on hard-breaking balls from right-handed pitchers. Earl also began playing switch-hitting outfielder Donny Buford full-time. Buford was not a good defensive outfielder, but he knew how to get on base and could steal 30 bases or more a year. He played left field against southpaws, against whom Curt Blefary had big trouble, and center field against right-handers, against whom Paul Blair had big trouble. Blair was the best center fielder in the league, but Earl gave up some defense to score more runs.

Even though I still wasn't swinging the bat well, I tried other tactics to generate runs. In the first week after Weaver took over, I slid headfirst into bases three times because it's the quickest way to get there. And once, on a shallow fly to left field, I tagged up and scored the winning run in the ninth inning with a headfirst slide.

Earl Weaver definitely got us moving, all the way up to second place as we won 91 games. I finally began to see the ball a bit better in late September and began diving into the ball again. But while the double vision was not as marked, it wasn't totally gone and I was still concerned about how long I could play.

Earl Weaver had managed Santurce in the Puerto Rican league the last two winters. Late in the season a few of us were sitting around talking to Earl when he said, "The Santurce club's got to find another manager this year."

I quickly said, "What about me?"

"Are you serious?" Earl asked.

"I'm very serious," I said. "I'm thinking about becoming a manager when I eventually retire, so I might as well start getting some experience."

We were in New York at this time, for the last few games of the season. Earl had his wife Marianna with him, and they had a dinner date that evening. But I found out afterward that he blew it waiting in his hotel room for the owner of the Santurce Crabbers to return his call. Earl later said, "I was making $28,000 and blowing a dinner date trying to get a winter job for a ballplayer who's making $115,000." Thanks, Earl.

I talked to the Santurce team owner, Hiram Cuevas, and got the job. This made me the first American black ever to manage an integrated professional baseball team. It was a job I came to love so much that I kept it a total of nine years. Working for Hiram Cuevas will always remain one of the most enjoyable and enlightening experiences of my life.

7

⑨ *MANAGING IN PUERTO RICO*

I was aware that—in addition to Earl Weaver—Cal Ermer, Preston Gomez, and Larry Shepard had in the last four years gone from managing in Puerto Rico to managing in the major leagues. So if I did well in the 70-game '68 season, it had to help my résumé. I was expected to do well because I had a very fine team, and I did. At one point we tied Earl's league record by winning 14 straight games, set a record with 49 wins for the season, won the pennant by 5½ games, and I was voted "Manager of the Year."

But I realized from the start that I had a lot to learn about managing a ballclub. As a veteran player I had thought it would be relatively easy, but I was surprised at how many split-second decisions I had to make—I mean instantly—during a game. You had to constantly think ahead and anticipate your opponents' potential moves so that you could counter them, and you could not afford to forget anything.

In one game we were losing 4-0 early and cut the lead to 4-3. The other team got two men on base, and I had a left-hander and a right-hander warming up. A right-handed hitter was coming up, so I signaled for my right-handed pitcher to come in. Then one of my coaches said, "Frank, he was just loosening up because he has a little stiffness in his arm." He had told me that earlier, and I'd forgotten.

I had to bring in the left-hander, who promptly gave up a hit, and we went on to lose, 8-4. As a player when I made a mistake or went into a slump, I never took the game home with me. But it seemed that as a manager I took things home with me every night. It was hard to believe I'd forgotten that I didn't want to use a pitcher with a stiff arm and then called on him.

My biggest problem the first year in Puerto Rico—which probably took me two or three years to work out fully—was in handling pitchers. Elrod Hendricks, my Oriole teammate and my Santurce catcher, told me, "Frank, I think you have hated pitchers for so long as a player that you have trouble relating to them as a manager."

He was right. I did not take kindly to failures and to excuses for failures that some pitchers made. I don't think any good hitter has ever really felt like a pitcher is his friend. There is a natural animosity because you're always competing against a pitcher. He's trying to get you out of a ballgame without a hit, and you're trying to knock him out of the game. So it did take me a while to relate to the situation that a pitcher was in and the problems he faced.

Yet the only pitcher who tried to give me a hard time was the veteran Juan Pizarro, who had been doing his own thing for years. He had never thrown between starts and didn't want to. But the Oriole pitchers on my staff, Wally Bunker, Jim Hardin, Dave Leonhard, and Jim Palmer (who was working out arm problems of the year before), as well as 41-year-old Ruben Gomez, all threw between starts. I told Pizarro that I'd have to fine him if he didn't join the others in the prescribed routine. Juan finally came around and said, "I'll do whatever you want, Frank." We got along after that.

The only hitters who tried to give me a bad time were first baseman George Scott and third baseman Joe Foy of the Red Sox. When they weren't hitting, I naturally dropped them down in the batting order and they bitched and moaned. Scott thought he should be batting fourth no matter how poorly he was swinging the bat. Not on my team. I thought it was strange that here I was the first black manager and the only guys giving me trouble happened to be black.

I wasn't as loose as some of the other managers were with their ballclubs in Puerto Rico. I had rules that you had to be at the ballpark at a certain time, you had to be in uniform at a certain time, you had to take infield at a certain time, and you had to take batting practice at a certain time every day. Guys would show up a little late, I would challenge them on it, and they'd get upset. All the players were ostensibly there to improve their skills in winter ball. That was why the owners of their ballclubs wanted them down there. But there were always some players who looked at playing winter ball in Puerto Rico as a paid vacation.

George Scott had been to the plate 350 times for the Red Sox the previous season and had hit .171 with exactly three home runs. I thought he should have been more concerned with his hitting than with where he was listed in the batting order. After I'd made my point a couple of times, George settled down and became very productive at the plate.

No matter what I had to do to discipline a player for lateness, for not running out a ball or whatever, whether I fined him or sat him down for a time, Hiram Cuevas stood behind me from day 1. He let me run the ballclub the way I saw fit and never even questioned any of my field decisions. Hiram, who had bought the Crabbers from his father and who was the only independent owner in the six-team league, is a man I respect as much as any man I've ever met.

Hiram Cuevas was a good, solid businessman with a lot of baseball knowledge. We spent much time together talking baseball, and I learned a lot from him about the game. I also learned a lot about myself in talking to Hiram, because he had a great mind for reading people and understanding different personalities.

We would sit down and talk about life, and about people, and Hiram would speak openly and honestly about me. I think he helped make me a better person. He made me look at myself objectively, probably for the first time in my life, and I began to see myself more clearly than I ever had before. He talked to me about the way I carried myself, about the way I conducted myself, and about what people thought of me.

"I don't care what people think about me," I said to him. "I never have cared what people think about me."

"Frank, you're wrong," Hiram said. "Everyone cares what others think of them. You care what people think of you, but you've never admitted it to yourself. You've been afraid to let people get close to you, to get to know you as a person. People don't know you, and therefore they are put off by your manner."

"What do you mean?" I asked him.

"Frank, you never smile," Hiram said. "You always look so serious, so intense, and people take you the wrong way. They stand back from you, are afraid to approach you. Just smile a little more, be a little more open, and people will be able to approach you."

Hiram Cuevas really helped me come out of my shell. I started trying to appear more relaxed, to be less off-putting to people and more inviting. I guess I'm still trying.

Hiram and I talked a lot over dinner after games, and several of our discussions that first year centered on our second baseman, Julio Gotay, of the Cardinals' organization. The Cardinals, who liked Gotay's bat, wanted him to work on his fielding, and I found out why. He did some very funny things on the field.

During our first game in Caguas, they had a tough, right-handed pull hitter, and we had decided to shade him heavily to left field, with Gotay playing over behind second base. But the first time the hitter came to bat, Gotay was playing him as if he were a left-handed pull hitter. I stood up and motioned him over toward second. Gotay shook his head no and didn't move an inch. I went running out to him.

"What's wrong, Julio?" I said. "You're supposed to be playing over behind second base."

"No, no!" he said, shaking his head and pointing toward the bag. There were two sticks on the ground by the base, one lying atop the other in the shape of a cross. By this time Elrod Hendricks had joined me.

"He's superstitious about crosses," Elrod said. "Julio won't go near a cross. Something to do with evil spirits. He believes in voodoo and evil spirits."

Now Gotay was nodding his head, as if to say, yes, if I go near that cross, the evil spirits will get me.

Hendricks walked over, picked up the sticks, and Gotay cried, "No, no, do not touch!"

Elrod looked at him disdainfully and said, "Bleep." Then he flung the sticks into the outfield.

"That's bad, very bad!" Gotay said. "You'll be sorry you did that. You'll see."

Hendricks moved back behind the plate, and Gotay moved over behind second where he belonged. Elrod gave the sign, the first pitch came in, the batter swung, and his bat came all the way around and smacked Hendricks in the back of his head. He was knocked out cold.

We all ran to him, and Julio Gotay said, "See, I told you!"

"Julio, get back out in the field," I said. "And shut up!"

Hendricks had to go to the hospital for X-rays, which proved to be negative. At least, I thought, the evil spirits didn't break bones.

In another game, in Mayagüez, there was a runner on first and a ball was hit to our shortstop, Leo Cardenas, who fielded the ball and threw toward Gotay, who was headed for second to take the throw on the bag, pivot, and go to first for the double play. But as the ball was coming at him, Gotay stopped in his tracks two steps from second base.

He caught the ball, let the runner go past him, turned, and threw to first for one out.

What the hell is he doing now? I wondered. I called time and went running out to Gotay. Before I could say anything, he was pointing at the bag. There I saw why he had refused to go near second base. Someone on the Mayagüez ballclub had heard about Gotay's superstitions and had neatly drawn a cross in the dirt by the bag.

I looked at Julio, who really looked scared, and I said nothing. I just walked over to the cross in the base path and wiped it out with my foot. "No, no!" he said.

"Yes, yes," I said. "Now let's play ball."

It got so that before each ballgame, I would run out to second with my infield and make sure that no signs of a cross were anywhere near second base. But I think that if I had been an outfielder playing against Julio Gotay, I would have glued two popsicle sticks into the shape of a cross, and any time he came running toward my base, I would have pulled it from my pocket, flashed it, and stopped him dead in the base path.

Even without a cross in evidence, Gotay did some peculiar things in the field. With a man on first base and the infield playing in, if a ball is hit to the second baseman, he normally tags the runner coming past him (even if he misses, the umpire usually signals out because the runner has gone out of the baseline) and then throws to first for the double play. But Gotay would catch the ball, step up to tag the runner—and get run over by him. I mean, knocked head over heels on his butt. This happened five, six, seven times.

After each incident I would go out with Julio the next day and say, "You don't let the man run into you." Then I'd show him how to catch the ball and swipe at the man coming past.

It wasn't until the last few weeks of the season that Gotay finally learned how to make the play without getting clobbered by the base runner. Of course, by that time he was bruised and scraped all over.

I think I showed a lot of patience with Gotay, particularly after one playoff game. Both teams were scoreless in the final inning, and the opposition loaded the bases with one out. I went to the mound and called my infielders over. "If you get a hard-hit ground ball, go for the double play," I said. "If there's a slow-hit ground ball, throw to the plate." The only player I looked at, to be sure he understood, was Gotay.

I ran back to the dugout, the count went to 3-and-2, and then the batter hit a grounder to Gotay. He scooped it up, stepped in, and started to throw home, where the runner would have been out easily. But then he suddenly turned and flipped the ball to Cardenas at second for a force-out... as the winning run crossed home plate.

I was too mad to ask Gotay why he had done that. In fact, I was so mad I was afraid that if I got near him, I would kill him.

But it was fun managing in Puerto Rico, even though it became apparent to me after three or four years that the players who caused me the most problems were invariably black. Elrod Hendricks noticed it too and said to me, "These guys have always been used to having white coaches and managers telling them what to do. Now they've got you, a black manager, and it's like they think they're free at last, that they can do whatever they want to do."

There was no question that some of my black players felt they deserved some favoritism from me, some special treatment because I was black. What they didn't understand was that I looked at everybody not as a black player or a white player but simply as a ballplayer. If I felt a guy was wrong, I came down on him no matter what color he was because I didn't notice what color he was. It was a problem. Blacks tested me far more than whites. They felt they would have it much easier with me, that they wouldn't be watched as closely, wouldn't be disciplined as hard, wouldn't have to worry about abiding by the rules, such as being prompt as I required.

Mickey Rivers, then of the Angels' organization, played some outstanding ball for me with the Crabbers, but he was always testing me. Rivers later became notorious with both the Angels and the Yankees for his love of gambling on the horses. In Puerto Rico he loved to gamble in the casinos. Sometimes he gambled into the early morning hours, which tended to result in his being late to the ballpark in the afternoon.

"Mickey, you know that's gonna cost you," I'd say.

"I think I feel a little feverish, Frank," he'd say.

"You look fine, Mickey. Get out on the ball field in the fresh air, and you'll feel fine."

Nobody put on a suit in Puerto Rico unless he was going out to a nightclub, a fancy restaurant, or a casino. Otherwise the guys dressed casually in sports shirts and slacks. One day Rivers called me at the ballpark, Hiram Bithorn Stadium in San Juan, and said he was sick, too sick to play. "I think I've got some kind of tropical flu, Frank."

"Well come to the park, and we'll have a doctor check you out," I said.

"I can see a doctor right near where I'm staying," he said.

"No, come in and have the team doctor check you."

Ten minutes later Rivers arrived at the stadium dressed in a suit and tie. "Were you gonna have a doctor at the casino look you over?" I asked.

"No, no, I just thought I'd feel better if I got dressed."

"If you're well enough to put on a suit, you're well enough to suit up," I said. "Get your butt out on the ball field." Rivers went out and got three hits and stole two bases that night.

Another problem I often faced in Puerto Rico was having to talk some players out of quitting midway through the season and going home. Guys would get discouraged if they weren't playing well in winter ball, which was closer to AAA ball than the major league level. The teams could have no more than 8 "imports," and the other 15 players had to have at least one parent who was born in Puerto Rico. So I generally had a team of pretty good young players and eight imports who played regularly; some of the talents included Reggie Jackson and Dave Kingman, who played winter ball to work on their hitting.

While I was usually successful in talking players out of quitting, I failed with Dave Kingman. He came down to try to improve his hitting against breaking balls. But after a couple of months of flailing away at breaking balls that he seldom made contact with, Kingman said he was going home. It seemed like we had an unusually large number of good curveball and hard-slider pitchers in the league that winter. I told Kingman that it would be difficult for us to get a replacement for him two months into the season and that I would work with him on his hitting if he'd stay. But Dave Kingman was always a stubborn ballplayer, and he went home. He hit a lot of home runs in his career, but very few off good breaking balls, I'm sure.

Reggie Jackson also wanted to quit on me in 1970. Reggie had hit 47 home runs in 1969 and batted .275 with 118 RBIs in 1969. But in 1970 he batted .237 with only 23 home runs and 66 RBIs. He had held out deep into spring training while battling with Oakland A's owner Charley Finley over his contract. Reggie had known nothing but success until that off-season in 1970, and he decided he'd like to play for me that winter and see if he could get his hitting stroke back. He contacted Hiram Cuevas, who was overjoyed at the prospect of having Reggie Jackson aboard to pull more fans into our games.

Now, Reggie Jackson has always been cocky. He's a little more subdued these days, but he still maintains a very high opinion of himself and he likes to play by his own rules. When he joined the Crabbers, he let me know early on that he didn't feel the need to play by my rules. In one of our first games Reggie hit a high pop fly to the infield. He stood in the batter's box watching it come down.

Reggie came back to the dugout, and I said, "Next time you don't run a ball out, it'll cost you $200."

In his next at-bat, Reggie popped up and did not run. "That's $200, Reggie," I said.

A few days later Reggie grounded out to second, took three steps up the line, and turned into the dugout with a disgusted look on his face. "That's another $200 out of your check," I said.

"I've had enough of this crap," Reggie said, and he stormed off toward the clubhouse. "I'm gonna pack and get out of here."

I followed him, knowing Reggie was really mad at himself after not having a hit in five straight games. "Wait for me," I said. "The way you're playing, you'll need somebody to help you pack up."

"Frank, I'm not running out on you," Reggie said. "It's my eyes; I want to go home and get fitted for some glasses. The ball's jumping all over the place on me, and I can't follow it."

"Great idea," I said, nodding. "One thing, though, Reggie. Make sure you get those special curveball lenses. They'll straighten those snakes right out."

Reggie laughed, and from then on he never failed to run out a ball he hit.

But Reggie didn't hit many balls anyplace during the first half of the season. He had only three home runs, his batting average was under .200, and he was leading the league in strikeouts. He was totally confused and frustrated, and he came to me and said, "I've had it, Frank. I'm not doing myself any good or the ballclub any good. I might as well go home."

"Reggie," I said, "If you're willing to listen and work hard, I'll help you with your hitting. I have a mental picture of the way you hit two years ago, and you're not hitting that way now. You're just gonna have to have confidence in me. But you'll have to start all over at the plate. You're gonna have to crawl before you walk, and you'll have to walk before you run."

"I'm willing to do it, Frank," he said. "Just tell me what I have to do."

Reggie and I went out to the stadium an hour early every day with a pitcher to throw him batting practice. And Reggie worked very, very hard. During the games themselves, I had Reggie sit next to me after each of his at-bats, and I talked to him about what he had done right and what he had done wrong at the plate. I went over every aspect of his hitting point by point: stride, head position, bat speed, pitch selection. And gradually he started hitting the ball the way Reggie Jackson should hit it. He ended up hitting 20 home runs in 57 games, and 3 more in the playoffs. The last man to hit as many as 20 home runs in the Puerto Rican league was Williard Brown, who hit 26 in the '40s, but never had an opportunity to play major league baseball because he was black.

Barbara and the children were with me in Puerto Rico through the Christmas holidays. When they went home, I invited Reggie to move into my two-bedroom apartment with me. After the season and the playoffs we went on to the Caribbean series, so we didn't go home until the first week of February. Reggie and I spent a lot of time together talking baseball and also talking about him as a person.

Reggie had a lot of high praises to heap on himself. He felt that his ballclub, the Oakland A's, could not be successful without him. "If I don't hit, the team can't win," he said. "I should be captain of the team."

I had to kind of tear down Reggie. Nobody could tell him anything if he didn't respect the person, and he's still basically the same way today. But he told me he had a lot of respect for me, for what I had done and was doing as a player and a manager, so I was very honest with him.

"Reggie, you can't ram yourself down people's throats," I told him. "If you want to be captain of the A's, you can't campaign for it. Number 1, your teammates have to respect you. They really watch the way you carry yourself, the way you conduct yourself on and off the field. You have to watch what you say. You just can't keep pushing yourself and get the respect you need from your teammates.

"And one player does not make a ballclub, no matter how good he is. You have an awful lot of talent on your ballclub. You've got Catfish Hunter, Blue Moon Odom, Sal Bando, Joe Rudi, Rick Monday, Rollie Fingers, Gene Tenace—a team full of solid ballplayers."

It took a while and a lot of conversation, but I thought Reggie not only improved on the ball field but as a person. He began to get his head together a little bit and developed a better outlook on how he should carry himself and on how he should treat other people. I told him he had to cut down on some of his arrogance and pushiness. "Let people approach you; don't always push yourself on others," I said.

We had many long, long talks into the night, and we got along very well together. A number of people asked me then and I hear the same question today: "How in the world can you be friends with Reggie Jackson?"

"Easy," I say. "Reggie is not a bad guy."

He listened. I remember one game in which Reggie struck out three times and then he angrily threw his bat. I took him aside and said, "Hey, if you're going to be a leader, you can't have 30 good days and then act like a kid when you have one bad day. You don't want to throw away in one day what you've accomplished in the preceding 30 days."

Reggie never threw his bat again while he was playing for me.

As it happened, the Orioles met the A's in the playoffs at the end of our next season, 1971. In one game Reggie hit two home runs against us, and as he rounded first base running out the second homer, he tipped his cap to me in right field. Later he said to me, "That was a gesture of appreciation for what you've done for me."

I smiled and said, "You're welcome, Reggie." He'd had a good season, hitting 32 home runs and batting .277. I could be magnanimous because we swept the A's in three games.

About ten years later I ran into Reggie and mentioned that I was planning to buy a VCR. A few days later he sent me one of the VCRs that Panasonic advertised as "Reggie-Vision." Enclosed was a note that said, "Thanks, Frank."

8

PLAYING FOR EARL WEAVER

W_{HEN} I returned from Puerto Rico for spring training in 1969, writers asked me if I hoped eventually to manage in the major leagues. That was a job a black man had never been offered, but the times seemed to be changing, and there was now regular speculation that Willie Mays, Henry Aaron, Elston Howard, and I among others, were "candidates for appointment as the first Negro manager in the major leagues." I acknowledged that I wanted that opportunity when my playing days were over.

The late columnist Milton Gross asked me if I regarded my winter job as a step forward toward my goal. "I don't see it as a step forward," I said. "It's not a step backward, but the managing job wasn't in the States. If it was, it would have been a step forward. It was just a tremendous opportunity for me that doesn't come every day to a man who is still playing. I was handling major leaguers, minor leaguers, American players, and Latin players, a composite of personalities. I certainly know the game. What I wanted to prove was that I could handle men. Mainly I wanted to prove it to myself. I do have a reputation of being a hothead."

We were talking in the clubhouse, and just then Paul Blair came by and said, "Hey, Frank, you going to be the first Negro manager?"

Milton Gross corrected him, saying, "It's black, not Negro."

I smiled and said, "Either way, black or Negro. In the past it's been one, now it's the other, but skin has nothing to do with the job. I'm bucking to manage in the majors, but color has nothing to do with whether you can get the respect of the men and know what you're doing. If you're black, white, or whatever, if you're not doing the job, you should be fired.

"I think the fans are ready. Bill Russell [the first black man to coach or manage a major sports team in America] proved that with the Boston Celtics [in 1966]. The world is ready now. It'll judge an individual by the job he does. In the past an individual was judged by his color. Black ballplayers had to be twice as good as white ballplayers to get a job. The players are ready. There would be no trouble if they felt you were qualified and knew what you were doing. Big league players are grown men, and you treat them as such, but no manager can keep 25 players completely happy over a 162-game season."

Earl Weaver did that better than any manager I'd ever known. He knew how to use all 25 men on the roster, and he wasn't afraid of being criticized for using the twenty-fifth man. He kept everyone relatively happy because you just didn't sit on the bench with Earl—you got to play. He had regulars, platoon players, and role players, and the latter might sit on the bench for three weeks and then be called on to play the next three days. Buford, Blair, and I were the regular outfielders, but a youngster named Merv Rettenmund replaced Blefary, who was traded to Houston for left-handed pitcher Mike Cuellar. Cuellar won 23 games for us in 1969, and Rettenmund broke into the outfield part-time and then hit .322 the next year. Earl Weaver got the most out of his players.

Earl used Mark Belanger as much as he could even though he might be hitting only .218, because Mark was the best shortstop in the league. But Earl didn't hesitate against certain pitchers to start Chico Salmon— who had steel hands if I've ever seen them—at shortstop, or second, or even at third. Salmon was an excellent offensive player who could step in on a moment's notice and get a base hit or two. Earl didn't worry about the fact that Chico might give up a run with his tin glove.

Weaver also kept precise statistics on how each of us hit against every pitcher in the league. The boos would rain down at Memorial Stadium when in the ninth inning Earl would send up Belanger to pinch-hit against someone like Nolan Ryan or Goose Gossage. But the fans in the stands didn't know that, while Belanger was hitting only .218 overall, Mark was hitting close to .400 against those power pitchers. Earl had the figures on the 3-by-5 cards he referred to in the dugout throughout ballgames.

In 1969 my eyesight was about 90 percent back to normal. My vision would never be what it was before the injury, and I could never again pick up a pitch as quickly as I used to. I would guess that even that slight vision loss ended up costing me, conservatively, 60 to 70 home runs over the last six years of my career.

But I was just happy to be seeing the ball as well as I did, and I got off to an unbelievable start. I hit 12 home runs in the short month of April, and the Orioles moved into first place and stayed there. I ended up batting .308, with 32 home runs and 100 RBIs. Boog Powell led the club with 37 home runs and 121 RBIs.

But the major difference in the ballclub that year over the preceding year was that we all started doing little things to generate more offense, giving ourselves up to move a runner along. Pitchers were throwing me more curveballs on the outside, and I began punching the ball to right field far more than I ever had before. Overall, the Orioles were a much looser group of guys in the '69 season.

Right after the All-Star break third base coach Billy Hunter came up with an idea that everyone enjoyed. He put in a kangaroo court and named me the presiding judge, and it convened after every game we won. At first all the charges brought concerned baseball matters: fielding errors in infield practice or in a game, throwing to the wrong base or missing the cutoff man, not knowing the number of outs in an inning—the list was endless. Each person filing the charge had to have a witness to the crime, and no more than three cases were heard at each session. Those who were convicted had to pay $1 fines, appeals that lost cost $2, and defendants very, very seldom won a case. The fine money—almost $1000 by season's end—was given to the children of Cincinnati catcher Pat Corrales, whose wife had died in childbirth that summer.

I presided over the court at my locker after games, donning the white head of a mop as a judicial wig and banging on the floor with a bat to get everyone's attention. It was a lot of fun and everyone participated, including manager Earl Weaver, who was charged with a crime every other time he made a move that didn't work. Usually the coaches got Earl. If he put in a defensive replacement late in a game when we were ahead and the player made an error, Billy Hunter would usually charge him.

"Your honor, I have to charge Earl Weaver with mismanagement for sending in a defender who did not defend."

I would look around the room and say, "Jury, how do you find?"

Everyone would yell "guilty" and show a thumb turned down. "I'm guilty and I'll pay the fine," Earl would say.

Brooks Robinson was once fined for yawning on the bench, and when

I looked at him to ask how he wished to plead, he had his eyes closed. "Obviously he's guilty," I said.

As the kangaroo court convened after victories, we had a lot of sessions in 1969 because we won 109 ballgames. That was the first year of divisional play, and we met the Minnesota Twins in the championship series. We swept the Twins in three games and then won the World Series opener against the Mets, 4-1, as Mike Cuellar beat Tom Seaver. We got good pitching in the next four games, but we couldn't score enough runs and we lost 2-1, 5-0, 2-1, and 5-3. Everyone talked about the miraculous catches made by Tommie Agee and Ron Swoboda, who had a Chinese grandfather, and the home run hit by little Al Weis (yes, the same guy of the double-vision incident) as the reasons we lost. But the reason we lost was that we didn't hit. Boog Powell was our only regular who batted over .200; my average was .188.

My 1970 contract called for a $10,000 raise, which increased my salary to $130,000, a nice figure. I was looking forward to another big season, and we certainly had it as a team. We won 108 games and finished 15 games ahead of the Yankees in the Eastern Division. But I feel my vision declined a bit again, and it affected my production at the plate. I just wasn't able to connect with the long ball the way I used to with runners on base. That was reflected in my RBI total (78) and home runs (25), even though I did hit .306.

But one game in Boston stands out in my mind. We were losing 7-0, then I hit a home run, and we came back to tie the game in the ninth inning. In the thirteenth Reggie Smith led off with a shot headed for the seats down the right-field line at Fenway Park. I had shaded Smith toward the line, not wanting to let a ball get past me for an extra base hit. I raced back, leaped, smashed into the wall, and somehow came down with the ball. Earl Weaver later told the press: "It's just such plays that give you an idea of what being super is all about." Thanks, Earl, I thought.

But when I hit the ground after the catch, I had to lie there for some five minutes while trying to get the breath back into my lungs. The muscles in my back, bruised and very sore, had tightened up by the time I went to the plate in the fourteenth. I knew I couldn't swing the bat, but we had the bases loaded, so I laid down a bunt against the drawn-in infield. I beat it out, and the winning run scored.

We went on to beat Minnesota in three straight playoff games; then we defeated the Cincinnati Reds in five World Series games. I homered twice and drove in four runs, but this was Brooks Robinson's series, and he dramatically won MVP honors. He not only made one spectacular play after another in the field but also had nine hits, including two home runs and two doubles, and a .429 batting average.

At the All-Star Game in 1970 one of the writers noticed that I was the only black player in the starting lineup for the American League, while the National League had five black starters. "I might not even have made the National League All-Star team," I said. "When you're competing against guys like Hank Aaron, Willie Mays, Roberto Clemente, and, this year, Rico Carty, well, that's a pretty tough outfield lineup.

"But it seems to me the National League has done a better job of scouting and signing better young players. That's not to suggest the American League is short of good, young talent, but the National League has more because it signs more black players. The Orioles are a good example, and this is in no way to knock my club. But look at our roster. We've got eight blacks and only two of them—Paul Blair and Curt Motton—were developed in our farm system. The other six blacks were either traded for or, in the case of Elrod Hendricks, signed after he developed elsewhere. And the farm system does not suggest that it's going to change significantly."

This situation had been bothering me for a while, and I just decided it was time to speak out. "People go to the park to see the best players, black or white," I continued. "The National League recognized that some time back. Each team over there seems to have more than its share of superstars, and a lot of them are blacks. In contrast, I think there are fewer big names, and therefore fewer blacks, in the American League."

To me, the biggest factor to this day as to why the National League has dominated the American League in the All-Star Game for years, as well as won more World Series, is that its teams make much more of an effort to find and sign the best young black ballplayers.

I was managing Santurce to another championship in the fall of 1970, but persistent rumors that I would be traded reached all the way to Puerto Rico. When I returned home, the Orioles having been unable to cut a deal for me, I was offered a $5000 raise, which I accepted. Once again we had not drawn a million fans at home or even sold out our playoff and World Series games. Brooks had to be brought up to the $100,000 mark, and Boog Powell was due for a big raise too.

I asked Harry Dalton, in lieu of a higher raise, about adding an attendance clause in my contract that would give me additional monies if we drew over a certain number of fans, or writing in other bonus incentives for performance totals.

"We don't believe in those things, Frank," Dalton said. "We just don't do anything like that on this ballclub."

"Okay, if it's against club policy," I said.

Later I found out that he had lied to me. Brooks Robinson had bonus incentives built into his contract for items like games played and total assists. When I found this out, I realized why Brooks would never come out of ballgames, no matter how far ahead we were, no matter what injuries he had, no matter what, unless he was so deep in a slump that Earl would send in a pinch hitter for him. Brooks wanted to earn that bonus money for games played and assists. I couldn't blame him for earning every dollar he could.

In 1971 I fared much better in picking up our base runners, hitting 28 home runs and driving in 99 runs, though my average dropped to .281.

We again won the pennant going away, finishing 12 games ahead of Billy Martin's Tigers and sweeping the A's in the playoffs. Then we jumped off to victories in the first two games of the World Series against the Pittsburgh Pirates, and we were all fairly confident that we'd win our second successive world championship. But the Pirates won the next two games, tying the series, and shut us out in game five 4-0.

Jim Palmer gave up only two runs through nine innings of game 6, and we went into the tenth tied. I led off the inning with a walk. The Achilles tendon in my right leg, which had troubled me quite a bit that season, was very sore. But when Merv Rettenmund grounded a single up the middle, I gave it everything and headed for third because Pirate center fielder Vic Davalillo did not have a strong arm. I dove in to the outside of the bag and beat the tag. Brooks hit a fly to shallow center field; I tagged up as Davalillo caught the ball, and again I beat his throw. We won 3-2.

But we lost the seventh game of the World Series, 2-1, a very painful loss.

At least we went off on a nice vacation three days later, a 31-day tour of Japan in which we played 18 games against the top Japanese teams. I knew it would be the last time I played ball with the Orioles. The rumors that I would be traded, which had started a year ago and resumed in the spring, had emerged again before we left. I had already discussed the situation with Harry Dalton, who was now in California negotiating to become general manager of the Angels. On the trip I said the same thing to Frank Cashen, who would take over as Orioles GM, that I'd said to Dalton.

I told him I knew that Don Buford or I, or both of us, were going to have to go. I had turned 36 on August 31 and Don was 34, making us the two oldest players on the ballclub. Room had to be made for outfielder Don Baylor, who had hit over .300 and averaged over 20 home runs and 100 RBIs with our AAA club at Rochester the past two years, and also for infielder Bobby Grich, another 22-year-old power hitter. I said I didn't want to be traded, but if I was, I hoped to be sent to a team near my home in California. Both Dalton and Cashen said that if I were dealt, they would try to accommodate me.

The other rumors that swirled around my name focused on various major league managing jobs that came open. Every time they did, writers would ask me if I had been contacted by the team that was looking to replace its manager. My answer was always no, because no team ever contacted the Orioles to seek permission to talk to me. I got so disgusted with this persistent scene that I finally said I was no longer interested in managing as a career.

"I'm sick and tired of all the fuss this is making," I told a writer. "They're not going to let a black man manage in the majors, that's all there is to it. Why should I bother getting my hopes up every time I'm mentioned as a candidate for a major league managing job?"

I still wanted to manage in the majors, but I didn't think it would ever happen, so I went to Japan determined to put the future out of my mind and just have fun. We lost only two games over there, and Barbara and I really enjoyed ourselves. We ate in the finest restaurants, and the Japanese threw parties for us everywhere as we traveled around the country by train.

During one train trip between cities, Boog Powell and his wife, Jan, Barbara and I, and a few other couples were sitting in the club car while having drinks and chatting. One of the Japanese writers traveling with us noticed that Boog had a seemingly endless capacity for drinks.

He walked over to Boog and said, "I know one drink I can drink more than you, big Boog-*san*."

"Is that right?" Boog said, nodding his head and smiling faintly. "Have the bartender set 'em up."

The bartender lined up five little sake cups in front of Boog and the writer and filled each cup with the steaming Japanese rice wine. "Okay, let's go," Boog said, raising the cup to his lips and sniffing. He knocked down one cup, two cups, three cups, four cups, five cups before the writer had drained two of his.

"I hope somebody's keeping count," Boog said, letting out a small burp.

When the writer had finished his fifth cup of sake, the bartender jotted the score and refilled the cups. Once again Boog resembled a machine as his hand went out and up and the sake went down, one cup after the other, like so much water. This went on for about 30 minutes. Then the writer said, "You very fast, but I drink more in the end."

Barbara and I went back to our coach seats. About an hour later, the writer came staggering into our car, babbling, "Boog-*san* very good drinker." Then he grabbed the overhead luggage rack, swung his feet up onto it, and began making jungle sounds as if he were Tarzan.

Boog came in behind the writer, stood at the head of the car and smiled as if he had just homered with the bases loaded. "What's wrong with that guy?" he asked. "Say, anyone want to hit the club car for a drink?"

9

⑨ *THE ALSTON MYTH,*
THE ANGELS'
GRIND

D*URING* the major league winter meetings in Phoenix that December, I was traded along with relief pitcher Pete Richert to the Dodgers for four young prospects; the only one of them who excelled, as it turned out, was pitcher Doyle Alexander. At least I would be playing for a good organization on a team that had finished only one game behind the Giants in the NL West, and Dodger Stadium was only a 20-minute drive from my home in Beverly Hills.

So I was looking forward to playing for the Dodgers—until I went to see general manager Al Campanis. I was ushered into his office at the stadium, and he said, "Hello, how are you Frank?"

"I'm fine, thanks," I said, and waited for him to welcome me to the ballclub.

Instead, Campanis silently walked over to a shelf on the wall, and pulled out a booklet, and handed it to me. The title of the booklet was *The Dodger Way to Play Baseball.* I looked at Campanis, who was back behind his desk, dropped the booklet on a table, and took a seat.

"Excuse me, Mr. Campanis, but if I don't know how to play baseball by now, after 16 years in the major leagues, I never will."

That was my first insight into the rarefied intelligence of Al Campanis, Dodger vice president. He had traded for a player who had been

MVP in both leagues, yet Al wanted me to read a book on how to play the game.

Worse than that, I had made $135,000 in 1971, and I told Campanis that, naturally, I expected a raise. "We can pay you what you earned last year, Frank, but I don't see how we can possibly give you a raise," Campanis said. "You know, $135,000 is a lot of money. Besides, you haven't done anything for the Dodgers yet that would justify a raise."

"I haven't done anything for the Dodgers yet because I haven't *played* for the Dodgers yet," I said. "But obviously you expect me to play well for you, or you wouldn't have traded for me, and you can't really expect me to play for last year's wages."

"Frank, we have players who have performed for the Dodger organization many years," Campanis said, "and nobody's making close to $135,000."

"But you traded for me, and you knew what I was making in Baltimore, with a team that doesn't approach the attendance totals of the Dodgers." I mentioned my stats and said, "You know I did whatever I could over there to help the Orioles win, and we won four pennants and two World Series. I should not be penalized for being traded."

We went back and forth for almost an hour, the discussion very cordial, but neither of us would budge. Then I had to leave to appear on the television game show *Sports Challenge*, which I had been competing on. In fact, I was undefeated in six appearances on that show when it was abruptly taken off the air.

At the show's taping that day I met the agent Ed Keating, who was there with two of his clients, Larry Csonka and Jim Kiick. The next day, while paying a friendly visit to Harry Dalton of the Angels, I met Keating again when he came in to negotiate a contract. I told Ed I was having trouble in my negotiations with Al Campanis. Keating said he would take over the negotiations, if I liked. He only charged 5 percent of any increase he produced, so I signed on with him as my representative. Ed Keating walked in to see Campanis and came out with a $17,000 raise for me. That made me the highest-paid Dodger player in history, and I liked such historic moments.

I was happy with my contract but disappointed with the Dodgers when I saw what was going on in spring training. I had always heard—and still hear—that the Dodgers were very sound fundamentally, that they worked hard on fundamentals in the spring and therefore made few mental mistakes during the season. With the Orioles, particularly under Earl

Weaver—who would be out on the field showing you what to do, how he wanted plays executed—we worked on fundamentals for hours day after day. The Dodgers, under the legendary manager Walter Alston, virtually ignored drills on fundamentals. One day Alston said we would work on hitting the cutoff man on throws from the outfield. So all of us outfielders ran out to the field. Balls were hit to us, we made a few throws, and suddenly the drill was over. We had worked all of 15 minutes.

Walter Alston ended up managing the Dodgers for 23 years, signing one-year contracts year after year. I wondered, did he have his outfielders practice hitting the cutoff man for only 15 minutes *every* year?

Once the season started, I decided the answer was yes. In game after game center fielder Willie Davis would charge a ball hit out to him—and he was very quick getting to it—scoop it up, and, with a man on base, come up throwing. And time and again the ball would sail over the cutoff man's head, allowing the base runner to advance.

"What in the world is wrong with Willie?" Walter Alston would say.

Coach Danny Ozark would say, "I don't know why he keeps doing that."

The other coaches on the bench would also gripe every time Willie Davis fired the ball over the cutoff man's head and gave the opposition a runner in scoring position. But not once through the '72 season did I hear Alston or any of the coaches say anything to Willie Davis about his overthrows to the cutoff man. Not once.

Willie Davis had tremendous natural ability. I don't know if I've ever seen a player go from first to third faster than he did, and he covered an enormous amount of territory in the outfield. He could hit for average, had fair power, and could steal at least 20 bases every year. But one reason why he didn't make the All-Star team until his eleventh season in the league, 1971, was that he wasn't a good baseball player. He didn't pay attention to basics, and I have a feeling that was because nobody corrected Willie and really forced him to tune into the game.

I remember a doubleheader we played in St. Louis that was a perfect example of the way Willie Davis's mind wandered and of the way Walter Alston reacted to Willie's drifting. In the first game we were down by three runs in the ninth inning. Willie led off, and the count went to 3-and-0. Walter Alston put on the take sign. Willie looked down at third base coach Danny Ozark and stepped into the batter's box. On the next pitch he swung and popped up.

Walter Alston looked around the dugout and asked, "What was the count?"

The players looked at one another like, "What does he mean what was the count? It was right up there on the scoreboard an instant ago."

"Was it 3-and-0?" Alston asked.

"Yeah, it was 3-and-0," someone said.

Walter Alston just shook his head; then he said, "We'll have a clubhouse meeting between games."

I was all for it. We'd gotten off to a fair start, but then began playing the sloppiest baseball I had ever witnessed. Alston had said nothing, but now we were halfway through the season, and I felt he was finally going to chew us out. He started off strong, saying some guys were going to have to start worrying about their jobs if they didn't straighten up. Then Alston, who liked to go hunting in the off-season, said something very strange: "I don't care, I don't have to worry about a job. I've got enough shotgun shells."

He paused and then really started tearing into us for missing signs, missing the cutoff man, and various other mental mistakes. He was really building in his reaming, his voice raised, his eyes flashing fire.

I said to myself, "Come on, Walter, we really need this! Lay it on!"

He poured it onto the team in general for a few more minutes, then he turned to Willie Davis specifically, and I thought that might really be helpful. "What in the world were you thinking about?" Alston said. "We're behind by three runs, the count goes to 3-and-0, we give you the take sign—and you pop up the next pitch! That's the most ridiculous thing I've ever seen from you, Willie, and I've seen a lot of mistakes from you! It's about time you get your mind in the ballgame."

Willie was sitting with his head down, and I said to myself, "Come on, Walter, keep it coming."

Then all of a sudden Alston lowered his voice and almost apologized for having yelled at us. He walked into his office.

Willie Davis turned to me and said, "What the hell's wrong with that man?"

"What do you mean, Willie?" I said.

"Why did he single me out?" Willie said. "Why's he getting on me?"

"You mean you don't know why he's getting on you?"

"No."

"Well if you don't know, Willie, I'm not gonna be the one to tell you," I said.

Just before we went out for the second game, Alston addressed us again, saying, "At the start of this game, everyone is taking until you get the hit sign. Is that understood? Willie, do you understand?"

Willie nodded his head.

"We're taking, starting with the first pitch of the game," Alston repeated. "Okay, let's get to it."

Then, in the dugout, to further emphasize the point, Alston said he would levy a $100 fine on any player who swung before he had the hit sign.

On the first pitch of the game, Willie Davis swung and popped foul.

"Did you see that?" Alston cried in the dugout.

"Yeah, we saw it," a bunch of us chorused.

"That just cost him $100," Alston said.

On the next pitch Willie swung again.

"That's $200," Alston said.

Willie Davis took the next pitch, then got a hit. I don't know if Walter Alston ever actually took Willie's money. I tend to doubt it, because I do know that Willie Davis continued to miss signs and cutoff men. It seemed to be his style.

When I had played against Walter Alston's teams all those earlier years in the National League, I was always impressed by him. It wasn't until I joined the Dodgers that I realized that no matter how things may seem from the opposite dugout, you don't really know what's going on over there until you get there yourself. I always thought that Alston was on top of the game, that he made lots of good moves during ballgames, bunting runners over, playing the hit-and-run, stealing bases. From the way the Dodger players manufactured runs in a game without much hitting, you felt that Alston was calling the shots.

Then I became a Dodger and found out that Walter Alston didn't do much of anything as a manager, beyond write out the lineup. He had two favorite moves and he made them every chance he had—sending up Manny Mota to pinch-hit and bringing in Jim Brewer from the bullpen.

As far as manufacturing runs went, that was all up to the players when I was a Dodger. The players pretty much stole on their own, tried the hit-and-run on their own, and, unless they were pitchers, bunted on their own. Walter Alston said very little and did very little. He was a myth in his own time.

Alston was the only manager I ever came across who let his players call in sick and take a day off. Willie Davis did that on at least two occasions that I know of. Once he had his wife call the clubhouse man, and she asked him to tell Alston that Willie wouldn't be in that day because he had a cold. I figured it couldn't be a head cold, because there wasn't enough room in there for a cold.

Maury Wills phoned the clubhouse man and had him inform Alston that Wills had some personal problems that would preclude his appearing at the ballpark that day. When he returned from his day off, Wills didn't stop in to see Alston and tell him of his availability, nor did Davis. And good old silent Walter did not call them in to see how they were, either, as a manager normally would.

The Dodgers had a bad year, finishing in third place, 10½ games behind Cincinnati, and so did I, hitting .251 with 19 home runs and 59 RBIs. (The Orioles also finished in third place, incidentally.) I felt I would have improved my numbers quite a bit if Alston had not virtually benched me the last half of the season, when I got into only 25 games.

Writers asked me why I didn't talk to Alston about my lack of playing time, but that wasn't like me. "That's his decision," I said. "At the end of the season I'll find out why I wasn't playing. I don't rock the boat during the season."

At season's end I went to see Peter O'Malley in the Dodger front office and said, "If this is the way it's gonna be next year, where I don't know if I'm gonna be allowed to contribute, I'd rather be traded."

"We don't know if Walter Alston's coming back or not," O'Malley said. "If he does come back, you'll probably have to fight for a job."

"I don't want that," I said. "Trade me to a team where I'll get a chance to play, hopefully on the West Coast."

Several days later a Japanese team contacted the Dodgers, who asked me if I'd mind if they gave permission for the Japanese to talk to me about signing a contract with them. The Japanese spoke to Ed Keating and offered me a $500,000 contract for two years. We countered by asking for three years, but before the Japanese could get back to us, I was traded to the Angels. I was managing in Puerto Rico when I was told of the trade, and I was happy to be working once again for Harry Dalton. I was sure that I would be given the opportunity to play again.

"Any time a man takes you to four World Series, you've got to be close to him," Dalton told the press. "Sure, Frank's 37 years old and he's not the same player he was five years ago. But he's still a superstar."

Not only was it important to me to be playing for a general manager who knew what I could contribute to a ballclub, but I felt I would finish my career with the Angels and possibly be considered by Dalton for the manager's job if it came open. I signed a two-year contract with the Angels, calling for salaries of $168,000 the first year and $180,000 the second.

Bobby Winkles was the manager of the Angels in 1973. A very successful coach at Arizona State University, Winkles had resigned and taken a cut in salary to become an Angel coach in 1972, then he got his chance to manage in the majors during my first year with the club. For Winkles, like myself, becoming a manager in the big leagues had apparently been a long-time goal.

But looking back, I'm sure that had Bobby Winkles had a say in the matter, I would not have been a member of the Angels under him, because it eventually became very clear that he regarded me as a threat to his job. That was ridiculous. With every team I joined, I tried to do whatever I could to help it win. Any time you help a ballclub win, you help the manager. And I always tried to help the manager in any other way I could, particularly by talking to younger players who sought my advice.

For example, Willie Crawford, a 26-year-old outfielder who had been given a $100,000 signing bonus by the Dodgers eight years before, had come to me the previous season. Willie was having problems with his hitting because he tried to pull everything to right field. "Willie," I told him, "you can't be something you're not, and you're not a pull hitter. When the pitchers work you outside, drive the ball to left. You do that, and the pitcher will have to come back inside to your power and you can pull it."

Crawford played for me at Santurce after the '72 season, and he worked even harder in going to left with the outside pitch, and he hit for a high average and with good power too. At season's end a Los Angeles writer asked Willie if he thought I would make a good manager in the major leagues. "He'll be a tremendous manager anywhere," Crawford was quoted as saying. "There isn't any kind of player Frank Robinson can't help."

It was just that kind of quote that made Bobby Winkles uptight, I'm sure, though our initial relationship was excellent. Bobby asked me to talk to the young players whenever I could find time. "I'll make time if anyone comes to me," I told him. "I enjoy working with young players, with anyone, in fact, who thinks I can help them."

Bobby Winkles had a lot of new ideas that he introduced in spring training. One that proved to be very beneficial to all of us resulted in the Angels not having a muscle pull all season, which was virtually unheard of in baseball. He had us do daily calisthenics, not the hard-driving military type but slow stretching exercises. One player would slowly apply pressure to the back of another's outstretched leg, then they would reverse roles. By stretching your muscles very slowly, you'd feel them begin to give more and more. I have such a long inseam that I had always had great difficulty touching my toes. But after only one week of those exercises, I could touch them easily.

I broke a toe in spring training and couldn't do anything for ten days. So I left our Palm Springs base and went home. I wondered why not only my toe but the soles of both my feet hurt. Then I realized it was because Winkles had us doing so much running at the training camp. We had to run to and from the clubhouse and diamond—which was quite a distance—every day. And we had to jog every place we went, from diamond to diamond. When we went to the outfield to work, we ran. When we came in to hit, we ran. We were out on the field four or five hours each day, and we ran everywhere.

The result was that, at age 37, I was in as good shape as I had ever been, and in better condition than I had been in recent years, as I was to discover late in the season. I had batted only four times in exhibition games before breaking my toe, but when I returned from ten days of idleness, I felt great. In my first at-bat in a game against the Padres at Yuma, I hit a home run.

Another thought that Winkles had which I agreed with was that base-ball games took far too much time to complete. So Bobby had the Angels running on and off the field between innings to speed things up. That didn't sit too well with some of the players, who also objected to the fact that Bobby tried to regiment the dugout. He wanted all the outfielders' gloves placed together, and all the infielders' gloves placed together. Players looked at one another like: "He's got to be kidding!" Some began complaining about "Winkles's rah-rah college style," and it was obvious that it was impossible to regiment 25 individuals in 1973. I doubt that it was possible back in 1963.

This was the first year of the designated hitter (DH) and I told both Dalton and Winkles that I didn't mind being the DH but that I wanted to play in the field once in a while just to stay sharp, if that was possible. The point was that no one knew how to react to performing as a desig-nated hitter. It seemed so strange to me at first, not playing in the field (I played defense in only 17 games). I looked at the job as pinch-hitting four or five times a game, and I soon got used to my role.

I saw other DHs leave the bench during games and go down into the runway or back into the clubhouse to swing a bat. I remained on the bench so I could stay on top of the game and study the opposing pitcher. Maybe I could pick up something for myself or something I could pass along to another hitter that might help us win a game.

My old buddy from Cincinnati, Vada Pinson, was with the Angels that season and often batted ahead of me in the third slot once again. It was nice to renew an old friendship and have someone to have dinner with on occasion when we were on the road. With the Dodgers I had always eaten alone.

It was ironic that the number 3, 4, and 5 hitters on the Angels, Pinson, me, and Bob Oliver, were black. We played in Anaheim, which was in conservative Orange County, and Angel management had traditionally not sought to sign black ballplayers. In the club's history, from 1962 through 1971, according to a press report, 211 players had performed for the Angels, but only 15 of them, or 7 percent, were American-born blacks. Small wonder that very few black fans ever showed up at an Angels' game, even though there was a large black population in nearby Santa Ana.

So rarely was a black seen at Anaheim Stadium that when a bottle flew out of the upper deck there and hit a Texas Ranger pitcher in the bullpen, he had no trouble spotting the kid who threw it. "He and his friend are black," Denny Riddleberger told the Angel official who asked him. "They have to be the only black kids in the ballpark."

We got off to a fine start in 1973 and actually moved into first place on June 27. I still wasn't seeing the ball as well as I wished, but from early July through August 20 I went on a tear and batted .344 with power. I finished with 30 home runs and 97 RBIs even though my average was only .266.

Unfortunately, the Angels collapsed in the second half of the season, and we finished fourth, 15 games out of first place. During this time I tried to show my teammates how to win, tried to tell the younger players what it takes to win, how you had to do that little extra and give yourself up for the team. But when players have never won, it's very difficult. Until you have tasted victory, been in a pennant race and in a World Series, you don't have that feeling of what it takes. And you can't pass on that feeling to someone else. You talk and talk, and the players say, "Yeah, yeah," and then do nothing. It can be discouraging.

And Bobby Winkles did not handle the ballclub's demise very well. One day late in the season he took me aside and told me he thought I was talking to other players too much and doing too much needling.

"All I've been doing is answering questions to the best of my ability," I said. "If you want me to stop talking to players, I will. But as far as my needling, that's just my style. I really only needle guys to be friendly with them, and I only needle players I feel I *can* needle, guys who can give it back to me. We just get on one another as a joke, just kidding around."

"Well some guys don't like it, Frank," Winkles said.

"You mean somebody's complained about my needling?"

"That's right," Winkles said.

"Who complained?"

"Rudy May," Winkles said.

I shook my head in disbelief. Pitcher Rudy May was a great needler himself, a guy who liked to have fun off the field. He was a tough competitor who wasn't doing well on the mound, and I just tried to help him relax. But if Rudy had complained about me, maybe I had gone too far with something I said.

A few minutes later, when I was sitting in front of my locker, Rudy walked by and I didn't speak to him. He came back and said, "Hey, you mad at me, Frank?"

"No, I'm not mad at you," I said. "But Winkles just told me that you had complained to him that I was needling you too much."

"What!" Rudy said. "I never said anything like that."

"Did Winkles say anything to you like he thought I was needling you too much?"

"Not a word. I thought he knew we were just kidding around. And if I had any problem, I'd damn well tell you. I wouldn't go to the manager."

"Yeah," I said, smiling, "I guess you're having enough problems on the mound." A gentle needle.

"I guess Winkles is just cracking under the strain," Rudy said.

"No comment," I said. "He thinks I say too much to my teammates."

"Say what?"

"You heard me right."

"I don't know why he's getting on your case," Rudy said. "You're the only guy hitting on this club."

I went to see Winkles and told him I'd certainly go along with any program he laid out but that Rudy May had denied complaining about me. Winkles rubbed at his face, paused, and said maybe he had misunderstood Rudy. Then he abruptly said, "Look, Frank, I know you are friends with Harry Dalton and, if it comes down to it, that he'll choose you over me."

And I knew right then where Bobby Winkles was coming from.

But I said, "I'm here to do anything I can to help this ballclub win, and that's all."

Obviously Bobby Winkles not only saw me as a threat but felt I was undermining him with general manager Harry Dalton. But Dalton never called me up to his office, and I never went there on my own to discuss the ballclub. I never once discussed Bobby Winkles or the manager's job with Dalton. The only time I ever talked to Dalton was around the batting cage or in the dugout before games when he'd ask me a question about myself or we'd just talk in general about baseball. I'm not the type to talk negatively about a manager to a general manager. A smart GM like Harry Dalton wouldn't think much of a guy who did that. And a player like me who was hoping to land a managing position down the road could not possibly do himself any good by suggesting that the manager he played for should be fired.

I suspect that Bobby Winkles's fears about my presence on the ballclub were fueled by the suggestions in the press that Dalton had signed me with the idea of naming me manager if Winkles fell on his face. Nothing was further from the truth.

By season's end, I was pleased to read in the papers that Bobby Winkles felt there were no problems on the Angels, specifically with me, and that we could be in the pennant race next year. "I think Frank Robinson and Vada Pinson are responsible for that," Winkles said. "They are very stable persons."

Vada Pinson may have been stable, but he was not an Angel in 1974. He was traded to the Kansas City Royals and had a good year. I did not have a good year, hitting .245 with 22 home runs and only 68 RBIs. The distractions in the clubhouse didn't help me at all through the first two months of play, and things didn't get a whole lot better thereafter when the Angels kept trying to dump me.

My relationship with Winkles deteriorated rapidly early in 1974 when he virtually stopped talking to me and I had nothing to say to him. Then, during the first week in June, Winkles called a clubhouse meeting in Detroit and announced that he had told Harry Dalton at the start of spring training that Frank Robinson should be traded. I was absolutely stunned. I think just about everyone on the team was embarrassed for Winkles.

"I didn't like it at all," I told the press. "To me, what Winkles was saying was that he couldn't manage with me on the team. He didn't want me here. But I haven't asked to be traded, and I wouldn't like for him to be fired."

A few days before the June 15 trading deadline, Dalton worked out a trade that would've sent Rudy May and me to the Yankees for Roy White, Bill Sudakis, and Dick Woodson. As I had to approve any trade of me, I told Ed Keating: "If I'm gonna move to New York, I want the living expenses above what it would cost me here covered, plus I want a contract for 1975, which would give me 20 years in the major leagues. If you can get that, Ed, I'm gone."

Gabe Paul, the Yankee general manager, would not meet my terms. It might have proved interesting contending with the Orioles, who finished only two games ahead of the Yankees. I just might have won a few games for the Yankees. But I really couldn't see uprooting myself to go off and try to help a team win the pennant, only to be dropped by it at season's end. So I bit the bullet and, rather than go to a good ballclub, I continued to play for Bobby Winkles.

Not for long. Winkles was fired on June 28. "I was fired for my inability to manage Frank Robinson," he said, adding he would do it all again but saying, "I just wouldn't manage the club with Frank Robinson on it. It would be a matter of having an understanding beforehand, but I don't think I could get an understanding with Robbie. I don't want to rap Robbie. I've always been very complimentary toward him. He should be a manager in the big leagues. It was my own fault that I didn't handle him right."

I wished he had stated what he had against me, because Bobby Winkles was not fired as a result of his inability to handle me. He was fired because of his inability to manage major league ballplayers. He really wanted major league players to conduct themselves like college players, and there was no way he could make that happen. Winkles was an excellent instructor with some good ideas, and he would make an excellent coach on the major league level. But in my estimation that was as far as his abilities went.

It was a shame that he never called me into his office and confronted me with his thoughts about me, how he felt about my being on the team and what he expected of me. I think if he had expressed his feelings and let me explain my feelings, we could have sorted everything out or at least made the situation easier on both of us. After that scene in Detroit, I suggested to Dalton that he meet with Winkles and me. But maybe at that point Dalton had already decided to dismiss Winkles.

One thing is certain: Given my desire to manage eventually, I did not need all this controversy about disharmony between me and my manager.

It increased speculation that Dalton was going to replace Winkles with me. But Harry had all but told me that I was not among his managerial candidates under any circumstances because I would not be back with the club the next year. That was why he tried to trade me. So I couldn't be disappointed when I didn't get the Angles' managing job; I was never considered for it.

To this day, though, no matter where Harry Dalton is employed as general manager—and when he left the Angels he took over the Milwaukee Brewers, where he still works—every time one of his managers seems to be in jeopardy of losing his job, my name pops up in the press among the candidates. I guess I should say, "Harry, I'm just waiting for a good offer."

As I've said, I don't regard Bobby Winkles as a good manager. But even a superb manager could not have made winners out of the 1973 and 1974 California Angels. Ideally, in building a contending ballclub, you play veterans and bring in one or two young players, then gradually add more until you've developed a good team. But the Angels went around in circles. They would bring in some veterans, add some youngsters, bring in more veterans, then try more youngsters. They didn't have a solid plan.

In 1973 we had a pretty fair pitching staff led by Nolan Ryan, who could have won with any lineup given the heat he was throwing that season. He won 21 games for us while striking out 383 batters, which is still a major league record for a season. We used 14 different pitchers that season, a reasonable number. But 26 other players wore the haloed Angel uniforms in 1973 as the front office scrambled to try to find eight everyday players who could actually play the game.

In 1974 we were even worse. Nolan Ryan again excelled (22-16 and 367 strikeouts), but we called on 19 other pitchers and 22 nonpitchers while playing .420 baseball and finishing in last place in the Western Division.

Whitey Herzog, the former Texas Ranger manager who was our third base coach, took over as interim manager for four games before the Angels hired Dick Williams to manage the club. He had superb credentials, winning the AL pennant in 1967 with the Boston Red Sox and then leading the Oakland A's to victories in the World Series in 1972 and 1973. Fed up with interference from Charlie Finley, the owner of the A's, Williams had tried after the World Series to accept an offer to manage the Yankees. But he still had two years to run on his contract with the A's, and Finley would not release him. Speculation had it that Finley let him go to the Angels only because they were 11 games out of first place and, according to one writer, Charlie decided, "If Williams thought he was such a good manager, let's see what he can do with that bunch."

One of the first things Dick Williams did upon joining us was call me in and say, "I'd like you to be captain of the team, Frank." I said that was fine with me and asked what my duties would be. He said once in a while I would take the lineup card out to the umpire at home plate and help him in any way I could.

"Normally a captain is paid $500," Dick said. "It's not a lot of money, but that's the standard. Usually the ballclub pays the fee, but if it doesn't, I'll pay the $500 personally."

"I appreciate that," I said, "but I won't be acting as team captain just for the money."

A little while later at the press conference in his honor, Williams announced that he'd named me his captain and said, "I'll be glad to pay the $500 out of my own pocket."

"You fellows are taking notes, aren't you?" Harry Dalton interjected to the press.

"There's too much Frank Robinson can give us beside his bat," Williams continued. "Frank was very instrumental in helping me develop a strong association with Reggie Jackson in Oakland. Frank's a leader and a winner. If Frank has something to say, I want the young players to listen. And if he wants to make suggestions on the bench, *I* will listen."

It all sounded good, and I appreciated Dick's confidence in me after what had gone before with Winkles. Williams read the situation and acted promptly. One writer wrote, "It is because baseball relationships are so intertwined, with lives cutting across each other repeatedly, that a feel for emotional undercurrents can be so important to a manager."

I realized then, and far more so once I became a manager, that the feel for emotional undercurrents on a ballclub was crucial to a manager and his team. Yet a manager has to stand off from his team to a degree because he controls the destiny of most players, deciding whether they will play or not and therefore whether they will have a chance to advance and excel. A manager who gets too close to his players may tarnish his ability to judge their capabilities objectively.

But Dick Williams kept himself farther from his players than any manager I've ever known. When he had a message for a player, he would not deliver it himself but instead sent a coach to do so. Always. I was a veteran player and the team captain, so Dick would talk to me. Certain players would come to me with gripes about lack of playing time, say, and I would take them to Williams. "So-and-so is a little upset that he's not playing," I'd say. "Maybe you should call him into the office and talk to him before the situation gets out of hand."

Dick would say he'd see to it, then he would have a coach speak to the player. That didn't sit well with many of the guys. To do their best, I believe that most players have to feel comfortable around a manager, that they can get fairly close to him if they need to, although they know he's the boss and that he can't be a friend. It's a thin line that most managers draw.

Dick Williams erected a fence around himself. He was a hard-driving, hard-nosed, no-nonsense-type manager who was a tough guy to be around. He could be gruff, sarcastic, abrasive in the comments he made about players, many of whom hated his guts.

But he reportedly had always been like that, while demonstrating that he was a very good strategist and a manager who won in Boston and Oakland, and later in Montreal and San Diego, before he began rebuilding the Seattle Mariners. Dick Williams's intimidating presence succeeds for a while until his players turn against him, not unlike what happens to Billy Martin. I like Billy, who was my teammate one year in Cincinnati, and he, too, wins everywhere he manages for the first year or two—in Minnesota, Detroit, Texas, New York, and Oakland. But once the players' fear of Martin wears off, he is gone.

After serving as captain for almost two months and not receiving the $500 I had been promised, I mentioned it to Harry Dalton. "We've never had a team captain here before," he said, "and we're not going to pay for one now."

I figured Dalton was worried about the club's finances. He had reportedly signed Dick Williams to a $100,000-per-year contract, which made him the highest-paid manager in the game. Bobby Winkles, whose salary was a miserly $28,000, had been the lowest-paid in baseball.

I went to see Dick Williams and told him that Dalton said the club would not pay me for serving as captain.

Williams shrugged his shoulders.

"You said if that was the case, you'd pay me the $500 fee you mentioned," I said.

"I said *I* would pay you?" Williams said. "I don't remember that. The team pays the captain. Always has."

I walked away. Our relationship was a little strained after that.

A few days later the Angels tried to trade me to the Red Sox. Since it was beyond the trading deadline, I had to be put on the waiver list. The Orioles promptly claimed me for the $25,000 waiver price. I agreed to join them if they would cover my living expenses and sign me to a 1975 contract. Frank Cashen wouldn't go for that. He just wanted my bat for the race in the east, which the Orioles ended up winning; then they lost three games out of four in the playoffs to the A's.

But I told Barbara, "It's obvious they don't want me here and they won't have me back next year. So the next team that claims me, I'm gone. It's got to be better elsewhere than it is here playing for a manager who lied to me and for a last-place team."

One thing became very clear to me at this time. It didn't matter how good a manager was if he had a bad ballclub and a poor organization that could not turn it into a solid team. I had never played for a last-place team before, but I saw there was nothing Dick Williams could do given what he had to work with. In 1975 the Angels finished last again. Williams couldn't make the Angels a winner in 1976, either, when he was finally fired. With Montreal in 1977 and 1978, Williams's Expos were under .500, but they were building, and for the next two years they finished second, two games behind the Pirates in 1979 and one game in back of the Phillies in 1980. When they faltered in 1981, Williams was fired, and his players turned on Dick and his abrasive manner.

Still, he was right back managing again in 1982, taking over the uninspiring San Diego Padres, and by 1984 he had them in the World Series. No complaints from the players were heard about Dick Williams then. Of course, when the Padres fell to third place in 1985, the players had few good words to say about Williams.

In fact, a survey of the players conducted by Phil Collier of the San Diego *Union* revealed that most Padres did not want Williams to return as their manager in 1986. "It's bad when you have the players saying they'll pass the hat and help buy out [the final year of] Dick's contract," one player said. Another said, "I love playing for Dick, but when I get out of the game, I'm going to run over him with a car."

Williams didn't bother to show up for the opening day of spring training in 1986. When he did arrive, he resigned. Apparently he had hoped the Padres would buy out the last year of his contract, no small consideration, as he was reportedly to be paid $250,000 for his gruffness. "You bet I'm glad to see him go," said pitcher Andy Hawkins. First baseman Steve Garvey said, "I think Dick deliberately misled the fans and the media [that he would return as manager] in order to inflict the most harm on our team. Leaving like this...was his way of trying to burn the players."

A serious charge, one that might cause another team to pause before hiring Dick Williams as manager. But Williams went back to work before the '86 season was over, becoming manager of the Seattle Mariners.

Dick Williams and Bill McKechnie have been the only managers who won pennants with three different teams. With that kind of credential on your record, I guess you don't have to worry much about getting a job. But Williams was no easy man to play for.

As pitcher Frank Tanana said when Dick Williams was fired by the Angels: "It's tough when a guy makes absolutely no attempt to communicate with his players. He wants nothing to do with them. That's the way the man went about his job. It's a lot easier to get guys to play for you if you show you care a little about them once in a while."

I was never one to run the streets at night after games like some players, but I did break curfew a number of times. The only manager who ever caught me was, you guessed it, Dick Williams. It happened on August 31, 1974, which was my thirty-ninth birthday. I had played that day and figured I'd play the next day, so I decided not to celebrate. In truth, I really had nothing to celebrate. I was lying on my bed getting ready to order from hotel room service, when coach John Roseboro called and asked if I wanted to have dinner in the hotel restaurant. I was friendly with John, not real close, but we both liked to talk baseball, so I said I'd meet him.

We sat down about 10:15, ordered a drink, then ordered dinner. The service was very slow, and we got caught up in our conversation and lost track of the time. All of a sudden I said, "Wow, John, it's 1 A.M."

I went up to my room, and the phone light was blinking. I asked for the message and was told, "Dick Williams called at 1 A.M., and you weren't in your room. He said see him tomorrow about it."

"What chickenshit!" I said to myself. "We're 20-some games out of first place with a month left in the season—and Dick's checking on me! On my goddamn thirty-ninth birthday! When I'm not doing anything but having a meal in the hotel restaurant!"

At the ballpark the next day, I went right to Williams's office. "Dick, you called me last night about 1 o'clock."

"Yeah," he said, "but I wasn't calling to catch you out. I was calling to catch those two relief pitchers who blew the game yesterday. But they were in, so I had to call everybody to make it look good."

"Well, look, I wasn't really breaking curfew," I said. "I was downstairs having dinner with John Roseboro and—"

"Hey, I'm not gonna fine you, Frank; don't worry about it," Williams said. "But don't let it happen again."

I didn't have to worry about anything to do with the Angels ten days later. The Cleveland Indians claimed me on waivers, and Ed Keating told me that general manager Phil Seghi would give me a contract for the '75 season. "Then I am an Indian, Ed," I said. "Wha-hooo!"

10

THE FIRST BLACK MANAGER

I reported to the Indians for the last three weeks of the season and signed a contract calling for the same $180,000 salary in 1975. And I saw right away that this team had a problem. Coach Larry Doby and all the black players on the club would seat themselves at the far end of the dugout, while manager Ken Aspromonte and all the white coaches and players sat at the near end. I sat in the middle, observing.

I knew that Larry Doby, who had been the first black to play in the American League back in 1947, also wanted to manage. But standing off with the black players, apart from the whites, was no recommendation for a manager. Yet he continued to do so, even when I made it a point not to join the group, and even when things began to get real tough for Aspromonte as the Indians fell from second place in late August to fourth and rumors had it that Ken would be fired.

After his retirement in 1959 Doby had been out of baseball until he joined the Montreal organization as a troubleshooter in 1968, a job he held three years, then he became a coach for the Expos under Gene Mauch. Larry had joined the Indians that season, and it looked like he felt he may have had a shot at the manager's job if Aspromonte, as rumors suggested, were to be fired. But Larry certainly wasn't doing anything to help Aspromonte by standing off with the black players.

Pitcher Gaylord Perry presented another problem. Perry had averaged over 20 wins per year in each of his three seasons with the Indians, but he was far more concerned with himself than he was with the ballclub as a whole. That was apparent between games of a doubleheader in Shea Stadium against the Yankees. George Hendrick had played center field wearing a heavy wrap on a pulled hamstring in the first game. We were tied in the ninth, 4-4, when the Yankees got a man on first and Thurman Munson hit a drive that split the gap in right center. By the time Hendrick, who couldn't run very well, got to the ball, the winning run scored.

I went into the clubhouse to get something to eat between games, and Gaylord Perry was in there screaming his head off. "If a guy doesn't want to play, he shouldn't be playing!" he hollered, throwing his glove into his locker. "If Hendrick's in the lineup for my next turn, I won't pitch! I don't want him in the outfield ever again when I'm on the mound! He won't even make an effort to run after a goddamn ball!"

Gaylord was a big man, 6-foot-4, 220 pounds, with a big voice, and he hollered at the top of his lungs for several minutes. His locker was right outside the open door to Aspromonte's office, and I lost some respect for Ken when he didn't come out and settle down his pitcher.

I looked around the room for George Hendrick, wondering what his reaction was to the tirade. He wasn't there. Sometimes a guy gets upset with himself over a play and sits in the dugout for a couple of minutes to unwind. But then I realized, as I looked around, that I was the *only* black in the dressing room. Oscar Gamble, Charlie Spikes, Tommy McCraw, Rico Carty, and Doby were also out in the dugout. They must have felt that Perry would explode and didn't want to hear it.

I thought it was wrong for Larry Doby to sit out there with the group. It would have been better if he had encouraged Hendrick to come in and face Perry and clear the air right then. But Perry flew home after the game, as he did after each of his starts, returning the next time he was to pitch.

And the next two times that Perry pitched, Ken Aspromonte did not play George Hendrick. Then, before the last game of the season in Boston, Hendrick came into the locker room early, as I did. He hung his suit bag in the locker next to mine, then went to check the lineup posted on the wall. He came back and slung the suit bag over his shoulder and said, "I'm out of here."

"What do you mean, George? We have a game to play." I said.

"He's got me in the lineup, and I'm not playing with Perry pitching. I'm gone."

"Are you sure you want to do that?"

"Yeah, I'm catching a plane."

I was the only one Hendrick talked to, and when Aspromonte looked for George in the dugout, I said, "He's on his way to California, Ken." That's why the air should have been cleared immediately between Hendrick and Perry.

I also had a problem with Gaylord Perry. He told the Cleveland writers he was looking for a big raise the next season. "I want to earn one dollar more than Frank Robinson," he said. Perry went on to say that he didn't see why the Indians were paying me for what I had done in the past, that they should pay me for what I could do now.

I was really angry when I walked into the clubhouse the next afternoon. Carrying the sports section with his quotes in it, I went directly to Perry, who was seated at his locker. I shoved the paper under his nose and said, "Are these quotes straight?"

"Yes," he snapped.

That infuriated me, and I yelled, "I don't care how much you make next season. The important thing to me is not that I'm the highest-paid player on this club. The important thing to me is that I'm satisfied with what I'm making. But I don't want my name dragged through the papers by you or anyone else. I don't want you to negotiate your contract in the papers through me. If you want to use my salary behind closed doors to try and get more money, fine. But not in the papers."

"I'm looking out for the young kids on the ballclub," Gaylord said calmly, not raising his voice. "If I don't speak up for them, they're not gonna get the money they deserve. Me and the other pitchers have been here longer than you. We deserve ours."

"Are you going to make sure the kids get what they want before you sign?" I yelled. "You're not worried about the kids, Gaylord, you're worried about yourself. I'm telling you this time—don't use my name in the papers again. Next time I won't tell you."

I was mad enough to fight him right then, but we didn't come close to that, even though the papers had it that "we almost came to blows." Just then Ken Aspromonte came in and called a meeting at which he announced that he had resigned as manager, effective at season's end, in a week.

Once again people were writing that I would become the first black man hired to manage a major league team. I had heard that rumor so many times over the years that I was almost afraid to get my hopes up. Baseball had not only never had a black manager in the majors, it hadn't even had a black third base coach. In fact, only three blacks had ever managed in the minor leagues.

But this time I learned my dream was about to come true. We were in Cleveland preparing for our final three-day road trip of the season, to Boston, when I was called to go up to the office of general manager Phil Seghi. My agent, Ed Keating, whose office was in the city, was waiting for me with a big smile on his face.

"They're gonna offer you the job of managing the ballclub next year," Ed said.

"I guess I'll listen to the offer," I said, smiling.

Ted Bonda, the executive vice president of the Indians, was in Seghi's office. We all shook hands and took seats. Then Phil Seghi started talking, saying they were going to change managers and that they wanted me to manage the club and also to play. Phil, seated at his desk and puffing on his pipe, never looked directly at me when he spoke. He looked at his desk, looked at the ceiling, looked over my right shoulder, looked over my left shoulder, but he never looked me in the eye.

"I'd prefer not to be a player-manager," I said, "but if that's what you want, fine. But I want you to know that I will use Frank Robinson just like any other manager would. I'll play when I feel like I should play, no more, no less. But the foremost thing in my mind is that I'll be a manager. The player Frank Robinson will come second. I will take care of the 24 other players before I take care of Frank Robinson."

Phil and Ted said that met with their approval, then we started discussing my salary. I had signed a 1975 player's contract for $180,000—and that was the figure they now offered me.

"I've already got that salary as a player," I said. "What you're telling me is you want me to manage for nothing."

That, I was told, was the offer.

"Well, I don't want to accept that, and I'm not going to," I said. "At least you could offer me a small raise. I wouldn't expect you to add to my player salary the figure you were paying Aspromonte or anything like that. But at least you could offer me a $20,000 raise."

In essence I was told, take the offer or leave it. Ed Keating asked if he and I could be left in private to confer, and Phil and Ted stepped out.

"Frank, this is your chance, the opportunity you've been waiting for for a long time," Ed said. "It doesn't look like they're going to budge. If you don't want to take the job on their terms, we can tell them no. But if you want to manage, here's your chance."

"Damn, Ed, this is awfully small-minded on their part," I said. "They actually want me to manage for nothing. If they were to release me right now, I would get $180,000 over the next year. If I take the job, manage the ballclub, and also play, I get the same amount. But they've put me in a position where they know I almost can't refuse their offer. If I refuse, there's no telling when I will ever get another chance to manage in the major leagues—or if I will. If I turn down the job, that would just give other owners an excuse not to hire me or other blacks."

"I think you're right," Keating said. "This is the first time a black man has been offered the job of managing in the majors, and it may just open the door for others to follow through."

"Okay, I'll accept the offer," I said. "But I just want you to know I don't like it, and that next year we'll stick it to them."

Having gotten the annoyance out of my system, I was happy finally to be a manager in the major leagues. Ed asked Phil and Ted to come back in, I signed the contract, and Seghi said my appointment would not be announced until after we returned home following the last game of the season in Boston. "The club will fly back here, but I want you to fly to Chicago, Frank, so that everyone thinks you're going home. In Chicago you'll meet Ed and fly in here later. Then we'll have the press conference here the next day."

I didn't understand the need for all the cloak-and-dagger stuff, but I went along with the plan. The only problem turned out to be that the ballclub's flight from Boston was delayed and it landed at the same time mine came in from Chicago. My teammates saw me and started hollering, "What are you doing here? We thought you went home."

"I decided to come back and visit some people," I blurted, barely able to keep a straight face.

I doubt that any press conference introducing a new manager was attended by as many members of the media as was mine. My appointment was a historic moment. It was a great day for baseball and also one that caused many writers to examine the game's abysmal record in hiring blacks for management positions. It had been 27 years since the late Jackie Robinson had integrated baseball's playing fields. Thus it had taken the major leagues more than a quarter of a century before summoning up the decency to hire the first black manager, and that was a disgraceful situation. When I think of all the black players who contributed so much to the game and then, with so much more to offer, left it only because they were given no chance to manage a team or work in a front office or even coach third base, I have serious doubts about the integrity of many of those who run our national pastime.

One reason the owners and general managers of major league teams have cited as to why no black manager had been hired sooner was that blacks did not have minor league managerial experience. But, of course, those same ballclubs would not hire blacks to manage in their minor league systems to get experience, which is the traditional route most managers take to the majors. In baseball's 25 years since 1947, through the 1972 season, major league clubs had farm teams that played 3491 seasons. In that time, exactly three black men—Gene Banks (two years), Tommie Aaron (two years), and Hector Lopez (one year)—managed teams for five of those seasons: 5 of 3491 is 0.14 percent.

But in that same 25-year period, approximately 20 percent of major league players were of black or Hispanic heritage. And the black and Hispanic players produced almost 70 percent of the most noteworthy career performances in the majors during that quarter century. In hits, 10 of the top 13 were black or Hispanic players; in runs scored, 9 of the top 12; in total bases, 8 of the top 11; in runs batted in, 7 of the top 12; in home runs, 6 of the top 10; in base stealing, the top 4. Among pitchers, the two top winners were Bob Gibson (black) and Juan Marichal (Hispanic). They joined Ferguson Jenkins (black) as the only pitchers who won 20 games in five or more seasons.

Some people were a little surprised when I refused to keep Larry Doby as a coach. He had given up a secure job in Montreal the year before to coach for the Indians, I'm told, in the hopes that he might become the Cleveland manager. Doby was certainly a popular figure in the city. But you like to see your coaches backing the manager, and Doby had not done that, had not rallied around Aspromonte. So I had to let him go. It wasn't an easy decision to make, because I know that Larry had gone through hell as the first black player in the American League, and I felt for him. But I didn't feel in my heart that I'd be doing the right thing in bringing him back. To this day when we happen upon one another, Larry Doby and I don't speak.

I didn't rehire any of the Indian coaches. I wanted to bring in my own staff and start fresh. When a club's been losing for years, you need to clear out the negatives and develop a new attitude among the players. If you keep the coaches, once you hit a rough spot the players tend to say that nothing's changed. A losing ballclub has to be changed.

As the first black manager, I was obliged to speak at a number of annual baseball dinners, as well as on *Face the Nation*. I also lined up my coaching staff quickly because I was committed to Hiram Cuevas to manage his Santurce team again, and I would never let him down even though major league managers were not supposed to work elsewhere in the off-season. I had to pass up the winter meetings, but I found out in subsequent years that I didn't miss much. At them you spend a lot of time rubbing elbows with other managers and general managers only to be told that they have super players and that yours are horse spit, but they sure as hell want to take some of your horse spit players off your hands and give you nothing in return.

One of the first coaching candidates I heard from was Jeff Torborg, the ex-catcher with whom I had played on both the Dodgers and the Angels. He had been coaching a college team and wanted to get back in the game. I had a lot of respect for Jeff's baseball knowledge and the way he worked with pitchers. I hired him as my bullpen coach.

I hired Tommy McCraw, age 33, as hitting coach. I had played with Tommy on the Angels, and he, too, had joined the Indians in 1974. He was a smart hitter who had batted over .300 in a part-time role, and I also planned to keep him on the active roster.

I asked around extensively about who would make an outstanding third base coach, and the name that came up most often was Dave Garcia. He had won four championships in 14 years of managing in the minors and had also won a championship managing in the Mexican Winter League. In addition, he had been the first base coach of the San Diego Padres for four years. From my first conversation with him, I liked Dave Garcia a lot.

I felt fortunate to get Harvey Haddix to leave his Ohio farm to return to the game as my pitching coach. I'd had a lot of respect for him as a pitcher in my early years in Cincinnati. Subsequently he had been the pitching coach for the Mets, Reds, and Red Sox.

Writers in droves descended on the Indians' spring training camp in Tucson, Arizona. Some of them wanted to know why I felt I had been hired as the Cleveland manager. I said I presumed that Phil Seghi, who had known me since 1958 and knew of my managing record in winter ball, had been the force behind my being hired. I later was to find out that Ted Bonda was actually responsible for my getting the job.

For years the Indians had been in financial trouble and were in fact near bankruptcy a couple of times, I learned, while I was the manager. I know there were several hotels that did not welcome us back in the second half of the season's play because our bills had not been paid from earlier visits. On charter flights, the airlines finally made the ballclub pay in advance. Once there were rumors that the club might not be able to make our payroll, but we were always paid on time. I guess Ted Bonda had to be a bit of a financial wizard to keep us afloat.

Bonda admitted that he had thought of hiring me as the Indians manager the year before, in 1973, when the team had attracted only 605,073 ticket buyers. (Being in the pennant race for much of 1974 had added over 500,000 ticket sales.) "I thought a black manager would be good for the city," said Bonda, as 35 percent of Cleveland's 800,000 population was black. "Only a few blacks have been coming to games, and I thought a black manager would attract more black spectators as well as awaken interest throughout the city. And I just thought hiring Frank was the right thing to do." But I disagreed with Bonda's view that a black manager would bring anyone to the ballpark; fans come to see players, not managers.

A number of writers speculated that a prime reason why Aspromonte was fired and I was hired was that George Hendrick would not play hard for Aspromonte but I would see that he did. I didn't anticipate having a problem with Hendrick. I had managed him in Puerto Rico after the '73 season and had helped him a little—George didn't need much help—with his hitting. He batted .362 and led the league in hitting.

George Hendrick had a style all his own. He did not bust his tail on a ball field at all times, and that annoyed fans, writers, teammates, and the front office. All I asked of George was that he give *his* 100 percent. It might not be the same as another player's 100 percent. People thought he didn't always run out ground balls, because George's running style did not feature flailing arms or anything like that. At times Hendrick seemed almost to stroll when running to first.

But I had no problem with George's style; it was not my style as a player, but then I did not expect anyone to play as I had. I expected each player to play within his own capabilities. So George Hendrick drew complaints from others, but on a baseball field he could do things better than most. He could go from home to third on a triple better than anyone else on the club, from first to third better, and he could make plays in the outfield better than any of our veterans. People felt he should play that way all the time, but that wasn't his style.

In one exhibition game George lined a shot deep to right and went into his home-run trot. But the liner sank and caromed off the fence. He got a double instead of a triple, but he had really been hustling all spring, so I didn't get on him between innings.

"I thought it was going out," George said to me, apologetically.

"I thought it was too," I said. "Just don't let it happen again."

I believe that baseball players do not do enough running, either in the spring or during the season. I hate to see a player hit a triple and have to stand at third bent over, with his hands on his knees, gasping for breath. So early in the spring I had all the players doing long-distance running from foul line to foul line in the outfield, the way pitchers run. We started with 15 repetitions and built up to 35. This exercise strengthens your cardiovascular system and your legs, and it increases your stamina. Many baseball players tended to be more than a bit worn down by the time the dog days of August rolled around. I hoped mine would be strong.

Player-coach Tommy McCraw forcefully supervised the distance running drills, and Rico Carty started calling him "Hitler." Veteran outfielder Ken Berry, who had played with McCraw on the White Sox and who was trying to make our club, said, "I baby-sat for McCraw's kids in Chicago, and look what he's doing to me!"

Players were encouraged to go hard on their runs, but no time limit was set as to how fast they had to cover the distance. As guys finished their repetitions, they could leave. Rico Carty was always the last player out there, running alone at his own leisurely pace.

As a player I always run a lot on my own: not in the off-season and not after the season began but in spring training. I did extra running without being told because I felt that if your legs were in shape, the rest of your body would take care of itself. Players today are doing far less running, and I don't believe they're in shape when the season starts. During the season, only the pitchers run regularly. But today pitchers don't run as much as they should, which is why they get tired and don't go nine innings as often as pitchers did in the past. Pitchers today think they falter because their arms get tired, but I think it's their legs that tire.

Once the players had some stamina built up, we had them concentrate on 90-foot sprints. Start, dash 90 feet, and stop. The distance between bases is 90 feet and that's what a baseball player needs to work on. We worked hard on the sprints, starting with 10 repetitions and building up to 35 each day. Most teams run 10 sprints without real effort. Guys will take maybe five strides before they get up any speed, run hard for about 45 feet, and coast the last five strides. They run ten like that and accomplish nothing for their conditioning.

The only two Indian players who complained seriously about our running exercises were Rico Carty and Gaylord Perry. They didn't complain to me, which was the worst part of it. Guys who keep bitching on the side are the worst kind to have on your ballclub, because they create bad feelings among the other players. Gaylord's comments could be particularly destructive, as he was the leader of the pitching staff, a veteran who had won 63 games over the past three seasons.

I had hoped that the problems with Gaylord had been worked out after I'd been named manager. He had congratulated me, and I had told him to forget about what had transpired between us, that as far as I was concerned, it was over. But when the pitchers reported to spring training, Gaylord told me that he wanted to do his own running program and that he'd always been allowed to do so. I told him that he couldn't do that with me as manager, that everyone on the Indians would follow the same program, and that it would be more extensive than in the past.

I laid out the program to all the pitchers and added, "I want all of you to run in from the bullpen when you're called to throw batting practice or pitch in an intrasquad game, and also run off the mound when you're finished. That will not only speed things up, it will benefit your legs."

The first time Gaylord was called to pitch batting practice, he strolled to the mound, and later strolled off it. Earlier, fooling around with pitcher Jim Kern during our stretching exercises, Gaylord accidentally gave him a scratch on the shin with his spikes. Next, he asked one of the coaches during the outfield running, "Why aren't any of the black players out here working out?" Charlie Spikes, who is black and an outfielder, was running on his own not 10 yards from Perry. "It's about time I moved to another team anyway," Perry said.

I finally called Gaylord into my office, closed the door, told him I didn't like his attitude, and said, "Apparently you want to be traded."

"That's baseball talk," he said. "You know I win my 20 games every year. You don't have anybody else to do that."

"You're right," I said. "But if you feel that's going to keep you here with a bad attitude, you're wrong. You know the players here look up to you. If they see you doing certain things, they're going to wonder why Gaylord can get away with those things. That pulls a ballclub apart."

"Well, if you're going to be watching every little move I make, maybe it's best that you trade me," he said.

"No individual is bigger than the ballclub," I said, which was what I told the entire squad. "Everybody will be treated the same."

Phil Seghi suggested that he meet with me and Gaylord. We did, and when Gaylord saw that I had the backing of the front office, he seemed to come around. Instead of being at the rear, his usual place, in our next running exercises, Gaylord was at the front. A good sign. I just hoped Gaylord would sustain that attitude.

Another of the Indian pitchers was anonymously quoted in the papers as saying, "Gaylord's lost a lot of respect around here."

I appointed shortstop Frank Duffy and center fielder George Hendrick cocaptains of the team, one to run the infield, the other to take charge of the outfield. Duffy told reporters that my run-in with Gaylord Perry had not caused any dissension on the club. "In fact, there is a closeness in this camp that we haven't had in the past," he said. "You can feel it, and I'm real happy about it."

As the spring wore on, I was happier about our chances to be competitive as a ballclub, particularly after we traded for Boog Powell. He'd had an off year in Baltimore, hitting only 11 home runs, but he was only 33 and I figured he'd bounce back. Boog did indeed, hitting 27 home runs, driving in 86 RBIs, and batting .297 for us. We had to give up our only front-line catcher in the deal, Dave Duncan, but he couldn't hit a lick.

Phil Seghi thought 23-year-old catcher Alan Ashby would develop, combining with John Ellis. Ellis was not a true catcher, Seghi admitted, but he had worked behind the plate 42 times in 1974, and Phil thought he would improve with more work. In 477 at-bats Ellis had hit .285 with 10 home runs and 64 RBIs, which was promising. But once we started playing exhibition games with John Ellis behind the plate, I had serious worries about our catching potential.

Early on in camp I emphasized at a clubhouse meeting that I wanted us to have a smart ballclub. "When I was with the Orioles we always played heads-up baseball, and I want us to play the same way," I said. "Physical errors I expect, but no bonehead plays."

We worked on fundamentals all through the spring, and it looked like we were going to have a fairly good defensive team that could play smart baseball. Except perhaps behind the plate. Neither Ashby nor Ellis would win any awards defensively at the time, though Alan has gone on to become a solid catcher who's still playing in the major leagues in 1988.

John Ellis had a peculiar problem for a catcher, one I had never come across before. John knew most of our opponents by their numbers, but he wasn't very good at placing names with faces. He seemed to have some kind of block in remembering who an opponent was by his face.

At one point in an early exhibition game there was a bang-bang play at the plate. The throw came in to Ellis, who swung around and missed the tag on the sliding runner, who hopped up and ran to the dugout. But from our bench we saw that the runner had missed touching home plate. Naturally, the umpire didn't make a call.

But we all started screaming at Ellis, "He missed the plate! He missed the plate! Go tag the runner, John!"

Ellis ran to the opposing dugout, but he didn't know which guy had been the base runner, because all the players had their backs, bearing their uniform numbers, to the wall. So Ellis started tagging everybody in the dugout.

Suddenly the runner leaped out of the dugout and headed for the plate. Ellis turned and threw the ball to our pitcher, who was covering home. The runner turned back toward the dugout and—in what must have been a baseball first—we had a brief rundown play between home plate and the dugout before the man was tagged out.

Afterward I said to bullpen and catching coach Jeff Torborg, "You think John Ellis heard my speech about playing smart baseball this year?"

Toward the end of preseason, Boog Powell told the press, "I didn't think Frank would have the patience to be a manager. He's such a perfectionist about baseball that when things aren't done right, it's got to eat at him."

People have a tendency to prejudge me because of the intensity with which I played the game. I knew what it took to be a winner, and I tried to instill that attitude in my players, to let them know what it would take, the sacrifices they would have to make to get to the top and help a ballclub succeed. But Boog was right about the game eating at me. I had no patience with bonehead plays and even less when they were repeated. I had no patience with a player who didn't strive to get the most out of his ability, who didn't give 100 percent, and that player heard from me.

I was a perfectionist as a player, and I tried to be as a manager too. But I did not expect perfection on a baseball field because I had never seen a perfect player. No one can be absolutely perfect all the time. Physical errors are unavoidable, and a manager has to accept a certain amount of mental mistakes. But the player who made the same mistake over and over again could not play for me.

Both Dick Williams and Earl Weaver said that I would not be able to play while managing. "I think that spring training will convince Robby he can't do both," Dick said. Earl said, "I'll make a bet Frank won't be playing after the first couple of months of the season."

I didn't devote a lot of time to preparing Frank Robinson to play.

Whenever I took batting practice—and I was always at the end of the line—my players would holler, "Stop hogging all the time in the cage!" It became a ritual that I enjoyed.

I concentrated more on Frank Robinson the manager and worrying about the other players. I was looking over a lot of young players who had been invited to camp, trying to get a line on my veteran personnel, and trying to select the best 25 players out of the group. Four youngsters that I knew would be Indians very soon were center fielder Rick Manning and second baseman Duane Kuiper, as well as pitchers Dennis Eckersley and Eric Raich.

Phil Seghi wanted me to play and kept insisting that I would. "I still believe Frank will be an important contributor to our offense," Phil said. "If I didn't, I wouldn't have signed him as a player-manager."

I just didn't think there would be much of a spot for me on the ballclub, beyond pinch hitting. I certainly couldn't play in the field and try to manage. Rico Carty, another right-handed hitter, was the designated hitter and a good one, who would bat .308, with 18 home runs and 64 RBIs in 1975. Seghi was remembering that, despite my low average in 1974, I had hit 22 home runs and driven in 68 runs. But there was no position that Carty could adequately play in the field.

When we prepared to break camp, I wanted to keep the four youngsters who had most impressed me. Dennis Eckersley was only 20, but he was a hard-throwing right-hander who knew how to pitch. I had to fight to get Seghi to put him on our roster, rather than give him more seasoning in the minors. Eckersley compiled a record of 13-7 with an earned run average of 2.60. I also wanted to keep Rick Manning, also 20, but a truly outstanding center fielder who would hit .285 and steal 19 bases for us in 1975 after we brought him up in May. I argued to retain Eric Raich and Duane Kuiper too, but Seghi said no on them, until May when veteran second baseman Jack Brohamer went out with a hip injury. Kuiper deserved to make the team in the spring, but Seghi didn't want to pay two salaries at second base.

I pleased Seghi no end on opening day in Cleveland when I showed him my lineup card. I was the DH batting second. "Why don't you hit a home run the first time up?" Phil said, smiling.

"Sure," I said and laughed.

A crowd of 58,000 was in the stands when we lined up in front of the dugout for the team picture. It so happened that the first four hitters in my batting order were black, the next five white. I noticed that John

Ellis was standing next to me, and I gave him a little shove. "Get down the end," I said. "This is a new deal this year. The colored guys are in front."

Then we went out for the introductions, and I couldn't believe the ovation I received. One hundred thousand fans could not have been louder. It was the biggest ovation I ever received, and it almost brought tears to my eyes. After all the years of waiting to become a major league manager—ignored because so many team owners felt that fans would not accept a black manager—I was on the job and people were loudly pleased. Thank you all, folks.

After Oscar Gamble popped out, I stepped in for my first at-bat. Doc Medich of the Yankees got two quick strikes past me. I fouled off the next pitch before taking two balls. Medich threw a fastball low and away, but I got the head of the bat out in front on it, and the ball sailed into the left-field stands for a home run. A fairy tale home run.

This time the ovation was even louder. Of all the hits I'd had and all the cheers I'd heard, that home run my first time up as a manager had to be my all-time thrill. I looked up in the loge and saw Barbara and my children clapping and yelling. When we went on to win the game, 5-3, it made for a perfect day.

Of course, that night, when Phil Seghi and his wife took us to dinner, all they kept talking about was that Phil had told me to hit a home run, what a great opening day it had been, and how everyone except the Yankees had gone home happy.

"I don't know what you're all so excited about," I said. "It was just another opening day." We all had a good laugh.

About ten days later I had my first problem with a player. It wasn't with Gaylord Perry but with his older brother Jim, a pitcher who had won 17 games for the Indians the year before and who had been totally cooperative with me and my program. I had told all the pitchers in spring training that when Harvey Haddix or I went to the mound to relieve them, they were not in any way to show us up. Just hand over the ball.

Jim Perry had pitched well in this game against the Brewers. We were down 1-0 going into the ninth, but then Jim gave up a home run to George Scott and a double to Don Money. On orders Jim intentionally walked the next hitter to set up a possible double play; then I sent Haddix out to relieve Perry. Annoyed, Jim kicked dirt on the mound before finally handing over the ball and stalking off to the dugout.

After the game I had Harvey tell Jim Perry that I wanted to see him in my office. I was annoyed with Jim, but I cooled down sitting there thinking about an incident in my rookie year when Birdie Tebbets had pulled me from a game for a pinch hitter. I slammed my bat in the rack. "Are you mad because I took you out of the game for a hitter?" Birdie asked me quietly.

"No, I'm mad you had to take me out because I'm not hitting," I said.

"Good," Birdie said, "because I just wanted you to know who's managing this team."

Harvey came back and said that Jim Perry was washing his hands, "But he said he'll come right in." When ten minutes had passed and he hadn't shown up, I told Harvey I was so mad that I'd wait to see Perry the next day. "Otherwise I'll probably say something I shouldn't."

What delayed Jim Perry from coming in was that he had been talking to the press. I read what he said in Russ Schneider's column in the next day's *Plain Dealer:* "I'm no rookie and I think I at least deserve the privilege of being asked if I still feel good, and if I'm still throwing the ball well. And if I had been asked, I would've told him I felt good. I'm out there busting my back and here comes Harvey to tell me I'm out of the game. At this rate, Harvey will be hated by all the pitchers by the time the season is over. Every time he comes out you know you're gone, without any questions about how you feel. They ought to know I'd be honest with them about how I feel."

Any time I spoke to my pitchers, in a group or in private, I had my pitching coach present, so Harvey Haddix stood by when Jim Perry came into the office the next day. I told him flat out that whenever he was summoned to my office, I expected him to appear promptly. "And any time I send Harvey out to the mound to take you out, I've made up my mind," I said. "I'm not sending him out there to ask you how you feel. Now I'm not going to put a muzzle on you about talking to the press. You can say what you want to say. But you're going to have some bad games and the newspapermen are going to come to talk to me. If you're going to rip me and my coaches when you have a decent ball game, I can do the same thing. If you want our protection, we want the same respect."

"I understand," said Jim, who had gotten the message.

In early May I had to remove Jim Perry from the rotation. He just wasn't getting the ball where he wanted it, his record by then was 1-5, and he was giving up an average of close to seven runs per game. Jim was not pleased by the demotion, but he didn't say anything.

None of the players was saying much as we kept playing sub-.500 ball, and in an effort to pull the team together a bit, I suggested that we have a kangaroo court similar to the one in my days in Baltimore. When I was with the Dodgers, they, too, had a kangaroo court. But neither that one nor ours in Cleveland was of much value. The players voted Oscar Gamble as our judge. He was articulate, but the judge in these affairs has to be a little witty, and Oscar was not.

In addition, the players kept bringing in cases that had nothing to do with baseball, which was what the court was designed to focus on and have fun with. If a guy happened to see a teammate someplace with an ugly girl, a silly charge was brought against him. That kind of case predominated in Cleveland. It suggested to me just how much my players were concentrating on baseball.

I also wondered if a kangaroo court could be effective with a losing ballclub. It was very hard to develop great enthusiasm among players who had been on losing teams for years, to say nothing of getting them to pay attention to the game every moment they were on the field the way players on winning ballclubs tend to do as a matter of course. In our first 26 games, players missed signs 15 times. I told everyone that from then on, anyone who missed a sign would be fined $100 and that outfielders who overthrew the cutoff man would be fined the same. Charlie Spikes, a prime offender in the latter category, was the first player fined.

"I understand," Charlie said. "I deserve it."

Most of the guys took the fines in stride and made an effort not to foul up again. John Ellis was not among them. He was fined $100 for missing a hit-and-run sign while batting. He was fined $50 for reporting late for batting practice. And for signing up for early batting practice and then not showing up for it, he was fined another $50. John complained to me and said, "I think I'd be better off in another organization."

"If you feel that way, you have my permission to talk to Phil and see if he can trade you," I said. "I don't want any players here who don't want to be here."

Ellis complained again when later I fined him $100 for missing the take sign in a game, and $200 for missing the take sign the next time up after I had told him about the first missed sign. I don't think I ever missed a sign. All it takes is concentration, which Ellis just couldn't seem to apply to his game.

By midseason I had had it with John Ellis. He was batting .217 when I sent up a pinch hitter for him, and John started throwing his catching equipment around the dugout. When he flung his catcher's mask, it almost hit me. I asked if he was mad at me, and he said he was.

"You're lucky even to be here the way you're hitting," I said.

"Yeah, and you're lucky to be here yourself," he snapped.

"I'll be here a lot longer than you will," I said, and immediately thought of how foolish Hank Bauer had sounded using a similar line when I was a player.

But I was so angry that I sent Ellis to the clubhouse, and even when he apologized to me after the game, I was still hot.

"You should've known I was upset," John said. "You shouldn't have said anything to me."

"*I* shouldn't have said anything to you? John, maybe you can't play for me."

"I guess that's right," he said.

"Well, since you feel you can't play for me," I said, "I don't want you to play for me. From here on out, you will not be my catcher. You'll still be on the team, but you won't be my regular catcher."

Looking back now, I probably should not have gotten on John Ellis so sharply in the dugout. And in later years I tried to hold my piece in such situations and make my points with the player in question when things had cooled down. That, I found, was a better way to deal with current players. But I had played for managers who responded in kind to angry ballplayers. Earl Weaver always chewed out a player for challenging his authority, usually on the spot and loudly. Most players tried not to infuriate Weaver again. Even those who yelled back at him continued to play if they could still contribute to the team's success. I just didn't feel that John Ellis, given his attitude, his .217 batting average, and his defensive liabilities, could help us very much playing regularly.

From the beginning of the season, it was apparent that, as constituted, the Indians were not going to be a competing club. Right after we had lost 10 out of 13 games in a stretch, we traded Jim Perry and pitcher Dick Bosman to the A's for pitcher John (Blue Moon) Odom and $25,000. We also waived two veteran outfielders and called up from the minors Rick Manning and Eric Raich. We had gone with older guys long enough, and I felt it was time to bring in youngsters who always had more enthusiasm and were not mired in a losing attitude. Young players have something to prove, and I wanted to give them a chance to show what they could do.

John Odom was a veteran who turned out to have a bad attitude. He came in saying, "I always wanted to pitch for a black manager." He was not thrilled when his black manager told him he would not be starting but pitching long relief. Next he threatened to leave the team if Phil Seghi didn't give him a raise in his $42,500 contract. If he left, I told him, he would be suspended without pay and fined for every day he was gone. Odom stayed but asked to be traded.

He didn't pitch particularly well, but on June 4 I needed another starter. I told Odom I had decided to give him a start, and he had a look on his face like I had just sentenced him to hang. "What's wrong now?" I asked.

Then I heard another baseball first. "If I do well tonight," Odom said, "is that going to mess up my chances of getting away from here to another club?"

I said no and told him that I expected him to go out there and give me 100 percent, which he did. John Odom threw a two-hit, complete-game shutout at the Royals, and we won 4-0.

Odom wanted to go back to the A's, and Charlie Finley was open to a deal but changed his mind. Seghi decided to meet with Odom in my office and hoped to change his attitude. When Phil said that Finley had pulled out of the deal for him, Odom said, "You're a liar."

"Don't call me a liar!" Phil fired back, and said he'd call Finley and let Odom hear from the A's owner himself, which he did. John heard the news and hung his head. I asked him if he could be happy pitching here, and he said only if he got a raise and could start. The next day he was traded to the Atlanta Braves for pitcher Roric Harrison, who had been an Oriole prospect when I was with the team.

In all we tried 20 pitchers and 25 nonpitchers in 1975 trying to find a winning combination. Just before the trading deadline, we sent Gaylord Perry to the Texas Rangers for three pitchers: Jim Bibby, Jackie Brown, and Rick Waits. We gave up Perry's $150,000 salary and also got $150,000 in cash for him. It helped our finances, and it helped the club's attitude. Gaylord was a cancer on the young pitchers, because there were guys who tried to emulate the veteran winner, who had gone 2-and-7 in his last nine starts for us, with an ERA of 4.22. He could have taught the young pitchers a lot. He had been a power pitcher in his younger days, occasionally throwing a greaseball. But he had become a smart pitcher in later years who knew how to work on hitters and avoid giving them anything good to hit. With us he just tried to do enough in 1975 to get by. I saw him throw his K-Y jelly ball only twice in two months.

We also brought up Duane Kuiper, and I played him at second base, where he fielded well, hit, and stole bases. All our youngsters made contributions, and I felt the trades had helped us, but we continued to lose more than we won until July, when we won 10 games out of 13 and became competitive. By that point I had gotten tougher on the players, instituting a curfew for the first time. But I was platooning John Ellis at catcher again, because I was so thin behind the plate without him.

I personally couldn't play as much as I wanted to. My left shoulder had been aching for months, and the doctor finally found I had a torn tendon that needed surgery. I couldn't damage it anymore, so I postponed the operation till after the season. I ended up batting only 118 times, hitting a career-low .237 with 9 home runs and 24 RBIs. One writer asked me if I put myself in as the DH when the opposition had a particularly tough left-handed pitcher starting.

"No," I said, "I put myself in only when there's a particularly easy left-hander in there."

I tried to lighten up whenever possible because I truly felt like I was under a microscope the entire season, that every move I made was scrutinized and analyzed. I was under tremendous pressure to win. The owners—and there were more than 50 of them—needed a winner to put fans in the seats. While drawing 1.1 million spectators in 1974, the Indians had lost some $400,000. And, of course, being the first black man to manage in the majors, I felt it was important that I win to keep the job and also to keep the way clear for other blacks to get the opportunity to manage.

Earlier in the season when we visited Texas, Ranger manager Billy Martin told me that he would be moving up to general manager next season. "When I do, I'll make you my manager, Frank," he said.

In July Martin was fired, but by the time we went into New York to play the Yankees on August 2, with whom did I exchange lineup cards at home plate but Billy Martin. We looked at one another and laughed.

"What's the secret, Billy?" I asked, and we laughed some more.

It was easier to laugh the second half of the season as the youngsters turned our ballclub around and we played much better baseball. After a horrendous start, we finished only one game under .500 with a 79-80 record. Late in the last game of the season in which we mashed the first-place Red Sox 11-4, Boston manager Darrell Johnson called me on the dugout phone and said, "I just want to tell you, Frank, that for the last two-thirds of the season, you were the best manager in the league."

"Thanks very much, Darrell," I said, "I really appreciate that."

This is me with the Reds, happy to be in the big leagues. *(Cincinnati Reds, Inc.)*

My wife Barbara and I enjoyed
traveling with our children, daughter
Nichelle (in my arms) and son
Frank, Jr.

Frank, Jr., enjoying a day at the ballpark.
(Herb Heise, *Cincinnati Enquirer*)

The great centerfielder Paul Blair and I
with our sons on Family Day in Baltimore.

Here I am with some mementos of a major league career.

This is a recent photo of my family: my wife Barbara, son Frank, Jr., and daughter Nichelle.

Barbara and I are proud parents at Nichelle's high school graduation.

The Baltimore Oriole old-timers have a reunion. Here are Barbara and I with: (TOP) Brooks and Connie Robinson,(MIDDLE) Eldrod and Meryl Hendricks,(BOTTOM)Boog and Jan Powell.

This is the Robinson family on the day of my induction into the Hall of Fame. *(Richard Collins)*

The Hall of Fame plaque looks mighty good to me. *(Richard Collins)*

Barbara and I enjoying a night out.

11 ⑨
⑨ *THE SCOUTING REPORTS LIST "RACE"*

ON August 25, 1975, Ted Bonda had summoned me to a meeting at his office in the Investment Plaza building. Phil Seghi was there, and they told me they wanted me back as manager and as a DH if my shoulder surgery permitted me to play. That took some of the pressure off me. A month later I signed an $80,000 contract as a manager and another for $120,000 as a player, health permitting. Ed Keating had also gotten me the same fringe benefits I had in 1975: a free apartment and use of a car during the season, plus round-trip airfare from Los Angeles for my wife and children.

When the announcement was made to the media, one of the radio reporters asked, "If you were Phil Seghi, would you have rehired Frank Robinson?"

I was so happy I decided to have some fun with the guy by saying, no, if I were Seghi I would not rehire Robinson. "Why?" the man asked, holding the mike toward me.

"The Indians finished fourth last year and they'll finish fourth again this year. The Indians did nothing the first half of the season. We started winning a few games now. But that's like being on a banana peel, sliding around and going no place. It just goes to show you again about *those people*. They can't handle responsibility."

That afternoon my coaches and I met with Phil Seghi to review the ballclub and assess our needs for next season. My coaches and I felt that our primary need was a good defensive catcher who could handle pitchers and also hit. Seghi wanted to keep Johnny Ellis, but I said he wouldn't do. Then Dave Garcia said, "Ellis is a bad person to have on your ballclub. He'll come off the trainer's table and tell Tom McCraw he can't play, then he'll walk over to me and say he can play."

I had gotten along well enough with Phil Seghi that season, regularly dropping by his office upstairs to discuss the ballclub and moves that I felt we should make. We didn't always agree on things, but I knew going into this job that a manager and general manager were never in total agreement. My assessment of John Ellis's abilities and Phil's different feelings were not atypical of our relationship.

He thought I should have pitched Jackie Brown more after we got him in the Gaylord Perry deal, and he pressed his point in one meeting with the coaches. As was his habit, Phil did not look at me but at the coaches when he said, "Brown won 13 games last year, why isn't he pitching more?"

"Don't look at the coaches," I said, not for the first time. "Look at me. I'm the manager who's not using Brown."

Then I explained once again that I wasn't using Brown as a starter because he wasn't pitching as effectively as he had the year before when I'd hit against him. Jeff Torborg was getting him back in line in the bullpen, and I expected Jackie to improve next year. I sometimes had the feeling that Phil, who had been a minor league manager for many years, still harbored ambitions of managing.

Seghi also seemed determined to keep me in the dark about key decisions in the organization, such as which amateur players we should draft. Nobody showed me scouting reports on players we considered drafting so that I could offer my opinions on our needs. I wasn't even invited to sit in on the draft meetings with Phil. I was pleased to hear that we had drafted a top catching prospect, Rick Cerone from Seton Hall, number 1, but I was not pleased to hear it from the writers rather than my front office. Then I wasn't informed that Rick Cerone was coming in for a workout with us until he appeared in the clubhouse, nor that he was going on the road with us for a few days before he reported to our Oklahoma City team. It was a very strange way of "communicating" for a major league organization.

Perhaps even more shocking to me was my reaction to the first reports on our opponents that I received from our major league advance scout, Dan Carnevale. The Cleveland Indian preprinted form listed not only player's name, height, and weight, but his race. I went flying up to Phil's office and told him that I thought it was time, over 100 years after the Emancipation Proclamation, that a man's race not be noted on our scouting reports.

"And I don't appreciate it when Carnevale throughout his reports uses the phrase 'this black boy' whenever the player's a Negro," I said. "He never describes a player as 'this white boy.' I don't think any such reference is necessary. Just tell Carnevale to tell me how to get a guy out or, if he's a pitcher, what he throws. I don't care what color a player is. As a matter of fact, when I see the player, I'll probably know what color he is."

Phil saw I was hot and quickly said, "I understand, Frank. We'll have the 'race' listing removed from our scouting report forms."

But he didn't do it. Phil just had the secretary white-out the race references on the copies of the scouting reports that were sent to me. Everyone else got the "colorized" reports. I understand the Indians still have a line on their forms that's headed "race." When I joined the Giants in 1981, their player forms also included race, but at my request new forms were printed that did not call for that information.

I'm sure, though, that to this day many major league organizations continue to make note of a player's race on all their reports. I know the Orioles listed race on their minor league player forms through the 1987 season. I don't think the Orioles have ever been among the most diligent organizations in scouting and signing black players, but I'm certain they haven't had a quota system where only a set number of minority players would be on the club at a given time. I have heard that some organizations have a maximum quota of blacks they will sign, but I don't know whether that is true. If true, those quota-restricted ballclubs would undoubtedly be found among the most unsuccessful teams in baseball.

Once the season ended, I had time to reflect on the problems I'd had with umpires. By June it had become apparent to me that certain umpires were so uptight about my being the first black manager that they wouldn't let me or my coaches say a word in defense of our players without threatening to throw us out of the game. After run-ins with several umpires—including one in which Jerry Neudecker pushed me twice while I was arguing that Charlie Spikes should not be called out on a foul ball that plate umpire Nick Bremigan ruled a fan had interfered with—I ended up pushing Neudecker. It was not unprovoked, though it proved to be unwise.

During another argument Neudecker bumped *me* and yelled that I had bumped him. I cursed him, and he ran me from the game. As he walked away from me, I hustled around him to get in a final word. Neudecker stopped short, thrust out his chest, and bumped me once, twice. I pushed him away from me with both hands. Rico Carty dragged me away, and I yelled at Neudecker: "If you think I bumped you this time, next time I'll knock you on your butt!"

I was fined $250 and suspended for three games by American League president Lee MacPhail. In his report he wrote, "Neudecker admits that it is possible that he may have bumped Robinson in the course of the argument but that if he did, it was accidental and unintentional." The umpire's bump was clear provocation, but MacPhail didn't see it that way. The umpire's bump was always accidental, but the manager or player always bumped an umpire intentionally, as far as the league office was concerned.

I was touched when my players rallied behind me and threatened to go on strike for three days to protest my suspension. They had all signed an agreement to do so and wanted to present it to MacPhail. I advised them not to, though I appreciated their support.

My second ejection came at the hands of Ron Luciano, the once-competent umpire who had turned himself into a clown and stopped paying attention to his job. Out of nowhere he once said to me when I was playing for the Orioles: "You're overpaid; you're not a real superstar."

"And if you were black and did what you do, they'd call you a clown instead of colorful," I said. From then on, Luciano didn't like me.

The incident in June occurred after Luciano, the first base umpire, called a checked swing by George Hendrick a strike. When Tom McCraw argued with Luciano, he said that if Tom kept it up, he'd be gone. I ran out and said, "You mean to tell me that a coach can't argue with an umpire?"

Luciano said that was right, that a coach couldn't argue on a checked swing. Then he said something that was very telling about the umpires' attitude toward me. "We can't be fair with you," Luciano said. "You won't let us be fair with you."

Ron Luciano admitted that the umpires were not being fair with me or my ballclub. For that inadvertent honesty, he should have been fired on the spot. But I did a very dumb thing with Luciano before leaving him. I pointed to the skin on my arm and said, "Is that why the call went against us?"

The first week in July I was ejected for a third time, and when you realize it took me 19 years as a player to be ejected three times, you might suspect something was amiss. This time my problem was with plate umpire Larry Barnett, who was squeezing Dennis Eckersley's strike zone on his sinkers. I yelled at Barnett a time or two, not screaming the way Earl Weaver does. Then when Barnett missed a third-strike call on Reggie Jackson, I hollered a cliché that everyone uses. "Poke a hole in your mask!" I yelled.

Barnett turned on me and said, "You're out of the game!"

I ran out to him to find out why I was gone, and Barnett said, "You don't tell me that."

"You've got to be kidding," I said. "Everyone yells that."

"Nobody yells it at *me*," he said.

I told the writers that no other umpire would run any other manager for yelling "Poke a hole in your mask." Russ Schneider of the Cleveland *Plain Dealer* asked if what I had meant was that I had been ejected because I was black. I said, "That's right." I also told him of the resentment and frustration that had built up inside me over the way the umpires were mistreating me and my ballclub.

The next day Russ asked me how many American League umpires I rated creditable, and I named ten who rated very good to not bad, including Larry Barnett. Then I named 13 others who ranged in performance from less than good to just plain bad.

Schneider's story was picked up all over the country, and within a week I received a visit from John Stevens, a retired umpire who worked for the league office as an umpire consultant. "What can we do to help you get along better with umpires, make things better?" he asked me.

"I don't want any special treatment," I said. "I just want to be treated like the other managers and not be subject to quick ejections."

Stevens nodded, then told me that *several* umpires had complained that every time I argued with them I ended up pointing to the color of my skin.

"I only did that once," I told him, "and I was wrong for doing it even once." I *felt* my skin color was a factor in some umpire's decision, but I never should have said it.

For the last two months of the season I cut down my yelling at umpires from the dugout and I stayed off the field as much as possible. When I did go out to argue, the umpires were much less defensive. I wasn't ejected from any more games in 1975. I decided that my beefs with the umpires may have been hurting the team more than helping it.

Near the end of the season, Schneider surveyed the umpires on their relationship with the league's managers and they agreed to speak anonymously. One umpire said of me: "Robbie has changed almost 100 percent since midseason. At first he'd start yelling at us on the first pitch of the game and he'd never stop. All of a sudden he went the other way. Maybe it's because the pressure of being the first black manager is gone."

I figured I knew how to handle umpires the next season, and I pretty much did—except for the Lou DiMuro crew of Rich Garcia, Bill Kunkle, and Dave Phillips. By July they had worked 15 of our games, and my team had suffered 12 ejections at their hands. We had only one other ejection in that time.

I regarded DiMuro as one of the worst umpires, but it was the other three members of his crew who ran me, my coaches, and players. Most of the ejections were absurd. Garcia got me first for simply yelling at him. I didn't curse once, yet he said, "I'm tired of hearing you yell at me."

Phillips was next. He was umpiring at home plate when I went out to talk to DiMuro about a play at second. I started to walk off, then turned back to Lou. Phillips yelled, "You can't go back."

"I can go back if I want to," I said, which is within the rules, but he tossed me anyway.

Bill Kunkle threw me out of a game in Chicago when I hadn't said a word to anyone. I was angry about a call at third base, but I remained sitting in the dugout waving a towel up and down. It was a hot day, and the towel slipped out of my hand, flew up in the air, and landed on the dugout roof, which is set back in Comiskey Park. It was strictly an accident, but Kunkle said, "You're gone." Later two of my coaches were thrown out of that game by DiMuro's crew.

Afterward, my mild-mannered third baseman, Buddy Bell—who normally never has problems with umpires but who had been ejected in a previous game by the DiMuro crew—complained to me. "It makes it tough when you can't get a gripe off your chest," Buddy said, which is true. "It's gotten so you can't have a conversation with those guys. If you say anything at all, they act like you're trying to show them up and they throw you out."

Phil Seghi made a request of the league office that the "Prussian-like" DiMuro crew not be assigned to future Indian games, a request that was ignored. Ted Bonda, now the club president, but a man who seldom spoke out, finally couldn't abide any more of the DiMuro crew members' treatment of us. "There is no doubt in my mind they have a psychological malice against our team," he said.

I think Ted was absolutely right. While DiMuro's crew had thrown 12 members of the Indians out of ballgames, it had ejected only 11 members of the 11 other teams in the American League.

I called a clubhouse meeting and said, "From now on we have to leave the umpires alone. I know it won't be easy on some calls. But we've got to ignore them because we just can't afford to lose players the way we have been. As for the DiMuro crew, I don't want to hear a word said to them. Every word any member of this ballclub says to a member of the DiMuro crew will cost $100—and that goes for me too. A $100-a-word fine should make us all keep our mouths shut." It did.

I still have no way of knowing if racism had any bearing on the way certain umpires came down on us without letup through the first half of my first two seasons at the Indians' helm. When we played in silence, as far as they were concerned, the umpires left us alone. But that is not the way baseball was supposed to be played. Leo Durocher used to kick umpire Jocko Conlan in his shinguards, and Conlan would kick Leo right back. Earl Weaver would yell at an umpire for five minutes, and the umpire would yell right back until he ran out of breath before ejecting Earl.

Everyone has got to make his points, right or wrong, and fans loved the show. But that show has been closed by the newer umpires.

12
LEARNING THE HARD WAY

DURING the '75 season we had gotten rid of 13 players from the 1974 squad and had improved. But I was aiming to bring the 1976 Indians in with a record over .500 for the first time since 1968, and more changes in personnel were necessary.

John Ellis, of course, had to go. We traded him to Texas for pitcher Stan Thomas and utility man Ron Pruitt, an excellent deal. In 37 appearances as a spot starter and reliever, Thomas had a 4-4 record and an ERA of 2.29. Pruitt was a great role player. I spotted him in all three outfield positions, at first base, third base, DH, and catcher.

Duane Kuiper was going to be my regular second baseman, so we sent veteran Jack Brohamer to the White Sox for infield reserve Larvell Blanks. He was a defensive liability but a good offensive player who had 20 extrabase hits in 328 at-bats and batted .280. I played him at shortstop against certain pitchers over regular Frank Duffy, a good defensive player whose batting average was only .212.

And we traded Oscar Gamble to the Yankees for pitcher Pat Dobson, who as my Oriole teammate in 1971 had won 20 games. A tough, take-charge guy, Dobson won 16 games for us in 1976. He was the leader of our staff and a solid influence on our young pitchers.

When Gamble got to New York, he immediately bad-mouthed me with the writers there, saying I was harder on the black players than I was on the white players in Cleveland. At first I was shocked. I had gone out of my way to try to make Gamble a regular player because he was a good power hitter but had a reputation as a butcher in the outfield. But I gave him extra work on his outfield play in the spring, and he won the starting job in left field, which he held for a month. Then he pulled a hamstring and was sidelined for a time. When he came back, Gamble couldn't reclaim the job full-time and I platooned him with Charlie Spikes and spotted him at DH. But evidently that was why Oscar ripped me. Of course, Billy Martin didn't play Gamble every day in the outfield either.

In addition to our player changes, we also changed a coach because Tom McCraw decided to become our roving minor league hitting instructor. He took a pay cut to be closer to his wife and two children in Huntsville, Alabama. I immediately called my old friend Vada Pinson, but he said he was staying with the job of first base coach for the Seattle Mariners. Vada thanked me for the offer but said he was happy where he was.

Then Rocky Colavito approached me at the winter meetings and said he'd like to work with me. Rocky, who had coached for the Indians in 1973, was a big favorite in Cleveland from his playing days, and I told Seghi I felt he'd be a fine addition. Phil hired him, and Rocky proved to be a very hard worker and a guy who always spoke his mind. I liked that, though Phil Seghi kept telling me he wished Rocky wouldn't keep after him about his salary. As he was being paid less than $20,000, I told Phil, "If you gave him a little raise, I'm sure you wouldn't hear another word from the Rock."

All my coaches were first rate. Third base coach Dave Garcia was unbelievably efficient. He knew my thinking so well it was almost as if he could read my mind on baseball. There were times in the heat of a game when I flashed him the wrong sign for a given situation, but Dave knew what I always wanted and put on the right sign.

In the two years Dave Garcia coached third for me, he made only one mistake—and it wasn't really a mistake. Ron Pruitt hit a ball in Milwaukee that caromed around the outfield off the fence. He went flying around the bases, and Dave tried to score him on an inside-the-park home run. Ron was running very well, but just as Dave released him, Ron stumbled slightly as he rounded third base and was thrown out. We lost the game by one run.

Dave took it very badly, but I told him after the game: "If our players made as few mistakes as you make, Dave, we'd win the pennant."

I made fewer mistakes my second year managing than I had in 1975, and I was a much better manager. I no longer felt that every eye was on every move I made and step I took; the circus surrounding the first black manager was over, and I was more relaxed. I knew the players now, and their capabilities, and I tried to be more open and communicative with them. Some players, like Rico Carty and Larvell Blanks, you occasionally had to push a little. Other players, like Buddy Bell and Duane Kuiper, you had to pat on the back occasionally, or they felt you were ignoring them.

Early in the '75 season Buddy had told me that and said he couldn't play for me. "You don't pat me on the back when I'm going good; you don't chew me out when I'm going bad. It's like I'm not here."

I corrected that situation, and near the end of the season Buddy Bell came to me and said, "I've enjoyed playing for you."

Phil Seghi told the press in the spring of 1976 that I had handled the players very well. "Frank did a superb job a year ago," he said. "We got real tough in the second half of the season, and the manager was in a large way responsible. He's one of the best in the business."

But to me in private Phil kept saying I had to do more to motivate the players, particularly George Hendrick. "You're not getting everything out of George that he has to offer," Phil said.

"Phil, I'm still trying to figure out how to get everything out of George Hendrick, and that just might be a lifetime task," I said. "But what we're getting is not bad, not bad at all."

I also told Phil that signing a player to a guaranteed four- or five-year contract was a motivation killer with some players. "The player knows he's going to be paid for four years no matter what he does on the ball field," I said. "All he has to do is show up. Then you tell me you want me to motivate that player. How do you motivate a player who's got a guaranteed long-term contract? Money has always been what motivates most ballplayers, and that motivation has been eliminated."

I realized that ballclubs that wanted to keep their best players had to sign them to long-term contracts after arbitrator Peter Seitz ruled that pitchers Andy Messersmith and Dave McNally, who had played the '75 season without a contract, were free agents. Now veterans would be able to sign with the highest bidder. It was a shame my former teammate Dave McNally had arm trouble and was forced to retire before he could get rich. I felt a bit sorry for myself that I had arrived in the major leagues too soon.

But I couldn't even open the season on the active roster. Phil Seghi wanted me to, and I certainly wanted to play. But I felt I had 25 better players than Frank Robinson because I was so busy in spring training that I hadn't had time to get into good shape.

Boog Powell suffered a severe ankle sprain in late April and had to be put on the disabled list for a month. I activated myself then, but I ended up batting only 67 times, serving as the DH 18 times, playing first base twice and in the outfield once. But I reinjured my left shoulder, which had been repaired surgically the previous October, and it affected my swing. I hit .224 with only 3 home runs and 10 RBIs for the season. I was just happy that in my final at-bat in the major leagues, I pinch-hit a single and drove in a run.

Big Boog also fared poorly in 1976, as he spent six weeks on the disabled list with a quadriceps muscle pull. He was 34, six years younger than I was, but we looked like two old soldiers at the plate. Boog had 9 home runs and 33 RBIs to go with a .215 average, a dramatic decline from the previous year. And that lack of production put added pressure on the healthy players, but we didn't have the kind of depth that could pick us up.

Still, team morale remained very good all season. The Indians showed a lot of hustle and worked hard. We were not overly talented, but we were a battling bunch, and the Indians finished three games over .500 with an 81-78 record. I felt I had done a good job.

I was particularly happy when Jim Kern became one of the best right-handed relief pitchers in the league. The Indians had been trying to make him a starting pitcher since 1968, without success. Jim Kern could throw the ball 95 miles an hour, and I thought he'd be more effective in the bullpen. I talked it over with Harvey Haddix, and he agreed with me. I believe in using young pitchers out of the bullpen so they can get used to working against major league hitters in small doses. Then they have a better chance of getting their confidence and succeeding.

When Kern arrived at spring training, he asked me what he had to do to make the club. "Throw strikes," I said. "And eliminate your curveball. It's a good one, but you won't need it coming out of the bullpen. That's where we're gonna use you, so just go with your fastball, hard slider, and an occasional change. That's all you'll need to work on a few hitters at a time."

Jim Kern liked the idea because he was successful right away. He turned in a 10-7 record with 15 saves and an ERA of 2.36. Kern combined with left-hander Dave LaRoche—who had 21 saves—to give us the best pair of left-right short relievers in the league. They were key factors in our compiling a winning record.

Two incidents marred the '76 season. The first involved Rico Carty, and I was at fault for the blowup, but I guess it was an incident that had been building for some time. Rico had made it clear from the start of our relationship that he didn't like me. The few times I played for him he didn't like it. He seemed to feel I was trying to take his job as the regular DH. That was ridiculous. If I had wanted his job, I could have taken it, but we were a better ballclub with Carty in the lineup. He batted over .300 and drove in over 140 runs in 1975 and 1976.

But I didn't much like Rico Carty either. He was a phony, a guy who put up a big front for the fans, saying he did everything for the team. Then he would hit a ball and not run it out. Rico also liked to make these little remarks half under his breath about managerial moves I made during games. He wouldn't openly second-guess me, but I knew that he was criticizing me to other players and that he was a bad influence on at least one player, Larvell Blanks. They became good friends,and then Blanks began to gripe and sulk whenever I didn't play him.

I certainly gave Blanks an opportunity to play regularly at shortstop because he was a much better hitter than Frank Duffy. I started Blanks at short in 56 games, but after a while I realized I couldn't have him out there booting balls and losing games for us. He just wasn't a good defensive infielder.

But the blowup with Carty occurred during that period when the umpires had been giving us a hard time and I had told everyone to cool it with the umpires. We couldn't afford to have players thrown out of games. Then early in a game Rico started arguing a called strike with an umpire. Everyone knows that you can't argue calls on pitches with the home plate umpire because he can and will throw you out of the game. Rico not only argued, he also cursed the umpire, and he was ejected.

I snapped at him when he came back to the dugout, "That wasn't called for, damn it, Rico!" He snapped right back at me, and we exchanged angry words for a few minutes before he stormed into the clubhouse. I should have held my peace until we both cooled down. But that was something I had to learn as a manager, not to speak out in the heat of the moment.

The second incident occurred in, of all things, an exhibition game we played with our AAA farm team in Toledo and involved pitcher Bob Reynolds. "Bullet Bob," as he was called because he threw hard, had pitched in the majors from 1969 through the 1975 season when, on my recommendation, we acquired him on waivers from Detroit. But he didn't make our roster in the spring. It was up to Phil Seghi to tell Reynolds that he was being sent down, because the morning the decision was made I left Tucson with the team at 8 A.M. on a road trip. But before Phil could get to Reynolds, a writer told him he'd been cut, and Bob got angry. The writer told me that Reynolds was upset that I hadn't talked to him. "How could I talk to him?" I said. "I would have had to bring him to the ballpark at 7:30 A.M. before I left. The general manager was supposed to talk to him."

We had a bus going to Toledo, but most of the guys, including me, drove their own cars to the exhibition game. I pulled into the parking lot and got out of my car just as Bullet Bob Reynolds stepped out of his. "How you doin', Bullet?" I said.

Reynolds grunted but refused to speak to me. He must still be mad, I thought.

The owners of the Toledo Mudhens had been after Rocky Colavito and me to each hit once in the game, saying they'd advertised that we would, hoping to put more fans in the seats. I said I wasn't going to play, and Rocky said that if I wasn't, he wasn't going to play either. But during the game the Mudhen owners kept pressing Rocky and me to hit, and Rocky finally said he would. So I also agreed to bat. It was announced in the third inning that we would be hitting in the fifth, and fans let out a cheer.

Reynolds had told several of my players that if he got in the game against me, he was going to "bean" me. I didn't take that seriously, and I couldn't be concerned anyway as Reynolds was not supposed to pitch. But the next thing I knew Rico Carty said, "Hey, Bullet's up throwing. I hope he doesn't come in here and start throwing at people."

Reynolds had a reputation for moving hitters back off the plate by throwing inside. But he came in and pitched the fourth inning without incident, throwing fastballs and hard sliders below the waist. The next inning Rocky pinch-hit one of those low fastballs for a single.

I stepped to the plate and Reynolds's first pitch was a fastball over my head that caromed off the screen. "You didn't even have the guts to come close!" I yelled at Reynolds. "You're gutless! If you're gonna throw at somebody, at least come close enough to knock 'em down!"

I stepped back in the box, and he got two strikes on me. "*Please* don't strike out," I said to myself. Because I wanted to hit the ball and then go across the field and tell Reynolds to his face what I thought of him.

Rocky had taken second on the wild throw, and on the next pitch I flied out to center field. Reynolds moved behind third to back up the throw-in. I ran to first, then turned in toward our dugout on the third base side. I arrived at the mound just as Bob Reynolds did.

"You're really gutless," I said, "throwing at somebody in a game like this."

"Well thanks a lot," Reynolds said. "At least you're talking to me now, you asshole. I should take care of you right now."

I hit him with a left and a right, and Reynolds went down. Jeff Torborg caught the 200-pounder before he hit the ground.

I was ejected from the game, and as I ran to the dugout the fans booed and threw debris at me. I went into the clubhouse and apologized to the Mudhens' general manager, Charlie Senger. "I apologize to you and to the fans of Toledo," I said. "It was an unfortunate incident, and I'm sorry it had to happen. But I've played the game long enough to know that that pitch over my head was no accident. Bob Reynolds had perfect control for one and one-third innings."

I was denounced in the press for decking Reynolds. The *Plain Dealer* even ran an editorial criticizing my lack of control. But the harshest words for me came from Toledo manager Joe Sparks, who ripped me in the papers for days. He later claimed that I was the reason his ballclub collapsed after the incident, which was a classic cop-out. If the team had surged after I popped Reynolds, would Sparks have credited me with sparking them? And what would Sparks and all of my other critics have said if I had ended up on the ground with a baseball stuck in my ear?

Toledo was part of the Cleveland Indians' organization, and I felt that the blather from Sparks was uncalled for. I should have realized, when Phil Seghi didn't back me and tell Sparks to shut up, that my general manager was no longer a supporter of mine.

That was apparent when Ed Keating approached Phil Seghi about discussing a new contract for me and was told that it hadn't been decided if I would be rehired for the '77 season. On September 16, Russ Schneider reported in the *Plain Dealer* that Seghi and Ted Bonda were engaged in a tug-of-war regarding me. "One source close to both, who insisted on anonymity, confided to this writer that Bonda thinks Robinson has done a commendable job and wants to rehire him," Schneider wrote. "But Seghi feels differently. The source said, in fact, 'If Seghi has his way, Robinson would have been fired long ago.'"

There was speculation in the media that I would not be rehired, which upset some of my players. Dave LaRoche criticized Seghi in the press for his seeming reluctance to bring me back as manager. Phil then called Dave up to his office and angrily chewed him out. Dave said afterward, "I told him I was sorry if I offended him, but what I had to say was my opinion and I'm entitled to that."

Seghi didn't agree, saying, "I told Dave that I respected his ability to pitch, but that he should leave the driving to me."

I didn't know where I stood until just before the season ended. The Indians finally offered me a one-year contract to manage, at the same $80,000 salary I'd received in 1976. But I had to retire as a player and give up the $120,000 I'd been paid as a player. Seghi seemed to think that in playing so little, I had ripped off the club, as if injuries didn't count. I was only 14 home runs from 600—did Seghi think I didn't want them? But what really annoyed me was when Phil said I would also have to give up my fringe benefits. The outlay for the apartment, car, and airline tickets for my family amounted to nearly $7000. Taking away those benefits after having given them to me twice seemed extremely petty to me, and I said so. But the terms were take them or leave them.

I said I would need a few days to decide whether I would accept the offer. But I had no choice. If I wanted to continue to manage, I had to stay with the Indians. No other offers were forthcoming. I did have some regrets about retiring as a player, only 57 hits from 3000, but I guessed it was time. Before heading for home at season's end, I signed the new contract.

Seghi said he expected me to be tougher on the players next season. "You didn't fine one player all season," he said. That was because I don't believe fines do much good. Once in a while you have to fine a player to maintain your authority. In 1975 we had a rule that no facial hair other than mustaches would be allowed. Near the end of that season pitcher Jim Bibby started growing a beard. Jim is black, and I didn't notice the hair on his face for a few days, but when I did, I told him to shave. A few days later I again told him to shave, and he defied me, saying, "Do what you have to do." I fined him $300. If I hadn't, other players would have defied the ballclub's rules.

Earl Weaver never fined players because he never had to. I talked to Earl about that, and he said, "If you feel like you have to fine a player to make him play better, then that player shouldn't be on your team." That made sense to me.

Having written that Phil Seghi had wanted to fire me, Russ Schneider pressed him on his relationship with me, and Seghi said, "There's always a certain amount of give-and-take between a manager and a general manager. But there never has been a rift between Frank and me, though there are times I question his judgment and I'm sure there are times he questions mine."

When he was asked if he was disappointed with the Indians' performance, Seghi said, "Yes, I thought our club was better. I thought we should have won more games."

I wasn't surprised when I read that. Phil Seghi always thought the ballclub was better than it actually was. Every year he predicted that we would be in pennant contention, and there was no way that was possible with the talent at my disposal. But I couldn't contradict Seghi. I had to be optimistic so that we could sell some tickets. We sold about 20,000 fewer tickets in 1976 than we had in 1975.

Seghi really seemed to believe that he was providing me with material that was good enough to win the division. I don't know if he believed that or if he was just massaging his own ego and trying to protect his job. But the message he kept putting out was that he was doing a wonderful job getting players and I was misusing them.

Still, I looked forward to the next season because I felt we could improve in 1977. Charlie Spikes and Boog Powell figured to bounce back from off seasons. It was Boog's history to follow an off year with a good one. Duane Kuiper was a much better hitter than he'd shown in 1976, and I really liked our pitching staff after we signed Wayne Garland as a free agent. He'd just come off a 20-win season with the Orioles.

But Phil Seghi cut one of the worst deals in history when he gave Garland a $2.3 million ten-year contract when no other team even bid for Wayne. He was a good guy, and I was happy to see him get whatever he could. But here we were—one of the poorest franchises in baseball—just throwing away money. Later, after Wayne injured his rotator cuff and couldn't pitch and the fans were on him as if he'd stolen the Indians' money, he said, "If you were walking down the street and someone offered you $2.3 million, would you turn it down? Of course you wouldn't. I couldn't believe the contract I was offered."

I remember when Wayne Garland hurt his arm that spring, though he wouldn't admit he was hurt at the time. I think that big contract put a lot of pressure on Wayne, and he tried to do too much too soon. I saw him throwing very hard early in the spring, even throwing his screwball hard. I told him to take it easy, to wait until his arm got loose and then gradually build up his velocity. But he kept pushing himself to prove that he deserved all that money. He got through the '77 season with a sore arm; then he needed surgery, and his career was, for all intents, over.

Phil Seghi made a host of bad deals that doomed the 1977 Indians. He traded George Hendrick to the Padres for two light hitters, outfielder John Grubb and catcher Fred Kendall, and nonhitting utilityman Hector Torres. When Seghi told me about the trade, I was sick. "You weren't getting the most out of George anyway," he said.

"I got out of George what he could give us," I said. "And is John Grubb going to hit .300 with over 20 home runs and over 80 RBIs? The answer is no."

Fred Kendall was not a frontline catcher, but we had to use him because Seghi traded both of our young catchers, Alan Ashby and Rick Cerone. Ashby and a minor leaguer were sent to Toronto for pitcher Al Fitzmorris. As we had lost Rico Carty to Toronto in the expansion draft ("I didn't think they'd take him," Seghi said in explaining why he hadn't protected our second-best hitter), Phil had to give up John Lowenstein and Cerone to get Carty back.

I couldn't believe it. Good young catchers were the most difficult talents to find, and Seghi had given up both of ours. Cerone, our number 1 draft choice of a couple of years ago, had played very well in brief appearances with us, and I had planned to platoon him with Ashby. An intelligent organization would never have lost the two of them.

Seghi did make one good trade, acquiring Andre Thornton from the Expos for pitcher Jackie Brown. Thornton got off to a very poor start, along with the rest of the team, though he eventually became a star. But Seghi made one more terrible trade in May, without consulting me, and I felt he'd lost his mind. Phil sent our best relief pitcher, Dave LaRoche, to the Angels for two part-time players. LaRoche had saved 42 games for us in just over two seasons. When I found out that Seghi had also received $250,000 in cash for LaRoche, I realized why he'd made the trade. Phil said the money was not the main reason he'd dealt LaRoche, but I didn't believe him for a minute.

As it turned out, when the Indians were reorganized and refinanced in December 1977, Ted Bonda admitted that the club had been virtually bankrupt. That didn't surprise me. When I arrived at spring training in 1977, I learned that our uniform laundry bill in Tucson had not been paid from the previous spring. The Indians' financial plight was undoubtedly another reason why Seghi got rid of a high-salaried player like George

Hendrick, which is not the way to build a contending team. And that we were not.

We were particularly inept on offense. Not only did we lose Hendrick's bat, but Boog Powell was unable to make a comeback. The hardest job I had to do as a manager was cutting a player, and releasing an old friend like Boog was one of the toughest cuts I ever had to make. Boog came to camp lighter and worked hard trying to regain his stroke, but it was a memory. I was just happy when the big guy hooked on with the Dodgers for one final go-around.

I knew in the spring that I was going to have problems with Larvell Blanks again. I wanted his bat in the lineup, but he was such a poor infielder that I asked him to try something else. One day during infield practice I walked out to him at shortstop and said, "You ever played any outfield?"

Blanks looked up at the sky and said, "No."

"You think you could play a little left field?" I asked.

He looked at the sky again and said, "I don't know."

"Well I think you ought to start working out in the outfield."

"Why?"

"Because that would give you another place to play and maybe I could get you some more at-bats," I said.

"Okay, I guess I'll try it," he said without enthusiasm.

Later he went to left field and worked out without enthusiasm. I couldn't chance using him in the outfield with that attitude. I kept trying to play him at short because we really needed his bat in the lineup in 1977. But I soon found I couldn't play Blanks much at shortstop. It didn't pay to have a guy there who might drive in a run and let in two with an error. And when he didn't play, Larvell sulked, or worse.

One day he yanked all his own clothing out of his locker and threw every piece into a garbage can in the clubhouse. Another day he broke several bats and a stool in the clubhouse. I called him into my office and said, "No more of that Larvell. I don't want to hear of you breaking up things in the clubhouse anymore." He nodded and walked out.

Blanks hadn't been playing for several days when I sent him up to pinch-hit in a game in Kansas City. He hit a low line drive to the shortstop, who caught the ball on one hop and threw to first. Blanks had taken only three steps up the line and turned back to the dugout. He stopped at our bat rack and started smashing it with his bat. I told him to quit, so Blanks grabbed a couple of bats belonging to other players and smashed them in the runway on his way into the clubhouse.

After the game I called him into my office. "Sit down, Larvell," I said, but he shook his head. He just stood with his back against the wall, looking angry.

"I think your attitude is very poor," I said. "You didn't even run out that ball you hit, and the shortstop had to make a throw."

"I thought he was gonna catch the ball," Blanks said.

"I don't care what you thought. You still run the ball out. Your whole attitude is bad. Your work habits are bad. You don't work hard on your defense, and that's what your game needs. And I told you before that I didn't appreciate your tearing up things. You beat up on the bat rack, and the bat rack didn't get you out. The pitcher did. Have you got anything to say?"

Blanks shook his head.

"Until your attitude changes and you're willing to come in and tell me that you're ready to do whatever I ask you to do to help this ballclub, I'm not gonna play you."

Blanks pushed himself away from the wall and walked out. But the next day he came to the bench wearing a strip of adhesive tape across his mouth. He sat at the far end of the bench with that tape over his mouth for the entire ballgame, acting like a child. That kind of thing does not help on a losing team.

Although he couldn't field the position, Blanks thought he should be the regular shortstop because he was hitting over .280 and Frank Duffy was barely over .200. But Frank, who committed only 10 errors in 1976, could make all the plays and never cost us a ballgame.

I later read in the papers that Blanks had a bonus clause in his contract that he would collect if he played in a certain number of games or reached a certain number of times at bat. Giving incentive bonuses to players is the most unfair thing a front office can do to a manager. It makes a player even more angry when he doesn't play, and this is a primary reason for many arguments and disappointments between players and managers in baseball today. And incentive bonuses can create problems throughout a ballclub. When two players are competing for the same position and one pops off about lack of playing time, it leads to tension and bad feelings. That apparently happened on the 1987 Mets when Mookie Wilson complained that he wasn't playing enough; then when manager Davey Johnson gave him more time, Len Dykstra, his other center fielder, was annoyed.

Larvell Blanks was annoyed with me, and he took his troubles to Rico Carty, who was rapidly becoming more of a pain in my neck with his little comments. They weren't loud enough for me to hear, but I could feel his animosity toward me. The two players who gave me the worst time, ironically, were black.

On April 24 we played a doubleheader against the Yankees and looked so bad in losing the opener that I closed the clubhouse door between games. "I was embarrassed by the way we played, and you should be too," I told the players angrily. "Sloppy fielding, poor base running, poor pitch selection, and some of you look like you just don't give a damn. From now on, I'm only putting guys out there who want to play the game the way it should be played. And if there's anybody here who doesn't like it, let me know." Then we went out and lost the second game.

Afterward I was asked by the press why we weren't scoring more runs. "Well," I said, "It seems like every time we get a man on base, we hit into a double play. We're just not driving in the runs when we have the opportunity." Rico Carty apparently took that as criticism of him personally, because he ripped me the next day before 600 Indians' fans, my players, Phil Seghi, and the media.

The occasion was the annual Wahoo Club awards presentation. Rico Carty accepted his tomahawk trophy as the Indians' Man of the Year in 1976. He thanked the fans, and then he started talking very emotionally in his deep baritone voice that was tinged by the accents of the Dominican Republic.

"They talk about the leader of the team," Rico said. "They mention this player, that player. Who is the best leader of the team? It's the manager. When he leads, we got a ballclub. Believe me. I'm telling this with all my heart."

At first I thought he was kidding, and everyone else did too. I sat on the dais smiling and looking out at the faces of people smiling in the audience. Some were quietly chatting, but then a hush came over the room when we all realized that Rico was serious.

"What do I read in the papers?" he said. "I see where 'we hit into double plays, we don't score runs.' Nobody wants to do that. If we could hit every time someone was on base, we would do it. I would get about 200 RBIs. But nobody can be perfect in this game."

I said to myself, "What is this guy doing?" And then I saw that what he was doing was sticking the tomahawk he had been awarded right in my back.

"I tell you, we need help from above," Carty continued, and he turned to face me. "We need your help, Frank."

He took a deep breath and said, "I ain't got nothing else to say, really." But he stared at me again. "If you don't help, we'll all be in trouble."

Afterward there was absolute silence that was finally broken by a scattering of what seemed to me embarrassed applause. I was shocked and furious. I looked over at Phil Seghi, who just sat there expressionlessly puffing on his pipe. When the writers came to him to comment on Carty's remarks, Phil characterized the speech which attacked my leadership as "a pep talk. It sounded to me like Rico just wanted to perk up the whole ballclub, all of us in the organization. I don't think he meant any harm. Maybe it will help give us the spark we needed."

Phil's words made me even more furious. He not only refused to defend his own manager, but he praised the slap at me. I knew I couldn't fire back at Carty. It would be like cutting my own throat because it would create a big schism in the ballclub, with guys choosing sides between me and Carty. I knew that a lot of his teammates thought Carty was a jerk. They saw the way he was always playing up to the fans and knew he was totally self-centered. As long as he got his stats in a game, he'd still be smiling if we lost.

But I sat there thinking, "If my general manager doesn't protect me in a situation like this, what chance have I got?" I realized for the first time that I was out there all alone, that I really had to watch my back. Seghi wouldn't take shots at me himself publicly, but he would encourage people like Carty to knock me. So it was only a matter of time—unless the team started winning and drawing fans—before Seghi convinced everyone else upstairs, including the club president, that I had to go.

My only remark to the press was, "I have no comment to make about Rico. Any player is entitled to say anything he wants about anything."

But pitcher Jim Kern told the press what I would like to have said. "I thought Rico was way out of line, and I told him so," Jim said. "If he feels the way he says he does, he should have enough respect for the manager to say it to him privately, not in front of 600 people."

But Rico Carty never had the guts to unburden himself to me in private. He may have had some good points to make that might have helped the ballclub, but I doubt it.

Third baseman Buddy Bell seemed confused by Carty's words. "At first I couldn't understand what Rico was saying," Buddy told the press. "You know he says a lot of things that don't always come out the way he means them. But I don't really think Rico meant to put down Frank. I think Rico meant well; it just came out bad.

"When you get right down to it, it's not all that big a thing, anyway. What is happening to us is something that we, the players, have got to pull out of ourselves. It's not Frank's fault, it's ours."

Ted Bonda had been on business in Germany. He returned the next day and came to see me in my office. Ted said he'd heard about the Wahoo Club incident, and he said, "Don't let this get you down, Frank. Just hang in there, your job is secure." He said that Phil Seghi had told him Carty's speech was just a pep talk. I came away from the meeting with the impression that what Ted had said was that he was the president of the ballclub and that he was behind me, and that it didn't matter what anyone else said or did. Ted Bonda also supported me in the media, which I appreciated. That's all I wanted Phil Seghi to do, but he never did, and I lost all respect for him.

Even before this incident I had felt a distinct change in my relationship with Phil Seghi. A coldness had set in. For two years I had often stopped up to see Phil in his office when I arrived at the stadium, just to get his thoughts and discuss what could be done to improve the ballclub. But in 1977 when I stopped by, Phil was distant and had very little to say to me.

Several people had told me that Phil had long harbored a desire to manage a major league team. He had managed in the minor leagues for ten years from 1946 through 1955. A general manager who would like to be a field manager is always going to heavily second-guess his own manager. And early in the '77 season Phil made it clear that was what he was doing.

Seghi's box was up over the third base dugout, across the field from our dugout, and we could see every move he made. Every time I glanced up at him, it seemed like Phil was ranting and raving and gesturing with his arms about something we did or did not do on the field. He'd slam a hand down and throw his head back in obvious disgust. I couldn't look up at him and keep my eyes on the ballgame too, but the players on the bench started watching Seghi. I kept hearing guys say things like, "Did you see what Phil did?" or "Look at Phil, he's going nuts again." It became a game with the players; it became a distraction for me.

I told Seghi, "I don't think it was right for Rico to pop off at me like he did."

"There's nothing I can do," he said.

As I left Seghi's office, I thought, "If he's going to back a player over his manager, he ought to fire the manager right now. The players know I don't have Phil's support—where does that leave me?"

Two days after the Wahoo whopping, we lost a 12-inning game to Toronto, 6-5. Then Phil Seghi struck again, this time through Joe Tait, the play-by-play announcer of Indian games on radio. "I don't think Robinson has the mental or emotional capacity to manage well," Tait said on the air at game's end. "I honestly don't think Frank will stay. I don't think the club's going to turn around, and I don't think he's the man to turn it around. A change has to come pretty quick."

Tait went on and on in that vein, and an announcer would never knock the team that controls his employment if the team's general manager didn't approve his sentiments. In fact, I read in the papers the next day that Tait had said on a sports talk show the previous fall that I should not be rehired as the Indian manager. When Tait saw Seghi the following day, all Phil said was, "I heard what you said on the radio last night." I thought, "Way to support your local manager, Phil."

By May 24 the Cleveland writers—who had always been very nice to me—were writing, "It is painfully obvious that Robinson soon will be fired," and that coach Jeff Torborg would be my replacement. I tried to keep the atmosphere light. When a couple of writers walked into my office on an off day, I said, "The vultures are arriving. You're never here on off days. Is something supposed to be happening?"

I kept a jar of M&Ms on my desk, and Torborg's sons, Greg and Dale, liked to come into the office for a handful. When they stuck their heads in the doorway, I said, "C'mon in, kids, and look around. You may have the run of the place tomorrow."

I winked at the reporters and called for Jeff Torborg to come in. He looked a little sheepish, but I smiled and rose from my chair, saying, "Sit down and try it out, Jeff. See how it feels. Think you'll want to make any changes in the office?"

Jeff laughed. I liked him a lot. I wasn't sure he was quite ready to manage then, but he had excellent potential. If I was going, I would just as soon see Jeff take over the ballclub as anyone else.

A writer said my status needed to be clarified by the front office quickly or I would be in danger of losing control of the team. I admitted that some of the players had not been going all out. "I give orders, and some guys don't respond," I said, which was why I finally had to fine Larvell Blanks for not running out balls. "Maybe some guys figure I won't be around long."

The players read the papers, and I could read their attitudes. I'd give orders to dissident players, and they might carry them out, but they'd look at me like, "Sure, buddy, we won't have to listen to you much longer." That is why I feel that any time a general manager wants to fire his manager, he should not tarry. Because the players know, and the manager very quickly loses full control of the ballclub. It's even more important that a manager has strong backing from the top on a losing team. Player attitudes on such clubs are bad to begin with, and they only get worse.

On June 1 Rico Carty went on the disabled list with a pulled hamstring muscle, but he was traveling with the team to get daily treatments. Five days later we were playing in Oakland, and I had a player bunt to try to move a base runner over. The ball rolled foul, and I could hear Rico's deep, resonant voice from the other end of the bench say, "Why are we bunting? I don't know what he's thinking about."

"Hey, Rico," I yelled, "you just be quiet, and let me manage the ballclub. You're a player. Don't worry about what I do, just keep quiet."

"Well, I don't understand what you're doing," he said.

"You don't have to understand," I said, glaring at Carty. "I tell you what, why don't you just go upstairs and get your treatment. As a matter of fact, you can stay up there. Don't even come back down here."

We won the game, 3-1, and I went into the clubhouse and told Carty to come into my office. I waited several minutes, and Rico didn't show up. So I went back out to him and yelled, "I don't appreciate your second-guessing me on the bench."

"I didn't second-guess you," he shouted. "I just said to a player, 'Why are we bunting?'"

"Well why don't you just pack your gear and go back to Cleveland," I said. "You're suspended. I don't even want you around the ballpark when we get home."

Then I told traveling secretary Mike Seghi to make arrangements for Carty to fly home. When the writers asked me if I was fining Carty, I said, "Yes, the biggest fine I've ever levied." I fined him $1000. And I told the writers, "I don't want Carty back until he straightens out his act."

Then Carty went home and lied to the writers in Cleveland about what had transpired. He also said I was hard to play for because I was always mad, which also was untrue. But he cited an incident in a game in Seattle before we got to Oakland. First baseman Bruce Bochte and second baseman Duane Kuiper let a fly ball fall between them in the infield. My reaction was to grab the folding chair I'd been sitting on and fling it to the dugout floor. I often did things like that when we made a dumb play, throw a chair or kick a watercooler. They were reflex actions, and once I got the anger out, that was it. I learned that from Earl Weaver. Don't rant and rave on and on. Get rid of your anger, and you'll never have ulcers. A manager can't let out his emotions on the field the way a player can, by sliding hard or diving for a ball or whatever.

When we got home, I didn't make my usual stop by Phil's office before the ballgame. It seemed senseless when he barely spoke to me anymore. But the next day I dropped in on him and said, "You see anything that'll help the ballclub, Phil, let me know."

He didn't even look up from his desk. He just said, "No, no, everything's fine."

I shrugged and said I'd see him later, went down to my office, and changed into my uniform. I was sitting at my desk writing out my lineup card when 15 minutes later Seghi and Ted Bonda walked in my back door, not through the clubhouse door that most people used. But I thought it was strange that Phil had come to see me when I'd just left him. Then he said he wanted to have a meeting with me and all the coaches.

"The coaches are out on the field working, Phil," I said.

"Well, bring them in," he said.

I sent the clubhouse boy out to get the coaches, who trooped in and sat on the couch. Ted sat in a chair, I remained behind my desk, and Phil stood up. He started talking and as usual didn't look at me.

"We're not playing good baseball," he said. He rambled on about a number of picky things that bothered him, including the all-important fact that players were not adhering to his order that they keep their hats on in the dugout at all times. Then Phil got to the point.

"I sit up there in my booth, and I see players at first base who don't get off the bag," Phil said. "They simply won't take a lead. Why not, Rocky?"

"Look, Phil," Colavito said, "we tell 'em. We work with the players and tell them to get off the base. They just won't take much of a lead."

"Well if I was the manager, I'd make them get off!" Phil said to me as he looked at Rocky.

But I was sitting there thinking, "Wait a minute! What does he mean, 'if *he* was the manager?' He's not the manager. I'm the manager."

"You've got to get those guys off first base, Rocky," Phil continued. "We have got to start stealing more bases. If I was the manager of this ballclub, I'd have those guys taking leads and stealing bases."

I spoke up, saying, "We practice taking leads, and the guys all take a proper lead in practice. Then they don't do it in games. What do you want Rocky to do? Push them off the bag?"

"I managed ten years in the minor leagues, and I never took stuff like that from players," Phil said. "When I told players to do something, they did it."

I was getting angrier by the minute, and after two more "if I was the manager" lines from Phil Seghi, I shot up onto my feet and slammed the desk so hard with the heel of my hand that I thought I had broken a bone. "That's it!" I yelled. "*You* are *not* the manager of this ballclub, Phil, and if you have anything to say to me, you should say it to me alone, not in front of these coaches. They work for me, and they work damn hard. They only do what I tell them to do. So if you have any complaints about them or their performance, make them to me.

"And I'm damn tired of this tirade from you about if you were the manager. If you want to manage this ballclub, here's the lineup. Fire me." I leaned over the desk and extended the lineup card to him.

"I don't want to manage the club," Phil yelled.

"Well that's fine," I yelled. "And until you can come down here strictly as the general manager, you can stay out of this clubhouse."

"I can come down here anytime I want to," he yelled.

"I didn't say you couldn't come down here. But if you're gonna come down here wanting to manage the ballclub, you can stay out. You're not gonna come down here with that kind of complaint again."

"I can come down here anytime I want to, Frank. I'm the general manager of this club."

"You're not coming down here with the attitude that you're gonna be the manager."

Ted Bonda finally stood up and said, "Okay, take it easy, you two. Let's calm down here." He paused a moment in the sudden silence after all the shouting, then he headed out the back door and Phil followed. Through it all, Phil had not looked at me. But I figured that Seghi went upstairs and really pushed Bonda to fire me, saying something like: "See, Frank Robinson won't listen to me even on something as simple as getting the players to take leads and steal some bases." Obviously Seghi had orchestrated the shouting match in front of Bonda with a purpose in mind.

The coaches didn't know what was going on. Rocky said, "What the hell's wrong with that man?"

"Don't any of you let this bother you," I said. "Continue to go out and do your work the way you've been doing it. You guys work for me, not for Phil Seghi."

Later that week we won games on Friday and on Saturday afternoon. Following the second victory I was in my office when Phil called and asked me if I could be at his office by 8 A.M. on Sunday. "Sure," I said, knowing Phil had never been in his office before 10 A.M. Then I went home and told Barbara that I was being fired at dawn.

13

THE WORST
PERIOD OF MY LIFE

PHIL Seghi was at his desk with his head canted down as I entered his office at 8 A.M. on June 19. His head came up, and he looked past me. "Good morning," he said, and lowered his head.

"Good morning," I said.

Phil's head came up, and he looked at the chair that was there for me and told me to have a seat. His head went down, and he said, "This is a tough situation, Frank. But we feel we've reached a point where it's imperative that we make a change. There's just too much uneasiness and unrest on the club, and we're going to have to let you go."

"Okay," I said. "Who are you hiring?"

His head came up, and Phil glanced at a corner. "Jeff Torborg."

"He's a good man," I said.

Phil's head went down, and he said, "We're having a press conference right after this." His head came up. "You're welcome to come to the press conference if you want to."

I stared at Phil's bobbing head and said, "I'm not going to the press conference. It's Jeff Torborg's moment, not mine. I don't want to throw a black cloud over his conference. Jeff's a friend of mine."

Phil's head came up and for the first time he actually stole a glance at my face, but he couldn't hold it. "What if the writers want to talk to you?" he asked.

"I'll be down in the office," I said. "I'm not gonna run away. When the writers finish at the conference upstairs, they can come down if they want to talk to me."

The writers seemed to be a little disappointed when I wouldn't rip anyone. I told them it had been a tough but enjoyable two-plus years and that I hoped to manage again sometime.

I went to see Jeff and wished him well. He asked if I wanted to speak to the players, and I did. I stood at one end of the clubhouse and said, "The ballclub has felt it necessary to make a change. I've been fired and Jeff's the manager now. These things happen in baseball. But I appreciate the efforts each of you has given me. I know you'll give Jeff the best efforts you can. Play hard, and I wish you luck the rest of the way."

I went around the room and shook hands with each player. I wanted to leave as a professional. Later I wrote a note to each of the writers who had covered the ballclub and said that I appreciated the way the reporter had treated me.

I had to laugh when I read Phil Seghi's comments in the paper the next day, particularly this line: "Frank had my backing at all times."

The truth was what *New York Times* baseball writer Murray Chase wrote: "Seghi could have stepped in and cut off the player criticism by showing support for Robinson. But he conspicuously refrained from offering such support, and the dissident players kept carping."

When I got home, I went through the absolute worst period in my life. I felt like a failure, and I had never had that feeling before. I'd finally gotten a chance to manage, I'd been fired, and I was afraid that I'd never get another chance to show that I could be a successful manager in the major leagues. I was devastated.

I don't let my feelings show—I always try to contain them, to keep everything inside and appear to be in complete control. That's what I tried to do when I got home. But I was completely lost, disoriented. For two weeks I never went out of the house. I just sat in front of the television set, having no idea what was on the screen. It was the first time I had been out of baseball since 1953—24 years. It was only the second time I was ever at home in June, the other being when I had double vision. But that was only for a month, and then I knew I'd be going back into the game. This time I didn't know if I'd ever get back into baseball, and that was the only business I had ever known.

Now I didn't know what to do, how to go about seeking another job in baseball. I had no direction, I was unable to make any decision. I just sat around, hardly talking to Barbara and the kids; I just listened to my insides trembling. I kept thinking, "I'm still a young man, 41, with maybe another 40 years ahead of me...and I don't know what I'm going to do with the rest of my life."

Barbara always knows when I need to be left alone, and that's what she did for two weeks. Then one day she said, "Frank, you've got to stop sitting in front of the TV and get out and do things. It wasn't your fault you got fired, and it's not the end of the world. You did your best in Cleveland. Other baseball people know you did a good job with the players you had to work with. You'll get another job eventually, and in the meantime you're still being paid. I'm taking a job in real estate so we'll be okay financially. Now snap out of it."

I realized that she was right. Other people had been fired and gone on with their lives. I got off my butt and started getting out of the house, doing some shopping, playing some tennis, taking my family out to dinner or a movie. I started living again.

True to her word, Barbara got a job with a Beverly Hills real estate agency and in a matter of months was becoming very successful in her new profession. Then on July 11 I received a phone call from Dave Garcia, who had given up coaching for me to join manager Norm Sherry's staff with the Angels. Dave wanted to work near where his family lived in California. He was calling to say that the Angels had fired Sherry and named him the manager, and he wanted me to come to work for him.

"Just as I began to make the adjustment to being out of work, you call, Dave," I said. "But you'll never know how happy I am to hear from you."

I joined Garcia as his hitting coach, and my main project was Don Baylor. Angels' owner Gene Autry had spent some $5 million to acquire free agents Bobby Grich, Joe Rudi, and Baylor. But Grich had been lost for the season following back surgery, Rudi was on the disabled list, and Baylor was hitting .220 without his normal power. Baylor was a lifetime .267 hitter who averaged over 25 home runs per season.

I looked at videotapes of Don when he was hitting well and learned that his position in the batter's box had changed from the way he had been standing then. He also no longer had his hands in the position he normally did when he was getting ready to hit. We made those changes and talked about Don's approach to hitting. It turned out he was trying to live up to his big contract and had his mind all messed up.

"I've got this huge contract, Frank, and I'm not doing anything," Baylor said. "I've got to have a $700,000 year, and I'm having a $7000 year."

"No one can have a $700,000 year, Don," I said. "No one. What you have to do is clear your head and forget about what you're making. Just go out and play the way you're capable of playing, that's all. Don't worry about your salary. You didn't hold anybody in a headlock to get that contract. The Angels gave it to you."

I think the main thing I did was get Don's mind clear. The mechanics of hitting came along gradually to the point where Don was back hitting the way he could. He had an outstanding second half of the season and finished with 25 home runs.

At season's end Dave Garcia said he would like to have me back, and I said fine, but he had to wait and see if he would be rehired. Under Norm Sherry the Angels were 39-42, .481, and under Dave the record was 35-46, .432.

It was interesting to check the Indians' records in recent years. The season before I took over the club it had played .475 ball. In 1975 we went up to a percentage of .497, then to .509 in 1976. During my time in 1977 we played .456 ball, but the club fell to a percentage of .433 under Torborg. Poor Jeff wouldn't fare any better in 1978 as the Indians' winning percentage was only .434. But looking at the records made me think I hadn't done a bad job at all.

I wanted to manage in Puerto Rico again, but Hiram Cuevas had another commitment. I wanted to manage somewhere, to keep honing my skills, and I finally landed a job in Culiacan, Mexico. The team was called the Tomateros, or Tomato Pickers. The industry of Culiacan consisted of growing tomatoes, growing marijuana, and committing murder. There had been 215 murders in the city the previous year.

The Tomateros were owned by a nice Chinese gentleman named Mr. Lee who, along with his brother, owned a string of supermarkets and shopping plazas. I've forgotten Mr. Lee's first name because that's what I always called him: Mr. Lee. He was generous and supplied me with two coaches, just as I had in Puerto Rico, so I could manage from the dugout. Hiram Cuevas had the only team in Puerto Rico with two coaches. But the Tomateros had only one home uniform and one for the road, which had to be washed after every game. As that wasn't always possible, I told Mr. Lee the players would really appreciate it if they had two home and two road uniforms.

"No one ever said anything about that before," said Mr. Lee, who promptly ordered the additional uniforms.

The caliber of the Mexican Winter League ball was about Class A. The good Mexican players played all summer and skipped winter ball. Most of our players were those the other three winter leagues—in Puerto Rico, the Dominican Republic, and Venezuela—didn't want. The ballparks in Mexico were not great, the playing surfaces rocky and uneven, and salaries were low. We got young players who were trying to improve, like Danny Goodwin and Ike Hampton of the Angels and Floyd Rayford from their minor league organization, and veterans like Bobby Tolan, who was near the end of his career.

The rest of my players were Mexican and didn't speak any English except for Felipe Montemayor, who played a little and translated a lot. All my pitchers were Mexican, so every time I went to the mound, I said, "C'mon, Felipe." And every time I argued with an umpire, I had to drag Felipe along.

I'd say, "Tell him he wasn't in position to make the call and that the runner beat the throw."

Felipe would tell the umpire, then turn to me, and say, "He say the runner was out and he still out."

"Tell him he better start hustling and get in the ballgame," I'd say.

Felipe would repeat my words in Spanish and then say, "He say you better get in the dugout if you want to stay in the game."

It was so funny that I finally stopped getting on the umpires. And what was the point in arguing when I never could win?

For the first month or so I got caught up in the excitement of baseball and I really enjoyed the experience of managing again. We were in first or second place all season.

But then the problems of living in Mexico began to get to me. The food and the water took 12 pounds off me in a month. I normally ordered my steak cooked medium, but every night at dinner I ordered a well-done steak, hoping the heat would cook out any problem that may have been lurking in the meat. All I drank was 7-Up. There were no U.S. newspapers or magazines in Culiacan. I'm more a TV person than a reader, but I soon tired of listening to John Wayne talk to me in Spanish on the tube. There was nothing to do in the off-hours but lie around my hotel room and watch the flies buzz around.

What got to me the most, though, were the bus trips—riding in straight-backed seats. Our shortest bus ride took four hours. The drive to Tijuana required 20 to 21 hours. I told Mr. Lee I couldn't make it and took the train round-trip.

In late November I received a call from Red Patterson of the Angels' front office. Harry Dalton had gone to the Milwaukee Brewers, and Buzzie Bavasi was the Angels' new general manager. When I told Red I thought it was strange that Buzzie didn't call me, Patterson said, "I'm calling because I know you, Frank."

"Buzzie knows me well enough to call," I said, knowing Red was not going to have any good news. He said the Angels were thinking about changing managers.

"We think the new manager should have a chance to name his own coaches," Red said.

"But you haven't fired Dave Garcia, have you?" I asked.

"No."

"Then why are you firing me? Dave said he wants me back."

"Well, we just feel this is the thing to do at this time."

"Okay," I said, "if that's your decision."

So I was out of work again. Within a week I abruptly found myself not concentrating during a ballgame. My mind was wandering, drifting. I thought about it for a day or so and said to myself, "This is not fair to the ballclub, to the owner who's been so nice to me, to the players. They would be better off with someone else."

I went to Mr. Lee and told him that. "We like the job you're doing and want you to stay," he said.

"No, I feel like I'm taking your money and not doing the job," I said, "and that's not like me. I've never quit on anything before, and I'm sorry, Mr. Lee. But I feel like I have to go."

He talked me into staying another week, my eighth. But when I still couldn't concentrate on the ballgames, I apologized to Mr. Lee, thanked him, and went home.

When I reached Los Angeles, I read in the papers that the Angels had signed free agent Lyman Bostock. In the story team owner Gene Autry was quoted as saying, "This is not to belittle Dave Garcia. He's a good baseball man. We have an understanding with him. We might make a change [in managers] if we can find someone with a little more zip... somebody who could get us a little more press."

Two days later Dave Garcia had apparently acquired some zip, because the Angels rehired him. The newspaper story said, "In a strangely worded announcement, the club said that Garcia would fulfill his 1978 contract, which is believed to give the Angels the option of naming him either a manager or a coach at a salary of $35,000." Talk about cheap! The story reiterated the fact that I had been let go and added that the Angels were looking for a first base coach.

The business of baseball does not encourage sanity in a thinking man. The Angels hired Bob Skinner to replace me as hitting coach. Skinner had held that job with the Padres, where Buzzie Bavasi had been general manager in 1977. Cronyism was more important to Bavasi than satisfying his manager.

Shortly after I had been fired in Cleveland, the Orioles' third base coach, Billy Hunter, left to become manager of the Rangers. At that time it was rumored in the papers that I would be added to the Orioles' coaching staff, a move that Earl Weaver said he was all for. But general manager Hank Peters rejected the idea, saying, "I don't want to invite suggestions that Robinson was being groomed as Weaver's successor."

That notion seemed silly to me, because Weaver wasn't going to retire for at least five years. Obviously Hank Peters didn't want me. But when I learned the Angels didn't want me back, I called Peters from Mexico and asked him to keep me in mind if any position opened in Baltimore, and he said he would. I didn't put too much hope in his answer until he reached me at home a month later and said that Earl wanted me as a coach. I was excited about returning to Baltimore. Earl Weaver was one of the few managers I could be around and still be myself because he was always secure in his job. I knew that he'd be a good man to work for, I'd contribute to the ballclub, and I'd learn something at the same time.

One of the writers asked me if I would be looking over Earl's shoulder. I said, "He's only 5-foot-8, I can look over his head."

Earl chuckled at that because he always liked to laugh. I considered him to be a friend, but Earl would never go in for cronyism in hiring a coach. Cronyism was a twofold problem for blacks. Not only were we shut out of jobs by whites in positions of power who hired their friends even if they weren't as well qualified as certain blacks, but we never had had a black in a position of power to apply cronyism for us.

The Orioles traditionally promoted people with long service in their minor league system to coaching jobs on the big club. Third base coach Cal Ripken and first base coach Jim Frey had spent years managing in the minors for Baltimore. Pitching coach George Bamberger had left to manage the Brewers, so minor league pitching coach Ray Miller had been moved up to the Orioles. Ellie Hendricks, who still played a little, was named bullpen coach. It's interesting to note that all of those coaches in 1978 except Hendricks, a black man who wants to be a manager, went on to become managers in the major leagues. In 1987 Hendricks was still bullpen coach.

Earl Weaver created the job for me, adding a fifth coach to his staff for the first time and making me outfield coach. The job paid only $25,000, but I didn't take it for the money. I needed the work and to still be in the game. Guys who leave baseball are soon forgotten. I was also paid money I had deferred when I played for the Orioles, $40,000 a year for five years, which I had begun receiving when I retired as a player in 1977.

Defensively the Oriole outfielders needed a lot of work. So I worked very hard with them all through spring training, and I felt very comfortable with the job. I loved to teach, and as a manager you just don't have time to work with individuals. I felt the Oriole outfielders were improving, although they had a long way to go before they would excel.

But once the season began, I just didn't have enough to do. Before every game I'd hit fungoes to the outfielders and talk to each of them. When the games began, though, it was strange. I was supposed to position the outfielders, moving them around for each opposing hitter, a job that Cal Ripken supposedly had handled the previous season. But I wondered how much moving he actually got to do.

Earl Weaver was funny. He would give all his coaches lots of authority, yet he kept his hand in everything. For example, in spring training Earl would go over the fundamentals himself the first time. He'd show the players how he wanted things done with the coaches looking on. Then the coaches would run the workouts. But Earl would jump in at any time and make his points.

For the first month of the season I sat next to Earl and tried to do my job. But if Earl saw something he didn't like, he'd say to me, "I think the left fielder's in too close." And before I could move him, Earl would be up on his feet whistling shrilly and pushing his hand at the left fielder to move back. That went on inning after inning, Earl mentioning something, then popping up, whistling, and waving to an outfielder.

In May, Ken Boyer resigned as manager of our Class AAA Rochester club to manage the St. Louis Cardinals, and Hank Peters asked me if I wanted to take over the Redwings. I told him I appreciated his thinking of me and that I'd think about his offer. It took me five days to decide that I would go to the minors. I felt it would be more of a challenge and that I would contribute more to the organization than if I stayed in Baltimore. And Peters said I could return as an Oriole coach next year if I wanted to.

First I consulted with Earl, who didn't want me to go to Rochester. "I know you want to manage again in the big leagues," Earl said. "You might just be risking your future with a bunch of kids." I guess he didn't figure his outfield would get much better without me around.

Before I left for Rochester, I talked to farm director Clyde Kluttz and asked if he wanted me to put an emphasis on teaching or winning. "Handle things any way you want to, Frank," he said. So I went off to teach and develop players for the Orioles, and we'd win if we could.

And that season in Rochester proved to be one of the nicest experiences I've ever had in baseball. The baseballs we used in practice were old and beat up. If one went over the fence, the players had to chase it down. We traveled everywhere on buses, and some of the trips took hours. I had no coaches. Earl Stephenson, one of the older players, coached at first base and I coached third. I had coached third a few games here and there in Puerto Rico, but this was the first time I coached on the line every day. It was a new experience that I enjoyed.

As a manager you're constantly flashing signs to your third base coach, who looks into the dugout for them. One of the writers said, "At least you don't have to look for the signs from the dugout."

"No," I said, "but I have to remember them."

You get a little spoiled in the majors, and you forget about the enthusiasm and eagerness of the young players in the minors. The kids are incredibly eager to learn, to absorb all the information and insights they can get. You go to the park early every day, and with no coach you're teaching all the time. I'd have extra instruction on outfield play and on infield play, and all the work fell on the manager.

But it was good work. I had 21 players, and we were together day and night, on the buses, in motels, in diners, in tiny clubhouses, and at the ballparks. There's such a closeness in the minors that you almost become like a family.

We didn't have a lot of talent on the ballclub, and we didn't play very well. Pitchers Sammy Stewart and Timmy Stoddard went on to the majors from that team and were still in the big leagues nine years later. But pitcher Dave Ford was the only other player from the 1978 Redwings who made the majors, I'm sorry to say. They were a good bunch of guys who never lost their enthusiasm even though we finished in sixth place. I've never seen a sixth-place team in the majors that demonstrated such enthusiasm.

At season's end Redwing general manager Don Labbruzzo asked me if I would be coming back in 1979. "Yes, I'd like to come back," I said, "unless I get an offer to manage in the majors."

I later heard that Labbruzzo got upset with me for not saying that I would definitely be back. Did he really think I would choose Rochester over a major league managing job? I felt Labbruzzo thought I hadn't put enough emphasis on winning, which was understandable. The Orioles did not own the Redwings, but had a long-standing working agreement with the ballclub. But the owners of the Redwings were more interested in wins that would attract fans than they were in developing players for the Orioles.

I was managing at Santurce in November when I received another of those dreaded phone calls. Clyde Kluttz was on the line to tell me that the Redwings didn't want me back, which was a blow. But all I said was "That's fine."

One thing that troubled me at Rochester, because it reflected badly on the Orioles' scouting, was that there were no black players on the team and only one Latin player. Teams were without black players generally because they were not out beating the bushes to sign them. The Boston Red Sox—the last American League team to sign a black player to a major league contract, in 1959—also had no black players on their Class AAA Pawtucket club in 1978.

But the worst mistake the Orioles—and most of the other AAA ballclubs I faced—made was in having no coach with their top farm team. Players are supposed to be taught in the minor leagues, but I had no instructor other than myself. There was a minor league hitting instructor who roved throughout the Orioles' system. He would show up for a day or two and then move on. But to be effective, a hitting instructor needs to observe a batter for more than a day or two at a time. In addition, no two individuals are going to coach hitting the same way. The player hears instructions from the manager and from the roving instructor, which often results in some confusion.

It seems to me that when baseball clubs are going to make huge investments in young players, they should then provide those players with enough instructors to draw the very best out of their talents. Many organizations have added pitching coaches to every level of their minor league system, if not to each team. But there still is not a batting instructor with every AAA ballclub, and that is very shortsighted, in my view. The hand-and-eye coordination that is needed to be a good hitter is harder to develop than are the skills required to become a good pitcher, as far as this old hitter is concerned.

Midway through the '78 season Larry Doby had been hired to replace Bob Lemon as manager of the Chicago White Sox. Baseball had its second black manager—only 31 years after Doby had integrated the American League. Baseball called it progress. Writers asked me how I felt about the appointment, and I said I was naturally happy. "Larry has wanted to manage for a long time," I said, "but I'm not happy for him because he's black. I'm happy for him because he's a human being, and every human being should have an opportunity to work at what he's qualified for."

Doby had coached for the Expos in 1976, then moved to the White Sox the next year. When they got off to a 34-40 record in 1978, White Sox owner Bill Veeck named Doby manager. Veeck was the man who had originally brought Doby to the major leagues, and they had remained friends. I read that when Doby joined the Indians in 1947, a number of his teammates refused to shake his hand and that it wasn't until seven years after his debut—not until 1954—that black major leaguers could travel without racial restrictions.

Larry Doby paid his dues, and he finally got his opportunity to manage at age 55, but for only 87 games. The 1978 White Sox, a weak ballclub, won just 37 games for Doby, finishing in fifth place, and he was fired. I thought, "It would be nice if someday a black manager could take over a contending ballclub. Otherwise there will always be people out there who say that blacks make poor managers because both of the guys who tried it were fired." But only a fool would contend that 87 games was a fair measure of anybody's ability to manage a major league team.

When I returned to spring training with the Orioles, writers asked me if I still hoped to manage again and I told them of course I did. "But since I was fired in 1977, the only job offer I've received in baseball was from Dave Garcia," I said. "And I don't have a calendar to figure out how many managers have been hired since then." But I could think of at least five in addition to Doby who had been hired during the '78 season.

I said that if I did get an offer to manage again, I hoped it was from a contending team. "I don't think I'd want to be in a situation where it might take five to seven years to develop a winner," I added. "I know I wouldn't last that long." That proved to be prophetic.

Earl Weaver named me baseball's first defensive coordinator in the spring of 1979. "I'm turning the outfield over to Frank," Earl told the writers. "He'll work with the players on every phase of outfield play. He'll have his own set of index cards showing where to play each hitter. Frank's going to talk to our pitchers before every game to find out how they plan to pitch the opposing hitters. Then he'll relay that information to the out-fielders. During games he'll sit with me in the dugout and be responsible for placing the outfielders."

Pitcher Jim Palmer, never one to mince words, had charged that the Orioles' outfield play in 1978 had cost the ballclub five games each month. I didn't know if it could be that bad, but my early coaching hadn't helped much. So I decided to go back to basics and work on the simplest funda-mentals, as if my outfielders had never played the position. I was con-cerned that established players might be skeptical, but not one outfielder ever questioned anything I asked him to do.

The regulars were second-year man Gary Roenicke in left, veteran Al Bumbry in center, and right fielder Ken Singleton, age 32. Singleton was one of the slowest outfielders I'd ever seen, and he'd gotten in the habit of letting Bumbry take every ball hit into right center and even some flies in deep right.

"Kenny, I want you to play a game with yourself in the outfield," I told him. "Try to see how many balls you can catch every day. Aim to be more aggressive, and you'll be more aggressive."

I think talking with Singleton spurred him on. It suddenly became fun for him to catch the ball. He didn't become any faster, but he became much more aggressive and a better outfielder.

The reserve outfielders were Benny Ayala, Pat Kelly, and John Lowenstein. "Steiner" had played for me in Cleveland, and he was the only good defensive outfielder in the trio going into spring training. But as we worked out day after day and once they had some success, all the outfielders gained confidence and began finding that playing defense could be fun.

"I don't like to see outfielders catch the ball one-handed unless they have to jump or dive for it," I said. "It's surer to catch the ball with two hands, and I prefer it. But if catching the ball with one hand is the only way you feel comfortable, fine. The only thing that matters is the catch."

Al Bumbry was very fast and very aggressive in center field. But the very first fly I hit to him in the spring landed several feet behind him because he misjudged it. But Al was an inexhaustible worker, a guy who had won a Bronze Star as a platoon leader in Vietnam, and he devoted hours to improving his judgment. We would come out 15 minutes early before regular outfield practice throughout the season. Most fungo hitters drive all long fly balls to outfielders. I would hit from only 150 feet away from Al, to an area about 60 feet wide. I'd start with ground balls that he'd come in and field with nobody on base. Then with a man on first. Then with a man on second, when Al would have to charge hard and come up throwing. The same with a man on third.

I went through this drill with the other outfielders. "I know fielding ground balls seems routine to you," I said. "But how about when the game's on the line and you charge as hard as you can, catch the ball, and come up throwing?"

We worked and worked. "Almost anybody can catch a high fly ball. But how about when a line drive is hit directly over your head and you have to turn and go get it?" I'd say. "Or when a liner is hit in front of you, do you dive for it or catch the ball on a hop?" I got good enough with the fungo so that the players had to go flat out and extend themselves to make the catch.

By hitting close to my outfielders I wasn't running them to death, and therefore we could get in a lot more practice than normal before a ballgame. You don't want your outfielders playing with heavy legs. But I feel the Oriole outfielders got stronger as the season wore on from all the effort they put out. Their stamina increased while players on other teams began to wear down in late August.

We also devoted a lot of time to throwing from the outfield to the cutoff man. And Oriole outfielders overthrew the cutoff man only five times all season. When we won the pennant in 1979, Jim Palmer said the major improvement in the ballclub was in the outfield defense, and I was proud of that. The Orioles did not lose a single ballgame to an outfield misplay in 1979.

Earl Weaver believed that an outfielder should catch any ball that stayed in the park and that no ball should ever be hit over an outfielder's head. A thousand balls could fall in front of an outfielder without comment from Earl, but he got upset if one ball went over an outfielder's head. I didn't want to disregard Earl's authority and his belief that our outfielders should play deep. But I believe that more balls are hit in front of outfielders than over their heads, particularly early in games and especially by the bottom third of the lineup. So I told our outfielders to play in three or four steps, which equaled 10 or 12 feet, and that made a difference in their getting to a lot of low liners.

"But during the course of a ballgame," I told the guys, "if Earl says to me, 'The outfielders are too close,' which he will at times, and either he gets up or I get up and wave you back, don't resent it. Move back. And when Earl sits down, slip back in a few steps. I want you to remember one thing: You guys are responsible to me, and I'm responsible for you. If you make a mistake during a game, I'll come down the bench and talk to you."

I did that and I also regularly talked to the outfielders about game situations and what to expect on the field before they went back out. I would defense an opponent before a game and throughout it. We talked a lot, and whenever one of my guys made a good play I made sure I went down and complimented him.

Al Bumbry was catching a lot of balls hit over the infield that he had been taking on a bounce the year before. People were saying, "How the heck is Al getting to those balls all of a sudden?"

Lowenstein, who played many games in left field against hard-throwing right-handers because he batted from the left side and was a good fastball hitter, also replaced Gary Roenicke late in many games. Steiner was fleet-footed and made a bunch of good defensive plays. He was excellent at coming in on dinks to left, sliding on his butt, and making the catch.

John Lowenstein was an ideal role player who always kept himself in top condition and never complained. He had a good perspective and a wry sense of humor that kept us all loose. Lowenstein claimed to have the largest fan club when he was in Cleveland, the "Lowenstein Apathy Club" (LAC). He said that everyone in the area who had no interest whatsoever in him was a member of LAC. Steiner said that the club was planning to hold a day for him when the Indians were on the road, but he's not sure if it ever came off. "I was on the road," he explained.

Steiner also said, "I have no need to be a star, but I'd like to twinkle a little." He twinkled a good deal for the Orioles. Now he does color commentary on the Orioles for cable television.

I got off a line that John enjoyed early in the '79 season. Second baseman Rich Dauer had been a notoriously slow starter at bat his first two seasons with the club. In his first 44 at-bats in 1977, Dauer had only one hit. He had 3 hits in his first 30 at-bats in 1978. His first time up in 1979, though, Dauer rapped a two-run single, and I said, "He's peaking too soon."

But that hit was symbolic of how the Orioles played baseball in 1979, going on to win 102 games and take the pennant by 8 games over Milwaukee. I got great satisfaction out of seeing my outfielders improve so much and helping the ballclub to the World Series. It was my first time in a Series as a coach, and it was not the same as being there as a player, but it was still a thrill.

We went ahead three games to one over the Pittsburgh Pirates, and I said to myself, "There's no way we can lose this Series." I would have bet my salary on our winning. We had Mike Flanagan, who would win the Cy Young Award as the best pitcher in the American League that season, going in game 5. He would be followed, if necessary, by Jim Palmer and Scott McGregor, pitching at our home park in Baltimore.

But, incredibly, none of them could win that one game we needed for the world championship. I went through more pain and anguish in this Series, it turned out, than I had in 1969 when the Mets beat us. In this one, all I could do was sit and watch.

14

THE NL'S FIRST
BLACK MANAGER

I had returned to manage for my friend Hiram Cuevas in the fall of 1978, and I did so again in 1979. It was my eighth season managing Santurce. Barbara and the kids had come to regard Puerto Rico almost as a second home. I loved working for Hiram, and I also felt that I had to keep my name before the public as a candidate for a major league managing job. But I wondered if anyone would ever give me another shot in the big leagues, no matter how much experience I acquired elsewhere.

I read that Maury Wills was now getting some managing experience in hopes of eventually getting a job in the big leagues. When Maury retired in 1972, he'd said he wanted to manage. The only job he could get at the time was in the Mexican Winter League, where he worked for two years. I thought he would make an excellent major league manager after I saw the way he worked with players when he coached base running for me in Cleveland during spring training in 1975.

But Maury was told that he needed to get more managing experience in the minors. Maury Wills had spent eight long years playing in the minors before he finally made the Dodgers, and he had understandably lost his fondness for bus rides. So Maury became a baseball announcer on television rather than a baseball manager in the minors, the broadcast job paying a whole lot more. When the TV jobs ended, in 1978, once again the only managing job Maury could land was in the Mexican Winter

League, where he was now making those 20-hour bus rides for the second year in a row.

But in the last few years, Joe Torre had been hired as manager by the Mets, Jim Fregosi by the Angels and Don Kessinger by the White Sox, all of them right off the playing field. Torre, Fregosi, and Kessinger were all white, and they weren't forced to go to the minors to gain experience. The situation was really beginning to get to me.

That was why, when a writer from *Sport* magazine asked me to do an in-depth interview in Puerto Rico, I decided to speak some truths. When I told Barbara that I was going to sound off on what was going on in baseball as far as blacks were concerned, she said, "You know it could hurt you in terms of becoming a major league manager again."

"Barbara, the owners and general managers are gonna do whatever they want to do anyway," I said. "I think it's best to just be honest about the whole thing."

The interviewer, Vin Gilligan, asked me about my frustrations in being unable to land another job managing in the major leagues after 12 years of managing experience overall. "Why aren't you managing in the major leagues?" he asked. And I said, "I can't answer that. But it makes you think, doesn't it?"

"Let's put it this way," Gilligan said. "If Frank Robinson was the same color as Brooks Robinson, would he be managing?"

"No doubt about it," I said.

"When is this going to stop?"

"I honestly don't see it happening any time soon," I answered. "Once the color line for managers was broken, I thought it would be a slow but steady opening up for others. But baseball has gone backward. It's like they've said to themselves, 'Okay, we've had our black managers, Robinson and Doby. The heat is off. Back to business as usual.'"

"Don't you ever feel like shaking someone by the neck and saying, 'What the hell is going on here?'" Gilligan asked.

I said I really didn't know who to shake. "You can't shake every owner and GM. I've been thinking a lot about this lately, about who to shake. Henry Aaron of the Braves' front office blasted commissioner Bowie Kuhn for his inaction on the ongoing situation. Until now I've been reluctant to stir things up, and I think that's true of black ex-ballplayers in general. But maybe it's time that a bunch of us like Aaron, Wills, me, and some other guys got together and made an appointment with commissioner Kuhn. Then sit down with the man and ask him, 'Why are blacks being excluded from managing and responsible front office jobs in baseball?'"

"Is it the commissioner's responsibility to see that blacks are given equal opportunity?" Gilligan asked.

"Definitely," I said. "When Willie Mays was hired as a greeter for a hotel that operated a gambling casino, the commissioner announced that it was his responsibility to remove Willie from active participation with any ballclub to protect baseball's integrity. He should feel at least the same responsibility to look out for baseball's integrity where human rights are concerned. He should lead. He should feel a moral responsibility to go before the owners and say, 'As a man of reason, I simply will not accept that in all of baseball there is only one black man, Henry Aaron in Atlanta, qualified for a responsible front office position and *no* black manager or black third base coach.' He should say, 'I don't want excuses. I want to see some black faces and soon.'"

I also said that we had just witnessed one of the most ludicrous examples of baseball's hiring practices. There was no room in the major leagues for a black manager, but when the San Diego Padres fired Roger Craig, they hired as their manager for the coming season their television announcer, Jerry Coleman. That was a slap not only at blacks but at every manager in the minor leagues who has paid his dues in hopes of rising to the big leagues.

"Les Moss played by the rules, was devoted to the Detroit Tigers' organization, and was very successful managing in the minors for years," I said. "So they moved him up to the big club last year and fired him after a third of the season. That's not even a shot. Detroit's treatment of Les Moss was one of the worst things I've ever seen in baseball."

I was in spring training with the Orioles when the interview came out. Barbara called to say she'd read it and liked what I'd had to say. Then she laughed and added, "But I'm glad you've got only one mouth."

Jim Frey had left the Orioles in 1980 to manage the Kansas City Royals. I can't say that I wasn't inwardly envious of Jimmy, who had the good fortune to get his first major league managing opportunity with a ballclub that was ready to win. (The Royals went on to win the pennant that season.) I was beginning to feel I'd never have the chance that Frey got.

Earl Weaver had me replace Frey as the first base coach and hitting instructor for the Orioles in 1980. It was interesting being out on the line for the first time, as we were in the pennant race right to the end, finishing with 100 victories, but that was second to the Yankees' 103 wins.

I continued to marvel at the way Earl Weaver got so much out of all his players, right down to the twenty-fifth man. Earl was a very keen judge of a player's ability, and even if a player could do only one thing, Earl had him do that thing and would win a ballgame. The Mets discarded Benny Ayala, who was a liability in the outfield if the ball wasn't hit near him. Earl not only got Ayala some time in the outfield, but it seemed like every time Earl sent him up to pinch-hit, Benny came through. Ayala was particularly tough at bat with men in scoring position.

John Lowenstein went from Cleveland to Texas, and his career seemed to be over there. But Earl picked him up on waivers and got a number of outstanding years out of him. Terry Crowley bounced around from the Orioles to Cincinnati to Atlanta to Rochester and then back to the Orioles, where he became one of the game's top pinch hitters for several years. Crowley's career was extended only because Earl recognized his capabilities.

Earl Weaver also kept all 25 of his players relatively happy, which is next to impossible. He would scream and holler at a player, and he allowed the player to scream and holler right back at him. Earl never held a grudge. The same guy who hollered at Earl one day and threw equipment around the dugout would be in the lineup the next day if Earl felt the player would help him win.

Some of Earl's classic confrontations with pitcher Jim Palmer were often right out on the mound before thousands of people. Earl believed in letting players express themselves, and Palmer never passed up an opportunity to do so. In their arguments on the mound everyone knew they were battling. Palmer would start waving his arms in anger, and Earl would gesture in kind. I know of no other manager who would stand for that, including me. It would be too embarrassing.

But Earl Weaver never felt embarrassed or that he was being shown up in an argument. He never even thought about it. All Earl ever thought was that he was right, which was his bottom line.

In late August I received word that there were rumors printed in New York papers that Mets' manager Joe Torre would be fired and that Frank Robinson would replace him. The stories said that Mets' general manager Frank Cashen, formerly of the Orioles, wanted to make the move. I got my hopes up for a couple of days. But then the *Daily News* reported that "it had learned from two sources" that there had been conversation between Cashen and Hank Peters. I knew right then that the rumor was false, or Peters would have told me of Cashen's interest.

In November the Red Sox, who had fired Don Zimmer, leaked a rumor to the press that I was one of three final candidates being considered to manage the ballclub. But the Red Sox never sought permission from Peters to talk to me. They just used my name to make people think they had considered a black man, which I felt was pretty shabby on the part of Boston's front office.

In December Giants' manager Dave Bristol was fired, and once again I was rumored to be a candidate for a job, along with three other former managers. I was reportedly well down on the list. But a few weeks later Hank Peters phoned to say that the Giants had sought, and he had given, permission to talk to me. That got my hopes up!

In two days Giants' general manager Spec Richardson invited me to fly up to San Francisco and meet with him and club owner Bob Lurie. Never having been interviewed for a job before, I didn't know what to expect. We met in a private room at the airport, and they wanted to hear my philosophy of managing and how I would communicate with players if problems arose. I said I had learned not to express myself to a player in the heat of anger but to cool down and wait until we could move behind closed doors.

I left the interview with a good feeling. I liked Spec Richardson and Bob Lurie as individuals and liked their straightforward manner of speaking. The thing that really impressed me was that they were not expecting to win a pennant in 1981. The Giants had finished 75-86 in 1980, and they were looking for a ballclub that played with enthusiasm and showed improvement over the season. Those sounded like fair expectations from what they told me about the talent on the team. In Cleveland the pressure to win had been extremely, and unfairly, intense, though I said nothing about it. Every manager in the majors feels pressure to win.

On January 14, 1981, I signed a two-year contract to manage the Giants, and I was very excited, even though my salary was only $75,000, $5000 less than I'd earned four years earlier. I wanted to manage again no matter what. The first black manager fired in the American League, now had a chance to be the first black manager fired in the National League. It was progress.

San Francisco had a problem with its ballpark that was even worse than the one I experienced in Cleveland. A lot of players did not want to play for the Indians because Cleveland Stadium seated over 76,000 people, but we often played before crowds of under 10,000. And the playing surface at Cleveland Stadium was the worst in the American League.

But the overall playing conditions at Candlestick Park had been by far the worst in the majors ever since it opened in 1960. I remember the first time I went there as a player. The wind was whipping in from left field to right. In batting practice I hit line drives that headed for the left-field fence and then fell straight down as if the balls had struck an invisible wall. I was in the 1961 All-Star Game that was played at Candlestick when Giants pitcher Stu Miller went into his windup, kicked his left leg into the air, and was blown off the mound by a sudden gust of wind. The umpire could do nothing but call a balk. The players on both benches could do nothing but shake their heads.

Every time I played at Candlestick Park, conditions were bad. Not only the relentless wind but the cold and dampness cut into your bones, and you just couldn't get loose as a hitter. No matter what you tried to do to warm up, you couldn't get loose. "Man, I'm just glad I don't have to play half a season's schedule in this stadium," I used to say. "Three games and I'm out of here."

Why did Horace Stoneham, who owned the Giants when Candlestick Park was constructed, agree to its going up on the edge of San Francisco Bay? He didn't know the weather conditions there. His general manager, Chub Feeney, discovered the truth when he inspected the ballpark one day during construction and was battered by gale winds. "Does the wind always blow like this here?" Feeney asked a worker.

"Oh no," the man said. "Only between 1 and 5 in the afternoon."

In 1972 I returned to Candlestick with the Dodgers after improvements had supposedly been made in the stadium. The City of San Francisco, which owns the stadium, had expanded its seating capacity for baseball to 55,000 by enclosing the bay side of the ballpark. The belief was that this would block the wind off the bay. It did not. The new design resulted in swirling winds that whipped dust into the eyes of the players and made the conditions even worse for them. You never knew from which direction the wind would blow, so you could make no adjustments. The swirling winds would change direction from inning to inning, from batter to batter, sometimes from pitch to pitch.

Giants' players were always bitching about having to play at Candlestick, so I knew I was going to hear plenty from my players. I read where someone asked Jack Clark, the team's best hitter, what he thought would improve the ballpark. "Dynamite," Jack said.

Even before I went to spring training with the Giants, I heard from players about the infield at Candlestick. "Please have the infield dirt replaced," they said. Actually, the infield dirt had already been replaced by ground-up volcanic ash. The groundkeepers felt the ash would not blow around like dirt, periodically blinding players, and it did not. But the volcanic ash was like rough gravel, and anytime a player dove for a ball on it or slid on it, he came up bloody. So I had the ash replaced by dirt.

It was understandable that the Giants found very, very few free agents who were willing to sign with them. They had made good offers to a lot of players without success, which was probably what had led general manager Spec Richardson in 1980 to sign free agent second baseman Rennie Stennett to a $3 million, five-year contract. That contract had the baseball world abuzz for weeks. Stennett had suffered a very bad broken leg with the Pirates two years before and was still limping when the Giants signed him. He no longer had any speed and could not drive the ball with his normal power anymore. Stennett was also limited in the field. My guess is that Richardson signed him out of desperation and in the hopes that Stennett's damaged leg would recover. Unfortunately, it never did.

Spec anticipated that in January 1981, because he signed free agent second baseman Joe Morgan to a contract. Morgan was asking more money than the Giants wanted to give, but twice he had been MVP in the league, so I pushed hard with Richardson to get him. Morgan was a winner, and I wanted him. He said he signed because he wanted to play for me and to be near his hometown, Oakland.

"The thing about Frank is that he really hates to lose," said Morgan, who at age 37 had left Houston on his own despite what he called "an attractive money offer to return" to the Astros. "And Frank makes it very uncomfortable to be around him if you do lose. A lot of people *say* they hate to lose, but they don't really mean it. Frank does. The Giants have some good players, but they haven't had the right attitude. Frank could make a big difference there."

I felt that Joe Morgan would make a difference too. After I had been hired, relief pitcher Greg Minton said of the Giants: "There was a disease on our club the last couple of years. People were always second-guessing each other, and it made for a bad atmosphere in the clubhouse. You have to find a way to win. We've weeded out some of the problems now, and we've got an astute baseball man. From what I'm told, if you're in the same dugout with Frank Robinson, your mind is on nothing but baseball."

One of the second-guessers, I was told, was pitcher John Montefusco, who had been traded. Also traded was pitcher Bob Knepper, who had been a member of a group of Born-Again Christians on the Giants. They had been nicknamed the "God Squad," and one of them reportedly had characterized a loss as "God's will." I was glad to be rid of Montefusco and Knepper, both of whom were said to be players more interested in their own stats than in the team.

In spring training I immediately put my position right on the table with the God Squad and told the players that I wouldn't deny anyone his religion but there was a time and a place for it. I said they could have their Sunday chapel meetings at the ballpark as long as they were held early enough so that they didn't interfere with the team's work. Gary Lavelle, I'd learned, had book racks in the clubhouse at Candlestick which he filled with religious pamphlets and other material he liked to make available to everyone. I told him I felt the clubhouse was not the place for his racks, and Gary understood. I had no problem with the God Squad all season.

I had one problem with the Giants before spring training that would plague me all season. I was told that the ballclub had re-signed all its coaches for 1981—Jim Davenport at third base, Vern Benson at first base, Don McMahon as pitching coach, John Van Ornum as bullpen coach, and Jim LeFebvre as hitting coach. I told Richardson and Bob Lurie that I could understand why I couldn't have all my own coaches as they wouldn't want to pay two sets of contracts. The Giants' attendance had dropped from 1.7 million to just over 1 million.

"But I would like to hire a third base coach I know because our minds have to be on the same page," I said. "For instance, if I flash the wrong sign to Jim Davenport, I expect him to give the appropriate sign for that situation the way Dave Garcia did for me in Cleveland. It really makes it more difficult working with a new man."

I was told I would have to wait a year unless real problems developed with Davenport. In February, first base coach Vern Benson suddenly quit and took a cut in pay to scout in the minors for another organization. I was told he left because "he was a Dave Bristol man." But I felt the man left because he didn't want to coach for a black manager. Good riddance.

It gave me a chance to bring in a man who wanted to work for me, my old teammate in Baltimore, Don Buford. He had played ten years in the major leagues and four in Japan before retiring after the '76 season. He had tried to get a job in baseball, but was unsuccessful until 1980 when Harry Dalton hired him as a part-time scout and minor league instructor for the Milwaukee organization.

Don Buford lived only ten minutes from me in Los Angeles, and we would get together in the off-season to have dinner or to take in a Lakers' basketball game. And, of course, we always talked baseball. I'd told him that if I ever got another managing job, I'd try to put him on my staff. But when I proposed that the Giants hire Buford, it wasn't automatic. I suggested Buford at a meeting with Lurie, Richardson, and Tom Haller, who was the director of player personnel. That duty had been taken from Richardson. The man who had been named National League Executive of the Year in 1978 had reportedly had his powers reduced as a result of the Stennett signing.

When I said I'd like to have Buford as a coach, Haller said, "Does this have anything to do with the fact that Buford's a friend of yours?"

I stared at him a moment, thinking, "I wonder if your question has anything to do with the fact that Don Buford is black?"

But I said, "I wouldn't hire anyone who couldn't do a good job."

"I know Don's been trying to get back into baseball for several years," Lurie said.

"I know that too," I said. "But I wouldn't hire him or anyone else who couldn't help me with this ballclub. Don Buford is a man who gave everything he had as a player. He's intelligent and articulate, and he'll be a great addition in coaching our outfielders on every aspect of their play and in coaching the entire ballclub on base running."

Buford was finally hired, but I wondered whether I would have had to do a selling job on my coaching candidate if he happened to be white. I found out a couple of years later when I suggested two other coaches that I wanted to hire. No questions were asked. Both men were white.

In spring training Buford taught outfield play the same way I had done it in Baltimore. The players all seemed to enjoy the new conditioning program I put in, particularly the slow stretching exercises I had everyone doing daily. I hired a woman who had been highly recommended to lead the exercises. I ran a loose camp, and there was considerable joking around, but everyone worked hard. The players told me that Dave Bristol had run a military-type camp and that they appreciated my looser approach.

March 16, 1981, would be another historic day in baseball. For the first time two black managers of major league teams would exchange lineup cards. On that day the Giants played an exhibition game against the Seattle Mariners, the American League team that Maury Wills had taken over as manager for the final 58 games of the 1980 season. He replaced

Darrell Johnson, who had managed the expansion team since its inception in 1977. Once again a black manager had been brought in to perform a miracle with a ballclub that had little talent. The Mariner winning percentage in 1977 was .395, in 1978 .350, in 1979 .414, and in 1980 .375 under Johnson, and it declined to .345 under Wills.

Maury had signed a two-year contract with the Mariners, and I hoped he would be given at least that length of time to turn the ballclub around. I had read a story in which Wills, on being hired, had said he'd grown skeptical of ever getting back into the game. After he'd lost his job at NBC, Maury said he wrote to the Dodgers seeking a position in the organization he had served for some 20 years. The Dodgers didn't even have the courtesy to answer his letter. I knew why. The Dodgers had become angry with Maury Wills in 1975 when he'd agreed to coach base running for me in spring training, which he had done for them in previous years. But in January when I called Maury, the Dodgers had not been in touch with him, so he figured he would put in two weeks with the Indians and then go to Vero Beach for the Dodgers. But Dodger president Peter O'Malley then wrote a letter saying that Wills had betrayed the Dodgers, and he never worked for them again. The attitude of the Dodgers in this instance may seem petty to some, but all too often that's baseball.

So Maury Wills, who waited eight years to make the major leagues, had to wait eight years after he retired to get back into the major leagues. "There was a lot of frustration waiting that long," Wills told the press. "I'd read the box scores every day and try to speculate on which teams might be ready to make a change in managers. I saw friends like Preston Gomez get three chances to manage in the majors and Dave Bristol get five chances. I grew frustrated, but not bitter, and now I'm totally prepared for this chance—mentally, physically, and spiritually. I honestly feel I'm not just going to be another manager. I think I can be an outstanding manager."

Maury Wills never lacked confidence. I remember what Maury said when I was named manager of the Indians: "Frank Robinson will do an outstanding job. The Cleveland Indians will never regret having hired him. But honestly speaking, I think I would have been the best choice. I say that arrogantly, confidently, and honestly."

It was nice shaking hands with Maury Wills before our exhibition game in Phoenix. We both had huge grins on our faces, and I said, "It's about time this came to pass."

"I wasn't sure I'd ever be here, much less managing against you,"

Maury said. "Now I just plan to make the most of the opportunity. You know something, Frank, I had a meeting with this team in the final week of last season. I had a coach go over our signs before a game—and five players didn't know the signs."

"It's tough getting guys to concentrate on the game when they've been losers for several years," I said.

I later read a quote in the papers from Maury Wills's book *How to Steal a Pennant:* "Give me a last-place club and after three years we would be strongly in contention, and by the fourth year we'd go all the way."

I wondered where he thought he was going to get enough outstanding players quickly enough to pull that off. Perhaps it was due to his bravado that Maury Wills, his Mariners bereft of topflight players, began to try and outsmart the opposition. In a rundown play, the idea is to chase the base runner back toward the base he'd left. But Maury, saying it was aggressive baseball, had his players chasing runners *toward* the advancing base.

Wills introduced another revolutionary idea when the Mariners were playing on the artificial turf at Seattle's Kingdome. If the opposition was likely to attempt a suicide squeeze of home, Maury wanted his pitchers to bounce the ball off the carpet to the catcher, and he had them out practicing it. Apparently he felt the batter would be too startled to try to put his bat on the bounced ball, so the catcher would grab it and tag the runner.

Maury Wills has a good baseball mind, but maybe he tried too hard. Certainly he did when, in late April, he had his groundskeeper make the batter's boxes a foot longer than the specified 6 feet, extending toward the mound. Wills later said he did it to end complaints from the Oakland A's that his outfielder, Tom Paciorek, stepped out of the box when he hit. It's more likely that Wills wanted his hitters way up in the box so they could swing against a sinker ball pitcher before the ball dropped. But it was all for nothing, because Oakland manager Billy Martin spotted the batter's box extension. Wills was subsequently suspended for two games and fined $500 by American League president Lee MacPhail.

Unfortunately, the attempt by Wills to cheat may have cost him his job, because ten days later he was fired. Mariner president Dan O'Brien said, "A manager is no better than his players. You have to have a cohesive performing unit, and when that happens, then the talent takes over and you start to win. And that wasn't happening.

"I can't say enough about how cooperative Maury Wills was to work with, how sensitive he is to people, perhaps too sensitive sometimes," O'Brien added. Then he said he felt Wills had been given ample opportunity to prove himself.

The Mariners had a 6-18 record when Wills was fired. Is 24 games really ample time for a manager to prove himself? If it is, why was Wills brought back by the Mariners after he had managed 58 games the year before?

Maury Wills made mistakes. Every manager makes a bunch of them in his first year on the job, and I think Maury would have improved if he'd been given a chance. He is a good baseball person with a sharp baseball mind, but he tried too hard. And being black, Maury Wills will probably never get another opportunity to manage.

His record would not spur owners to offer other blacks a job managing in the majors, either, and as of this writing, no black manager has been hired since Wills was fired.

I had my players working in the spring of 1981 on some ideas I'd had for some time. Certain teams tell players that when they are on second base with less than two out, they are to make sure that any ball hit in front of them goes through the infield before they advance to third. This puts a negative thought in the player's mind, and he freezes on a ball topped to third. Obviously on a ball hit slowly down the line, the third baseman has to come in on it and leave the base uncovered. I wanted my runners to react aggressively after they checked the third baseman and to take that base whenever possible.

On flies to the outfield, many teams have the runner on first go halfway and then return to the base unless the ball is dropped. But how often does a major league outfielder drop a fly ball? We worked at tagging up at first on long flies and taking the base. During the season we actually did that to help win a few ballgames.

Any manager who has been in the game for 20 years sees traditional baseball executions that he'd like to change simply because there are better ways to make a play. To this day I don't understand why, on a ball hit down the left-field line, the third baseman goes to the bag and the shortstop moves out to take the throw in. I had my third basemen practice going down the left-field line, because they had less ground to cover than the shortstop, who could slide over to cover third base. By saving a few steps, you speed up your defensive routine.

We worked on this new routine for several days, but then I saw it was not going to take hold. The players were so steeped in the old way of reacting to a hit down the left-field line that they couldn't make the change comfortably. We discarded my idea. But that's what a manager does in his first year with a ballclub: try his own things and keep those that work. Anything that doesn't work, you throw out. That's why it makes no sense to fire a manager like Maury Wills or Les Moss before he's even completed his first year on the job. Before he's got his feet on the ground, he's gone.

The individual I probably worked most with in the spring was outfielder Bill North. He was speedy and a good base stealer, but the rap against him was that once he got on base, he sometimes did foolish things. The coaches couldn't seem to reach him. They told me that in 1980, North had been on second base five times with Jack Clark up and two out—and Bill was thrown out four times trying to steal third.

I talked to Bill North, and at first he couldn't understand why I didn't want him to do that. He counted only the time when he successfully stole third. The throw was wild, and Bill scored the winning run. He was one of those players who count only the times when they're successful, not when they're unsuccessful.

"The percentages of stealing third with two outs are not good to begin with, Bill," I said. "And with our best hitter up, Jack Clark, you've got to give him a chance to swing the bat."

Bill North finally understood, and he made things happen on the bases for us, stealing 26 bases in the 37 games he appeared in. But by then North had dropped so many routine fly balls that I had to get rid of him. In fact, four of the fly balls he missed cost us ballgames.

If we had won those four games, we would have been 31-28 instead of 27-32 before the 1981 strike, which lasted seven weeks, and we would have winning records for both halves of the schedule.

But Bill North wasn't the main reason why the Giants did not have a much better record in 1981. Tom Haller saw to that.

15

A GM FOR NO SEASON

*F*OR a manager to succeed, it is all-important that he have a good working relationship with his general manager. And from the beginning I had a very close relationship with Spec Richardson, an outstanding baseball man for many years with Houston and the Giants and a nice, warm person who would always consider what I had to say.

For example, center fielder Chili Davis had a great spring with us, and though he was only 21, he was a switch-hitter and I wanted to keep him. Spec was afraid that Davis wouldn't play enough and thought he could use another year in AAA ball. "I guarantee you I'll get Chili 250 at-bats over the course of the season," I said.

"All right then," Spec said, "you can keep him. I just don't want him sitting on the bench. Chili Davis is gonna be a regular here for a long time."

When I couldn't play Davis much the first few weeks of the season, we sent him down. But the point was that the general manager had gone along with what I thought was in the best interest of the ballclub.

I exchanged ideas with Spec Richardson almost every day. We not only saw one another at the ballpark, but we regularly got together over breakfast and at dinner to talk. I think it's very important that a manager gets together socially with his GM. It's easier to get to know one another's thinking, to be open in a relaxed atmosphere over coffee or a drink.

On the road we would see one another socially three or four nights in a row. Spec would say, "What're you doing after the game, Frank?"

I'd sometimes say, "I'm pretty tired. I think I'm going right back to the hotel to sleep."

"Oh no you're not. Let's go get a drink and talk."

We didn't always have serious discussions about our ballclub. We would talk about all kinds of things concerning the game, the league, and what other clubs were doing. Very quickly we got to know each other's philosophy about baseball and about life. We grew close.

Any time I said I wanted to send a player down and bring up another, Spec made the move. If I needed a player who was not in our organization, Spec made every effort to get him. He tried, even if he wasn't always successful because the Giants did not have a lot of talent to trade. And when Spec wanted to trade first baseman Mike Ivie to Houston for outfielder Jeff Leonard and first baseman Dave Bergman, he asked me if I liked the deal. I readily approved, as I liked the scouting reports on Leonard for the future.

Spec Richardson tried to involve me in all aspects of the Giants' organization, from scouting right up through our minor league system. And Bob Lurie was all for my increased involvement with the entire Giants' organization. At the chamber of commerce luncheon for the Giants in San Francisco, Lurie said, "We've already talked to Frank about some of his ideas on the farm system. And although he lives in Los Angeles, he wants to spend time up here next winter and work with us." Specifically, I wanted to remodel our farm system after the very successful one employed by the Orioles, in which players throughout the minors were taught to perform exactly as everyone on the major league club does.

But during the strike, Bob Lurie fired Spec Richardson and named Tom Haller general manager. After retiring as a player in 1972, Haller had gone into the insurance business until he returned to the Giants as a bullpen coach in 1977. "I always had it on my mind to become a manager," Haller said. When he moved into the scouting department of the front office, he admitted he still wanted to manage, and he was disappointed when I got the job and he didn't.

Haller had sat in on the meetings I'd had with Richardson and Lurie, but we had never sat down and had a one-on-one conversation. I thought surely we would get together privately at the organizational meetings that were held during the strike, so that he could get a feel for me and for what I felt the ballclub needed. But instead of getting together with me, Haller seemed to purposely avoid me.

As it would turn out, in the more than three years that I managed the Giants, Tom Haller never asked me to have a meeting or a meal or even a cup of coffee with him alone. On the road I would see Haller take out one of the coaches, particularly Jim Davenport, with whom Tom had been friends ever since they had come to the Giants together. But the only times I was invited to dine with Haller were when all the coaches were also along or when Bob Lurie took Haller and myself out for something to eat while we talked business.

It was apparent that Tom Haller did not want to get to know me—and also didn't want me to get to know him. I kept wondering: What has this man got to hide? His admitted lack of experience as a GM? I might have been able to help him there, as I had some experience working with a general manager and an owner. But Haller didn't want my input. From the start he somehow seemed threatened by me and the rapport I had established with Bob Lurie.

Haller also seemed to suggest that he did not have much respect for my thoughts on trades. I told San Francisco *Chronicle* columnist Glenn Dickey, "I think the general manager and owner should have the final word on trades, but the manager's opinion should certainly carry a lot of weight because he's the one who has to use the players."

Wrote Dickey: "Haller says he plans to ask for several opinions within the organization, including Robinson's, before he makes a trade. I asked him what he would do if he and others wanted to make a trade that Robinson opposed. 'I'd make the trade,' he said."

I read that and said to myself, "Spec, I hate to see you gone."

Earlier in the strike, before Richardson had been fired, I had received permission to spend several days in Baltimore examining in depth the Baltimore organization: how the Orioles went about scouting players, developing them, and advancing them. Tom Giordano, the director of player development and scouting for the Orioles, answered all my questions and even gave me a copy of the organization's defensive book. It was a manual of defensive plays that had been used throughout the system since it had been prepared by Earl Weaver and Billy Hunter in the 1960s.

The Orioles were noted for developing well-disciplined, dedicated players, and I asked Giordano if there was such a thing as an Oriole type that the organization looked for. "No," Tom said, "we look for the best athletes we can find. They become Oriole-type players by coming up through our system." Giordano also gave me the Orioles' scouting manual.

The Giants' media guide was a sorry publication, so I met with Oriole public relations director Bob Brown and got a copy of the guide he prepared, which was the best in baseball, I felt. I wanted the Giants to become a first-class organization, and their media guide now resembles the Orioles'.

When I returned to San Francisco, Richardson was fired. Haller initially accepted the materials and the ideas I brought back, because he was new and because Bob Lurie liked the approach I proposed. But without Spec Richardson there, I lost the in-depth input I would have had.

Haller soon modified or abandoned the changes in the system that I had suggested. It was as if he feared that I was making a bigger contribution than he was in revamping the Giants and building a winning organization. From the beginning Tom Haller was more interested in playing power politics than he was in developing a successful organization.

After meeting with Lurie and Haller, I flew to Phoenix for a few days to look over our players at the AAA level. And I was appalled. Most of the players on our top farm team were deficient in such fundamentals as bunting, base running, and hitting the cutoff man. The Giants weren't putting enough emphasis on teaching fundamentals. That instruction should start in the Rookie League, be polished in A and AA ball, and be second nature by the time players reach Triple A.

But when I brought up catcher Bob Brenly in August, he said, "I hadn't bunted in two years at Phoenix."

While in Phoenix I watched a game against the Dodgers' AAA club, and I was impressed by that team's bunting. In situations where a bunt was called for, the manager had his number 3 and 4 hitters lay one down. In the same game, the Phoenix leadoff man didn't even bunt a runner over when it was called for. If a game situation *cries* for a bunt, every hitter in the minors should know how to do so. Because when the number 3 or 4 hitter in Phoenix gets to the major leagues, he may bat second or he may bat seventh, and then he's going to be called on to bunt from time to time.

Bunting is something players once learned to do in the minors, along with executing all the other fundamentals of baseball. But fundamentals are just not taught the way they used to be. Even the 1987 Orioles' organization, renowned for the well-schooled players it sent to the majors for over 40 years, was delivering players to the big club who were not fundamentally sound. Why? It's my belief that the problem started on the sandlots the last decade or so. The men who used to coach sandlot baseball had done so for decades. They knew the game and taught it well, then the players' skills were honed in the minors. Most sandlot coaching is now done by fathers who haven't had coaching experience. This is why there should be at least two good coaches with every rookie league, Class A, and Class AA club in baseball. The quality of play in the game has definitely declined, but that doesn't mean it has to remain slovenly.

After seven weeks of inactivity, the players resumed play on August 1. We had finished ten games behind the Dodgers in the prestrike standings. The team that finished first in the second half would play a best three-of-five playoff series against the Dodgers to determine the NL West champion. I told the writers honestly that we were not on a level with the Dodgers or the Reds but that the Giants were a better team than our record suggested.

"I think we're five or six games better than we showed," I said. "And if Jack Clark or Darrell Evans had hit anywhere near as well as they're capable of hitting, we'd be right on Houston's heels for third place."

Clark was hitting .224 with 6 home runs and 25 RBIs; Evans was hitting .223 with 9 home runs and 29 RBIs.

Then I made a casual remark about Jack Clark, based on his history and on what others said of him. "I keep hearing that Clark is the type of hitter who can carry a team for weeks at a time," I said. "I wish he'd show it. I've got to think he could have won five games for us himself."

Jack Clark had been very critical of earlier Giants' managers and had asked to be traded more than once, as had a number of his teammates. As I said, nobody liked Candlestick Park. But I had gotten along very well with Clark, who had said in the spring: "Whether we win or not, it's like a dream come true under Frank Robinson. We have no excuses anymore. We've got proven players at every position. Nobody's complaining or asking to be traded. I really believe this is the team to be on in our division—the team of the future."

But I came to find that Jack Clark could change his views at any moment.

A few weeks later Clark drove in four of our runs in a 5-4 victory over the Pirates. His second home run of the game in the thirteenth won it, but we had played sloppily, and I held a meeting in the clubhouse afterward. Clark, who was doing the postgame radio shows, was not present. But earlier, trying to put a stop to all the griping about having to play in Candlestick Park, I said, "If you don't want to play here, let me know. We'll get some people who do want to play here. In the meantime, stop complaining about the weather, because there's nothing anybody can do about it."

So at this meeting I was purposely low key. I started out by saying to the players, "I'm not getting on your cases. I just want to make these points before you go home because I want you to come here tomorrow in the right frame of mind and ready to play baseball. Against this ballclub tonight we made errors on two routine pop-ups, we missed signs, and we made base-running mistakes. We were fortunate to win because Jack Clark had a tremendous game. The Pirates were injured, and if you play that way against a good ballclub, we're not gonna win. I just won't tolerate those mistakes.

"Now I want you to go home tonight and get this out of your heads. If we play up to our capabilities, we may have a chance to contend for the second-half title."

I learned later that when Jack Clark came in after the meeting, one of his teammates said, "Man, you missed a good ripping from Frank." Apparently a couple of other players moaned to Clark too. I found that a number of his teammates liked to use Clark to pop off about whatever was bothering them.

When the writers came in, Clark was fuming. "Whenever we mess up, people are always coming down on us," Jack said, "but nobody ever says anything about his managing. Robinson isn't perfect. He's made lots of mistakes. Frank has to realize he no longer is a player, that guys on this club aren't gonna hit 500 home runs. He's always talking about getting rid of guys, but you gotta play with what you have.

"He criticizes me," Jack continued, "but his managing hasn't been all that great. I think he's more concerned about himself looking good. He takes it personally and thinks we're trying to make him look bad, but we're trying. Because of what Frank was as a player, I thought it would be different here this year. But it's the same old thing. We still don't communicate. He hasn't spoken to me more than five or ten minutes all year."

I was a little shocked by Clark's attack, which I was certain he never would have made had he been at the meeting. I called him into the office the next day and told him if I had known how he felt, I would have had him in earlier. "I didn't appreciate what you said about me, Jack, but the worst part was that you spoke out in public instead of to me face-to-face," I told him. "I've worked very hard to turn around the negative attitude on this ballclub, and I just hope your outburst doesn't disrupt what we've finally got going now. But I'm not going to accept mediocrity on the field. You have an opportunity of a lifetime—a chance to make the playoffs. But everyone on this team has to reach out and grab that chance."

It was a good meeting in which we cleared the air, and the ballclub began playing much more alertly. We extended our winning streak to four games, which put us four games over .500 for the first time—and into a tie for the division lead. The Giants were playing better than they had a right to, as Clark and Evans increased their production at the plate, and I thought we had an outside chance at finishing first in the second half.

The two hitters we brought up from Phoenix, Jeff Leonard and Bob Brenly, also made major contributions, as both batted over .300 and played well in the field.

Brenly was a total surprise to me as no one had told me anything about him. I'd seen him at Phoenix, where he was hitting over .300, and when I returned, I asked Haller about him. "Brenly's just a utility-type player," Haller said, shrugging. I looked into Brenly's background on my own, once it was clear that Haller wasn't able to or wasn't going to give me any information. Bob Brenly could catch, play third base, and play the outfield, plus he was a right-handed hitter. My regular catcher, Milt May, hit from the left side, so Brenly would give me the opportunity to platoon. Brenly, 27 years old, had never been invited to a big league training camp, and I hadn't even heard of him. But I said to Haller, "Let's give this guy a shot, Tom. Maybe he can help us."

He did, but I'm still amazed that the Giants' general manager knew so little about Bob Brenly that he would have stayed in Phoenix if not for me. Brenly went on to become the regular catcher for the Giants, a position he was still playing with distinction when the team made the playoffs in 1987.

In mid-September our hopes of staying in contention suffered a serious blow when Vida Blue was sidelined with a sprained thumb on his pitching hand. The left-hander was supposed to be my best pitcher, coming off a 14-10 record in 1980. But he showed up at the ballpark and said he couldn't pitch and held out his swollen thumb to me.

"What happened?" I asked, disappointed.

"I was getting out of my car and I stumbled," Vida said. "When I went to brace myself, the thumb went back against the car."

One of the coaches told me later that he'd learned what really happened. Vida had an argument with his girlfriend, who swung at him. He reflexively threw up his hand against the blow, and it sprained his thumb. Somehow, I wasn't surprised. Vida Blue had been acting strangely all season.

When I took the job, the coaches had told me that one thing I was going to appreciate was having Blue as leader of the pitching staff. They said he was a hard worker who would get to the ballpark early, run on his own, and then run with the other pitchers. They also said Vida was a high-energy guy, an outgoing person who would step out of the dugout at big moments in a game and start leading fans in cheers.

"That's great," I said. "I love that kind of player."

However, Vida had been nothing like that in the '81 season. He not only wouldn't do extra running, but didn't even want to run with the other pitchers. He often made excuses and stayed in the clubhouse until just before game time, saying he wasn't feeling well or whatever. And when he wasn't starting, Vida developed a habit of leaving the bench and going into the clubhouse during games. Worst of all, Blue's performance on the mound had consisted of one good game followed by one bad game. His record was 8-6. A pitcher who had been consistent for ten years was suddenly totally inconsistent.

I didn't know what was wrong. I had pitching coach Don McMahon look at videotapes of Vida Blue from the year before to check his mechanics. Had he changed his motion, his stride, his release? It turned out none of those things were his problem. His problem was cocaine, which we learned about when Vida's involvement with drugs was made public a couple of years later.

But even an inconsistent Blue was better than nothing. When I lost him, I immediately went to Tom Haller's office. That was the only way I could communicate with him, because Haller would never stop by the clubhouse to see me.

"Tom, Vida can't pitch, and we need some pitching help," I said.

"I'll get you someone from Phoenix," he said.

"I mentioned back in spring training that if we needed a pitcher along the way," I said, "we had no one at Phoenix who could really help us. Everyone at the meeting agreed with me. And from what I saw in Phoenix during the strike, that's still the case."

So Tom Haller brought up a pitcher from Phoenix who couldn't help us, and we finished 3½ games out of first place in the second-half schedule. What Spec Richardson had done when I needed help was show me a guy on the waiver list and ask if I was interested in him. Haller never did that, and I probably should have pursued him more. If we had come up with a pitcher who could have won four games for us, we would have met the Dodgers for the NL West championship. I probably didn't push Haller because I didn't want to make waves. I wanted to get along with my general manager, and I knew I wouldn't exactly make a hit with him when I asked that his good friend Jimmy Davenport be dismissed.

Jimmy and I were not getting along well as far as his coaching at third base went. He wasn't what I call real sharp in picking up my signs and understanding my intentions. We were not on the same page, and I felt I had to make a change. On our last trip to Houston, I brought this up over dinner at Trader Vic's with Bob Lurie and Tom Haller.

"I would like to make two coaching changes before next season," I said. "I would like to make a change at third base because Jimmy and I just don't have a good line of communication. I don't mean that Jimmy's not intelligent; it's just that he's not very quick about picking up the sign and relaying it."

"I know what you mean about Jimmy," Lurie said. "The only reason we kept him as the coach at third was because he had been under consideration for the job of manager. When you were our choice, we kept on Jimmy as a courtesy."

"You're right about Jimmy not being very quick at times," Haller said. "I know that from being around him for some 20 years. So you can make that change, and we'll try to find something else for Jimmy in the organization."

"Fine," I said. "I also want to make a change of pitching coach. Don McMahon's a good guy personally, as is Jimmy Davenport. But Don was a power pitcher himself, and that's what he tries to teach everybody, bringing every pitch right over the top. I want a pitching coach who can work with a variety of individuals, who can work with the skills they have and *improve* them."

"All right, Frank," Haller said, "you can make those changes at the end of the season. I'll tell Jimmy, you tell Don McMahon."

When we got back to San Francisco, I let a week go by before I went up to see Haller. "Have you told Jimmy that he's not gonna be back?" I asked.

"Well, we had a meeting, and I started to tell him," Haller said. "But Jimmy said he'd like to stay on for another year because he'd like to manage someday and he felt this was the best place for him to get exposure.

So he'd like to stay on, if you don't mind. But you can get rid of your pitching coach."

Speechless, I just stared at him. Here was a general manager who didn't mind saddling his manager with an inept third base coach. Haller had acknowledged Davenport's shortcomings, as had the team owner, yet they would still keep Davenport on the line.

I finally said, "No, Tom, I'm not gonna let McMahon go because I don't believe in changing a coach every year. There would be no stability on the ballclub, as far as the players were concerned. They'd be saying, 'What's going on here?' I'll keep Davenport and McMahon for another year. But at the end of next season, they both have to go."

The Giants played .558 ball the second half of the season and finished one game over .500. It wasn't a bad season, and on the last day my contract was extended two years. I would be paid $85,000 next year, go up to $95,000 in 1983, and jump to $125,000 in 1984. More important than the money was the fact that Bob Lurie was committed to me for three more years. I felt that would give me time to turn the Giants into legitimate contenders—if Tom Haller would cooperate and bring in the players we needed.

To the press, Haller was all in favor of my contract extension and said, "I think that was a good idea because it showed the players we have confidence in Frank—that his way is the way we want things done. It will be good for stability throughout the organization. Even the guys in the low minors will know that the brand of ball they're being taught is what they'll be playing in San Francisco."

But I was sure Bob Lurie, not Tom Haller, was behind the decision to extend my contract. I had suggested that the Giants hold an organizational meeting to which executives, managers, coaches, scouts, and instructors throughout the system would be invited, and in October we all assembled in Phoenix. It was the first full-organization meeting the Giants ever had, and it was one of the last ideas at that level I got through. During the proceedings Haller let everyone know that he was the boss, and he made it clear that—though he said, "I believe in communication"—he really wasn't interested in ideas from subordinates.

One man who seemed to have Haller's ear was Bob Fontaine, who ran the scouting and player-development staffs. Fontaine had been general manager of the San Diego Padres until 1980, where former relief pitcher Bob Miller had done a number of jobs for him. Right after I told Haller that I wanted to change pitching coaches, we played in San Diego, and Haller asked me to interview Miller for the job as Fontaine had recommended him. I talked to Miller as a courtesy, but I already knew the man I wanted as my pitching coach, Herm Starrett, who had done great work in the Baltimore organization.

Spec Richardson had hired Fontaine, and when Haller kept him on the job, I figured they had cut some kind of supportive deal. Fontaine was able to hire Bob Miller as our minor league pitching coordinator who would also scout and be training camp coordinator. The Giants loved to give people three or four jobs to do, saving money seemingly taking precedence over efficiency.

Ralph Nelson, age 26, had been our traveling secretary, public address announcer, and statistician. Haller promoted Nelson, making him his assistant; for this position Nelson had to learn the intricacies of contract negotiations, arbitration procedures, and collective bargaining. But Nelson would also continue to serve as traveling secretary and public address announcer at Candlestick. Needless to say, he would not be paid three salaries.

When I learned of this, I told Haller, "It's tough enough doing a good job as traveling secretary, never mind learning the job of assistant general manager."

"Look, Frank, Ralph can handle the work," Haller said. "And it never hurts to save the ballclub a few bucks. Ralph will learn the new job quickly."

Ralph Nelson was a friend of Haller's, he was white, and he was smart enough to learn on the job. A black man in Nelson's position would not have been promoted to a new position that he'd have to learn on the job. Haller and Fontaine both subsequently revealed what they thought of a black man's intelligence when they fired my friend Curt Motton.

On my recommendation, Curt had been hired in 1981 as a minor league outfield instructor, and everyone I talked to had said he'd done a great job. Even Fontaine had complimented Motton's work.

I was having breakfast the last morning of the organizational meetings when Bob Fontaine stopped at my table to say hello. Then he left, and I flew home. I no sooner walked in the door than the phone rang. "You won't believe this, Frank, but Bob Fontaine said he had to let me go," Curt said.

"I don't believe it," I said. "I just saw Fontaine three hours ago, and he didn't tell me. What was his reason?"

"Budget. He said he was firing the other three minor league instructors too."

"That's crap," I said. "You just hold tight, Curt, and I'll get back to you in a day or so."

I was annoyed. Bob Fontaine knew Curt Motton was a friend of mine, and he could have told me of his plans that morning in the coffee shop. Instead, he waited until I left, then went right over to see Curt, and canned him. I tried to reach Bob Lurie, but he wouldn't be available until late the next day.

The following morning I read Fontaine's explanation for firing Motton in the *Chronicle*. "Curt's a nice person, but because of budget considerations, we're looking for combination people as instructors," Fontaine said. "You use them as instructors a certain part of the time, then use them in other areas, maybe scouting. Curt could only instruct outfielders. A guy like Bob Miller can do four different things for us."

I was angry when *Chronicle* reporter Dan McGrath asked for my reaction to Motton's firing, but I held it in. "Working with the outfielders is all Motton was asked to do," I said. "If you want a guy to do other things and he needs training, then train him."

That's what Haller was doing with Ralph Nelson. And what gave Bob Fontaine the right to say "Curt could only instruct outfielders" when Curt had never been given an opportunity to do more? How the hell did Fontaine know that Bob Miller could be our training camp coordinator when he had no experience? Fontaine's statement that Miller "can do four different things for us" was just a smoke screen that he figured would allow him to bring in his friend and fire my friend.

Deciding I might as well let the world know what was going on in the Giants' front office, I let Dan McGrath know that I wasn't happy with the way Fontaine and Haller had orchestrated the Motton firing behind my back. I said, "I don't know if other managers get involved in things like this, and maybe it's not my area, but I'm supposed to be involved with setting up this system. I'm consulted in some areas, but I want to be kept up to date in all of them. I didn't know about Motton until I got home. I thought communication was one of the things we were going to try to improve."

McGrath reported, "Fontaine and Haller insist that Robinson and his coaching staff had plenty of input at the meetings, but the makeup of that staff is an indication that Robinson doesn't have the authority of a Whitey Herzog or a Billy Martin." Martin was then managing the Oakland A's across the bay.

The writer went on to point out that everyone knew I wanted to replace Jim Davenport and Don McMahon, but I had not been permitted to. When McGrath asked Tom Haller about that, he said, "Our manager will always have the authority to hire some of his own people. But we're also going to have some organizational men as coaches. You need that for stability, especially if you change managers."

So Haller was already thinking about changing managers, even though I had three years to run on my contract. It was more important for Haller to have organizational men as coaches than it was for him to give me the tools I requested that would help me make the ballclub successful. Obviously Haller wanted only his own people working for the Giants so that he could control everything.

McGrath went on to write: "It isn't realistic to expect Robinson to wield as much clout as Herzog or Martin, who are their own general managers. But Robinson is a strong personality who gave the Giants a sense of direction, something they desperately need."

I reached Bob Lurie that afternoon and told him that Curt Motton, one of our best minor league instructors, had been fired. "Bob, we really can't afford to lose good instructors if we're going to build a solid organization," I said. Lurie rehired Motton immediately.

I later found out that the new instructors Fontaine hired were not asked to do anything more than teach. Fontaine wouldn't do anything without Tom Haller's approval, so I knew he had been behind the attempt to dismiss Motton.

I shouldn't have been surprised by Haller's attitude. I had been to see him on several occasions during the season, but whenever we had mutually agreed to do something that he was to act upon, the minute I walked out his door he trashed my ideas. Once Haller told me a team wanted one of our players and was offering in exchange a player I thought would help us more. When I told him that, Haller nodded and I left the meeting thinking the trade would be made. It wasn't. And I heard through the grapevine that the other general manager said, "Yeah, Haller said he'd make the deal after checking with his manager, then he came back and demanded that we throw in another player as well. For a new guy on the job, he's awful greedy. I told him no deal."

Haller never told me why we hadn't made the trade, but that same situation was to occur several times in the future. Haller would tell me of potential trades which I approved, then he would go back to the other team and ask for more than had been agreed upon, and the trade would die. He not only would tell me he would do something and then not do it (as when he said he'd tell Davenport he was gone), but he would agree with me in private on certain things and then back off in public.

Haller had told me before the organizational meeting that we would discuss whether we wanted to use designated hitters on our minor league clubs. Teams throughout the minors had the option of using the DH or not, and Giants' farm teams had been using it. I wanted the DH dropped in 1982 because our pitchers had been coming up to the majors without having touched a bat in years. "That's totally unfair to our pitchers," I told Haller. "They come up here, and they can't bunt a runner over. Some of them can't even get out of the way of an inside pitch because they haven't batted in such a long time. Their reflexes aren't honed at the plate. That's not right. For them, or for us."

Haller seemed to agree with me that it made sense to have our minor league pitchers get used to batting and learn to bunt. But at the organizational meeting most of our farm club managers wanted to keep the DH. They were afraid that in playing without a designated hitter against teams that used one, they would lose. So Tom Haller decreed that the Giants' farm teams would continue to employ DHs.

I stood up and said, "I thought we were trying to develop players for the Giants. If winning games in the minor leagues takes precedence over developing major league players in our system, we've got the wrong philosophy."

I was even more stunned by Haller in mid-November when he traded starting pitcher Ed Whitson to Cleveland for second baseman Duane Kuiper. Haller never even asked me if I was interested in the deal. He had asked me at the World Series in Dodger Stadium what I thought of Kuiper as a player.

"I loved Duane at Cleveland," I said. "He's a gamer. But he busted up his knee real bad a couple of years ago, and I hear he's lost a lot of range in the field."

"The Indians want to trade him," Haller said.

"Who do they want for him?"

"Whitson."

"I don't think we can afford to trade a starting pitcher without getting one in return," I said.

A month later Haller made the trade anyway, and when the writers called for my reaction, I said, "Now what do I do with Joe Morgan? He and Duane are both left-handed hitters, and they both have to play every day to remain sharp. I'm less than enthused about the trade."

I was very concerned about Joe Morgan's feelings. He was a leader on the ball field and *the* leader of the team in the clubhouse, a guy who wouldn't let his teammates get down into the loser's attitude that had prevailed on the Giants. I had told Morgan that I wanted him back, and his agent was negotiating with the Giants, but he hadn't signed. I phoned him, reiterated that I wanted him to return, and said he was still my regular second baseman. I also asked him if he was getting in shape.

"Yeah, I'm in a regular conditioning program," Morgan said. "I've lost 10 pounds and I feel ten years younger."

I had told Morgan to lose weight and said that, at age 37, he now had to begin working out year-round. I had been after him in 1981 to make some adjustments at the plate to compensate for aging. Most older players fight adjusting at bat, because that means changing a style that had made them successful for years.

I'd asked Joe to move closer to the plate when hitting, saying, "They're pitching you outside, then busting fastballs inside on you."

"Nobody can throw the fastball by me," Joe said defensively. "I can hit anybody's fastball."

"I didn't say you couldn't. But they're throwing you outside, and you're trying to hook that ball over the right-field fence. And you don't have the strength of youth to hit the outside pitch over the fence, so you're popping out to left. Now if you move up on the plate, you can handle that outside pitch."

When I talked to Joe Morgan in November, he said he was going to try the adjustments at the plate I'd suggested and was looking forward to the '82 season. Right then I felt I was going to have my leader back with me. And Joe would end up raising his batting average almost 50 points to .289 and hitting more home runs, 14, than he'd hit since 1977.

As soon as Bob Lurie returned from a trip to Japan, I phoned him and told him about the trade Haller had made without my knowledge and explained why I disliked it. He said he'd already heard about my displeasure and understood my feelings. But he also said the press was having a field day reporting that there was a rift between his manager and general manager, and we couldn't have that.

"We have to be together here, Frank, and work in harmony," Lurie said. He told me he was going to tell the press there was no problem, and he asked me to put on that type of face.

"All right, Bob," I said. "But I want you to know that I wasn't consulted on this trade that has stuck me with two left-handed-hitting second basemen and minus one starting pitcher."

"I understand," Lurie said, "but I want you and Tom to find a way to work things out yourselves so the press isn't sniping at us."

I never went out of my way to knock Haller in the newspapers. But when writers asked me about situations that came up, I wasn't going to lie even if I couldn't reveal the full story. When I was asked about the rift between us, I said, "Tom and I have a working relationship." The writers saw a good deal of what was going on. Tom Haller and I were not at the place a general manager and a manager had to be if their organization was to rebuild successfully. Haller talked about communicating but made no effort to communicate with me. And that made it very difficult.

But at least my call to Lurie caused Haller to talk to me before the other trades he made in that off-season. We ended up trading our other starting pitchers—Vida Blue, Doyle Alexander, and Tom Griffin—and brought in a bunch of players who I felt would make us a better ballclub.

I was the deciding voice in one trade that brought me a lot of heat. I felt Jeff Leonard was a better outfielder, with a little more pop in his bat, than Larry Herndon. So we traded Herndon, our most consistent hitter in 1981, to the Tigers. I predicted that Herndon would hit more home runs in Tiger Stadium than he did with us. When Herndon hit 23 home runs and the pitchers we acquired for him were losers, I was blasted in the press. Of course, Leonard needed to play, and he eventually surpassed Herndon.

We had a chance to sign Reggie Smith as a free agent, but Tom Haller hemmed and hawed so long I feared we might lose him as negotiations continued well into the spring. The Yankees had offered Smith $500,000 a year for three years, but I knew he wanted to stay on the West Coast. I tried to push Haller to sign him, and I also called Reggie twice to tell him how much I wanted him on the Giants. I think those talks were the main reason why Reggie finally signed a one-year contract with us for $300,000. But Haller's delay deprived Reggie Smith of a lot of spring training when, at age 36, he should have been getting ready for the season.

I had a little problem with Reggie early on after he got upset when he was put on the disabled list without being told. Reggie's right Achilles tendon was very sore, and he couldn't do much without adding to the injury, so we put him on the disabled list for 15 days to allow him to heal. Tom Haller happened to mention it to a writer before he'd told Reggie, who didn't like being on the disabled list at any time and particularly didn't like hearing about it from a writer.

"I didn't like the way it was handled, and that's all I've got to say about it," Reggie said.

I asked him to come into my office so that I could talk to him in private, but he refused to see me. I didn't feel I had to track him down the next day.

Not long thereafter the team was busing to the airport after losing a game. The players had their portable tape players cranked up loud, and I told them to lower the volume. Reggie Smith popped off that he liked his music loud, and he kept it that way.

"If you don't want to turn it down, it's gonna cost you $100," I said.

"Fine me, I don't care," he said.

"And every time you open your mouth, it's gonna cost you another $100," I said.

"I don't care," he said.

"That's $200," I said.

Reggie popped off again.

"That's $300."

Again.

"That's $400," I said.

The fine went all the way up to $1200 before Reggie shut up and turned down his tape player. But that incident was not at all like Reggie Smith. He and Joe Morgan became the coleaders of the ballclub. By midseason they had taught the Giants how to lose without quitting, complaining, griping about Candlestick Park, pointing fingers at one another, and generally feeling sorry for themselves. That was the attitude on the club that I had been trying, with the help of Morgan, to turn around. The negative attitude is typical of losing ballclubs. By learning how to lose without whining, the Giants learned how to win, and we became a solid ballclub the second half of the '82 season.

Joe Morgan used a velvet-glove approach trying to reach his teammates with good counsel. He would take a guy aside and talk to him quietly. Or he would bring the guy's problem to me. Say our young backup third baseman, Tom O'Malley, was concerned about his lack of playing time. Joe would suggest that I bring him into my office for a private chat. I wouldn't do so right away, because the player might say, "I just confide in Joe, and he goes right to the manager." I would wait a day or two before sitting down with the player, explaining his situation to him, and trying to encourage him to stay ready.

Reggie Smith's approach to a player's griping was less subtle. Often Reggie would just yell, "All right, that's enough of that bleep. Let's get it together here as a team." And the case would be closed.

Joe and Reggie would walk into my office at any time, sit down, and talk. By doing so, they nipped a lot of potential problems in the bud, and I appreciated it. I took them out to dinner a few times so we could discuss things, but I couldn't do that too often for fear it might not sit well with other players. Any time I happened to be in a restaurant where players were eating, I'd have the waiter bring me their check. But I tried to stay away from places the players frequented, because a lot of guys don't feel comfortable being out in the presence of the manager.

Team leaders, particularly veteran players like Morgan and Smith, are tremendous assets to a manager, who doesn't have time to get very close to players. I think I was one of the most open, accessible managers in the game. My door was always open to players, and while some didn't like to come in, I had no qualms about going out and bringing a guy in for a talk.

16

MANAGER OF
THE YEAR

IF it hadn't been for my two bullpen stoppers, right-hander Greg Minton and left-hander Gary Lavelle, we would have been out of the 1982 race by June. Minton had a great sinker that could get anyone out. Lavelle had a 91 mph fastball, and his pitches tailed away from right-handed hitters, so he was death on them. We were playing .500 ball only because of my stoppers.

But we weren't hitting. In fact, in late May we had the lowest batting average in the league: .237. "We don't have more than two guys who are really fighters at the plate," I said, referring to Morgan and Smith, "guys who will force a pitcher to throw strikes, who will take the extra base, who will drop down a bunt to get something started."

Jack Clark, who was in a 4-for-40 slump, was being booed mercilessly. "If Clark isn't hitting at the top of his game, he can't help you," I said. "Shortstop Johnnie LeMaster tries to pull the ball all the time, doesn't bunt half as much as he should, and swings at the first pitch damn near every time. A lot of guys here talk a good game, talk about hustling, doing the little things, playing fundamental baseball, but they just don't perform. They don't seem to want to work to improve."

I wasn't talking about Clark, who looked at videotapes of himself hitting, responded to what he was told in practice, and then forgot what he'd learned in games. "Jack's taking a lot of pitches that he could hit, and he ends up getting only one swing," I said.

Darrell Evans was in a 5-for-28 slump and complaining that he wasn't getting any pitches to hit. That was because he was standing too far off the plate and pitchers were working him outside, and he was either taking strikes or hitting little fly balls to left. I kept advising Darrell to move in on the plate a couple of inches. "That'll bring the outside pitch in to the middle of the plate, and you're quick enough to still handle the inside pitch," I told him. Darrell had always been a pretty good .250 hitter, and he was reluctant to change. He had a nice controlled swing, he stayed in shape, and when he finally moved up on the plate the next year, Evans almost doubled his home run output to 30 and got his average up to .277. Five years later, in 1987, Darrell was still powering the ball for the Tigers, with whom he signed as a free agent in 1984. He became the first 40-year-old to hit over 30 home runs in a season.

But as players get older, they have to make some adjustments at the plate and most fight changing. The longer they fight changing, the worse off they're going to be. I know personally from going through the later years as a player that physically you can't do what you did as a kid. You're smarter at the plate, but you're not as quick with the bat. The first thing that goes is your consistency at bat, so your average falls. But if you play regularly, you can still hit 20 home runs and drive in 80 RBIs if you adjust at bat. I think that was the major problem with Reggie Jackson as he got older. He was reluctant to make changes, and those he made were not the right changes.

Reggie Smith, who had been sidelined, returned to the lineup hitting, and Jack Clark came out of his slump after attacking the Giants' front office "for not trying to build a winner" in late May. By July 9, Clark had 17 home runs and 57 RBIs, when he suddenly popped off again. "I'm having fun playing now," he said, "but I don't forget some of the things that have happened around here. Frank Robinson ripped me in the press, and he's never apologized."

I didn't apologize because I never ripped him. But I was annoyed that he was whining when we were winning. "It's all been said before, and I don't know what purpose it serves for Jack Clark to pop off now," I said. "When Jack wasn't going good earlier, we supported him and worked with him. Now it seems when Jack Clark is going good and the ballclub is coming around, he's not going to support us. If he didn't want to be here, he should have thought of that before he signed his big-money contract."

"It doesn't help when I'm batting cleanup and there's nobody behind to protect me," Clark told the writers. "Darrell Evans can drive the ball, but he's hardly playing."

When I heard that, I pointed to the statistics sheet that showed Reggie Smith had equalled Evans's RBI total in 105 fewer at-bats. I was sitting Evans more than I wanted to because he wasn't hitting, but he would still end up with over 450 at-bats for the season.

Jack Clark was a good friend of Evans's, who dressed next to him. I'm sure Darrell remarked to Jack that he wanted to play more, which prompted the pop-off.

I told the writers, "Jack should remember that he's paid to play and I'm paid to manage. If he doesn't like it, we can go to the front office and see about changing jobs—if we can also trade salaries."

Even that didn't shut up Clark, who said, "Frank and I are not close, and we won't be close. I thought I might learn a lot from him, but he hasn't taught me very much or even tried."

"The only thing I haven't done with Jack Clark," I replied, "is put my arm around him and tell him I love him, and I don't do that. I've told him I'll talk hitting or baseball any time, but he never comes to me. Each time I've reached out to him, he winds up stabbing me in the back or ripping me."

Jack Clark was not a bad guy, but he was very immature. In addition, it seemed like every time Jack ran his mouth in the press, he followed it with a barrage of base hits, so he kept popping off. He said getting things off his chest helped him relax. It didn't help me a whole lot.

Jim LeFebvre was our hitting instructor, but Clark didn't like him. He had told me earlier that he wanted to see Hank Sauer, our minor league hitting instructor, who had helped Jack when he originally signed with the Giants. I phoned Hank and asked him as a favor to me to come in and see Jack. When Hank left, I told Jack to phone him for advice whenever he wished.

Clark was no real problem compared to the trouble that umpires were suddenly giving me and my ballclub. During the '81 season I had been thrown out of two games and threatened with several other expulsions by umpires who said I left the dugout to argue too often. So I stopped going out unless it was really necessary, but that didn't keep the umpires from making some terrible calls against us in crucial game situations.

A lot of the players thought the umpires had it in for us and that they'd actually cost us four or five games. Clark told me that he'd be running to his outfield position and the umpires would be cursing me.

"The players and I can't question calls," I told the press. "I really don't know the reason. I hope it's not racial."

But some of the calls were so absurd that I felt there had to be some racism behind them. I would go out to the mound to talk to a pitcher, and the umpire would be right behind me saying, "Let's go, Frank." Other managers would stay out several minutes and not be rushed. When I'd continue to talk to my pitcher after being told to move, the umpire would say, "You've got five minutes to get off the field, or the game's forfeited."

Ironically, the two umpires who were toughest on me were black, Eric Gregg and Charlie Williams. In the first inning of a game I yelled about a pitch; Gregg ripped off his mask behind the plate and said, "One more word and you're out of here."

I walked out to him, crossed my arms over my chest, and, facing the outfield, calmly said, "I just hollered about a pitch, and you tell me one more word and I'm gone. That means if you call a pitch that bounces up here a strike, I can't say anything. You're not allowing me to do my job as a manager."

"Is that what you think I'm doing?" Gregg asked.

"That's right."

"Then that's what I'm doing," Gregg said, "because one more word out of you and you're gone."

I didn't get along any better with Charlie Williams, who always had a chip on his shoulder with me. Maybe a statement Eric Gregg made was at the root of my problems with both black umpires. "You know, you're really awful hard on me," Gregg said.

"I'm no harder on you than I am on other umpires," I said. "If I feel like you're not doing your job, you're gonna hear from me."

I had the feeling that Gregg and Williams felt that because we were all black, I should take it easy on them. But I didn't look at them as black umpires. I looked at them as umpires.

Jack Clark stopped talking to the press, which was fine with me. But he went on the Giants' radio talk show and said he wanted to be traded and that he couldn't communicate with me. "It's almost worse after going in to talk things out with Robinson," Jack said. "He just sort of looks at you."

I had to laugh at that statement. It was true that all I could do at times when Clark came in was stare at him, because he wouldn't let me get a word in. Jack would talk on and on and on without letup, and I didn't want to be impolite and break in. If Jack Clark couldn't communicate with me, he couldn't communicate with anyone. I talked to him more than any other player on the team except for Joe Morgan and Reggie Smith. I talked, but I'm not at all sure that Jack ever listened.

Jack Clark claimed to be a team player who was always in the ballgame, but periodically he would start running off the field with only two men out. And when I tried to get Jack to play first base on occasion, he refused, even though he would have been better there defensively and we would have had a more flexible lineup. Jack didn't want to replace his friend Darrell Evans at first when Reggie Smith was sidelined. Jack Clark became a better ballplayer in St. Louis when he became a first baseman.

I put Jack Clark and the Giants aside for a couple of days when, on August 1, I journeyed to Cooperstown, New York, to be inducted into the baseball Hall of Fame, in the first year I was eligible for the honor. It was the biggest honor of my life when 89.1 percent of the 415 members of the Baseball Writers Association voted for me. The only players who went into the Hall of Fame with a higher percentage of votes were, in order, Ty Cobb (98.2 percent), Henry Aaron, Honus Wagner, Babe Ruth, Willie Mays, Bob Feller, Ted Williams, Stan Musial, and Christie Mathewson. I finished just ahead of Joe DiMaggio, in very good company indeed.

On my plaque I asked that I appear in my Baltimore Orioles' uniform, as I had my most enjoyable years while wearing it. Six members of the Orioles' front office and two busloads of fans from Baltimore traveled to Cooperstown for the induction ceremony. Bob Lurie and my wife, Barbara, and children were also there beaming. Gabe Paul, who had run the Reds during most of my years with them, called me from his office as the Indians' general manager, and congratulated me. But the Cincinnati Reds, for whom I had played ten years, did not send a single representative to the ceremony or even call me. I considered that a slap in the face, and I later wrote to Dick Wagner, then the Reds' president, and asked him to remove my name from everything pertaining to the ballclub.

But it was a pleasure to be inducted into the Hall of Fame with Henry Aaron and Happy Chandler, and in the presence of Roy Campanella and Rachel Robinson, the widow of Jackie Robinson. Most people have forgotten that it was Happy Chandler, even more than Branch Rickey, who was responsible for Jackie Robinson's having been allowed to integrate major league baseball. Rickey cast the only team vote in favor of Robinson's being allowed to play; the other 15 major league club owners all voted against it. Chandler ruled for Rickey against the other owners, which cost him his job as commissioner, but he never regretted the stand he took.

"I told Mr. Rickey," Chandler said at the ceremony, "that someday I was going to have to meet my maker, and if He asked me why I didn't let that boy play and I said it was because he was black, that might not be a satisfactory answer. So I said, 'You bring him in, and I'll approve the transfer of his contract from Montreal [the Dodgers' International League team] to Brooklyn. I was just doing what justice and mercy required me to do under the circumstances, and if I had to do it over again, I'd do the same thing."

When Henry Aaron got up to speak, he talked about how meaningful it was for him to be standing in the same place where Jackie Robinson and his Dodger teammate Roy Campanella had been when they had entered the Hall of Fame. "They proved to the world that a man's ability is limited only by his lack of opportunity," Henry said, and I silently applauded.

But the thought crossed my mind: "I wonder if a black man will ever be inducted into the Hall of Fame not for his playing abilities but for the record he has achieved as a manager? Will a black man ever be given the longevity as a manager that would allow him to perhaps earn Hall of Fame consideration?"

When I rose to speak, my voice was choked with emotion as I thanked Barbara and my children for all the sacrifices they had made so that I could pursue my baseball career. It hadn't been easy for Barbara raising the children virtually alone, and it hadn't been easy on the kids with me away from home so much. Then I thanked Jackie Robinson and Roy Campanella for the manhood they displayed in taking abuse in their early years in the majors. Their courage gave the rest of us who followed a chance in an easier time.

"Without Jackie," I said, turning to Rachel Robinson, "I don't know if the door to baseball would have been open again for a long, long time. I know I couldn't have put up with what Jackie put up with."

When I rejoined the Giants, pitcher Greg Minton, who is called "Spaceman" because he is spacey, had hung a sign over his locker that read: "I can't be traded. Slaves have to be sold."

We went on a seven-game winning streak and moved within 6½ games of first place. Joe Morgan said, "Frank Robinson should get all the credit for our surge. We are not a team of great players. But Frank has always been a winner his whole life. We see him, and his posture says, 'I'm not a loser, you're not losers.'" I felt the players were beginning to believe that.

Even Jack Clark came around. He brought in his agent to meet with me and Tom Haller, and I told him what I'd been telling him all season. He could come and talk to me about anything, but I didn't want him complaining in public before he'd complained to me.

Clark was hitting but Jeff Leonard was not. He had batted .290 with Houston a couple of years before, he'd had a great spring with us, and he'd gotten off to a good start in the field and at the plate. But then he suddenly started overrunning fly balls, bobbling ground balls, and generally playing bad outfield defense. And Jeff had been a very good outfielder. He was a mystery to me.

The mystery was solved later when it came out that Jeff Leonard had been using cocaine, and that really saddened me. I liked Jeff, who was a nice individual, a hard worker, and a team player. But he voluntarily entered a drug rehab center in the off-season and came back to hit 21 home runs and lead the club in RBIs with 87 the following year.

But Joe Morgan, Reggie Smith, Jack Clark, Chili Davis, and Darrell Evans all turned in solid seasons. And our bullpen was the best in baseball, which was a blessing because our top starter, rookie Bill Lasky, won only 13 games. Our prime relievers, Greg Minton, Gary Lavelle, and Al Holland, combined to win 27 games and earn saves in 43 others. So they had a hand in 70 of our 87 wins. Since late June we had played the best ball in the major leagues, turning in a 52-31 record. We finished at 87-75, in third place, but only two games out of first.

After the Hall of Fame ceremony I thought managing in a World Series might be my next, if not last, honor in baseball. But at season's end, United Press International named me the National League Manager of the Year.

When I said good-bye to Reggie Smith, thanked him, and told him I looked forward to seeing him in the spring, he smiled. "I've paid my fines, Frank, and I haven't agreed with everything you did this year," Reggie said. "But I've learned from you, and I've enjoyed playing for you. One thing I'd suggest for next year. Be a little more cautious when you're discussing players with the press. The way guys are today, they take everything as a rip, even if what you said is the truth."

Joe Morgan, who had counseled me to come forward more with the younger players, told me he thought I had improved my communication 100 percent, and I was pleased.

One thing that bothered me was that Haller announced he still wasn't willing to let me name all my coaches. Earlier in the year Haller had decided that Jim LeFebvre could be both the major league and the minor league hitting instructor. I told him there was no way Jim could do both.

"Ted Kluszewski used to do both for the Reds," Haller said.

"Yeah, but that's when they were the Big Red Machine," I said. "We don't have those kinds of hitters throughout our lineup here, and we need a full-time hitting instructor. I know Jim can't handle both jobs."

"He says he can," Haller said.

"What do you expect him to say? That he can't do the jobs?"

LeFebvre may have said he could do both jobs, but by July 1982 he was still with us and our minor league system was without a hitting instructor. So I asked Jim when he was going down to the farm system. He went to Phoenix for three days, returned, and stayed with us until mid-September, when he left to manage our ballclub in the instructional league. He told me he would be a roving hitting instructor in the minors the next season and said he would be my eyes and ears on everything that was done down there.

"Jimmy, what have you been drinking or smoking?" I asked him. "You're gonna leave a major league staff to go to the minors? You gotta be crazy."

"No, I want to do this for you, Frank," he said, "because I think you're doing a helluva job here. And I want to make sure that everyone in the system is working on the same fundamentals."

But before that came about, I was informed that Tom Haller had named Jim LeFebvre director of player development for the Giants. In other words, he was head of the farm system. In addition, he would also be manager of the Phoenix ballclub. I asked myself, "How the hell can he manage a ballclub and perform the duties of a farm director at the same time?" Then I answered myself: "By not doing either job very well." That's what Jim LeFebvre did.

Haller next announced that, with LeFebvre gone, I would be allowed to name one new coach, and possibly two. "But managers come and go," Haller said. "If you let every manager name all his coaches, that shuts off any opportunity for your minor league managers to become coaches on the major league level, and you lose some good people for that reason."

A priority of most general managers is to see that his manager is confident of and happy with his coaching staff, which I hadn't been for two years because it was not doing the job effectively. Tom Haller was not like most general managers.

But I finally convinced Haller to relieve me of Jim Davenport. I thought of trying to hire a black coach to handle third, but I couldn't think of anyone who really seemed fully qualified for the job. I did arrange for Don Buford to get some experience coaching at third base for our team in the Arizona Instructional League that fall. We had our organizational meeting in Arizona at the time that Don was coaching for ten days. I was able to observe him in a number of games, and I was sorry to see that he wasn't quite ready to coach third in the majors with a ballclub like ours that was still scratching for an identity.

So I hired Danny Ozark, a former Phillies' manager and long-time third base coach for the Dodgers. Ozark had really impressed me the year I was with the Dodgers. He'd had different signs for every individual on the team, something I had never seen before. Haller immediately approved when I decided to bring in Ozark, and I also had no trouble hiring Herm Starrette as pitching coach. Both men are white.

But the man I wanted as hitting coach, Tom McCraw, was black. I had a big battle with Haller over bringing in McCraw, even though I pointed out that he had done an excellent job for me in Cleveland. I was beginning to get the feeling that Tom Haller was not fond of black coaches...to say nothing of black managers.

Haller said he was going to keep Jim Davenport with the organization by making him the guy who charts pitches during games and hits fungoes to the outfielders before games. "That's a lousy job for him," I said. "And Jim can't afford to take it."

"We'll keep him at the same salary," Haller said. "Jim'll take the job."

I couldn't believe that Haller would pay Davenport $40,000 to $45,000 for scout work. But before he could do so, our advance scout, Del Rice, passed away, and Jim Davenport replaced him. He had no experience scouting, but that did not concern Tom Haller. His main interest was in keeping his cronies in the wings.

Don McMahon got angry when he was fired, saying I had lied to him several weeks before the season ended. It was true. He had asked me if he would be rehired, and I told him it hadn't been decided. I hated to do that. I had been a coach, but I also didn't think it would be fair to the players to tell a coach before season's end that he wouldn't be back. You do that, and you might as well send the man home.

I liked Don McMahon, who had been nice enough to get me season tickets to the Oakland Raider games from his good friend Al Davis, with whom he'd gone to high school in Brooklyn. I liked Don as a person, I just didn't like his approach as a pitching coach.

So Tom Haller allowed me to make a couple of moves, and then he began making some player moves that totally destroyed the winning attitude that we had been nurturing on the Giants. Haller began negotiating with free agent Steve Garvey, the former Dodger, making him an attractive offer. But at the same time Haller ignored Reggie Smith, which ticked him off, understandably. When I spoke to Garvey, I was not convinced that he really wanted to play with us, and I told Haller to bring back Reggie. But Haller kept saying we were going to land Garvey to play first base.

The result was that Reggie Smith made a deal to play with the Tokyo Giants rather than the San Francisco Giants. The Tokyo Giants offered him close to $1 million a year; Tom Haller offered him nothing. I was in Hawaii at the winter baseball meetings when I heard we had lost Reggie, and I was shocked. "It didn't seem like the front office took Reggie very seriously," I said.

I was also disturbed by Haller's lack of progress in signing Joe Morgan. Joe had met his incentive bonuses last season and earned a total of $525,000. Now Haller was haggling with Morgan's agent over a difference of about $100,000, while letting it be known that he didn't want Joe's case to go to arbitration. That told me he was thinking of trading Morgan.

"Reggie and Joe made a tremendous difference on the club," I told the press. "Not just with the years they had, but the way they influenced other players. Their ideas got through to guys like Clark, Evans, and LeMaster. Joe and Reggie made them believe they could win. I don't want to make a big thing about this, but I think losing both Smith and Morgan would be a big mistake."

A couple of days later Reggie said, "You can't fault them for being interested in Garvey, but you have to ask, 'Is he really coming here?' With the San Francisco weather, the fact that it's a less glamorous city than Los Angeles for Garvey's career plans, you have to wonder."

Reggie went on to say that his only regret was leaving me. "I feel bad for Frank," he said. "He went out on a limb for me last year; he was the only reason I played here. I know if it were up to him, I'd be back."

The next thing Haller did was trade not only Joe Morgan but my most versatile relief pitcher, Al Holland, a guy who could be used effectively at any point in a game. Morgan and Holland were sent to the Phillies for a minor leaguer and starting pitcher Mike Krukow, who had won 13 games and lost 11 in 1982. At age 30 his career winning percentage was under .500—58 wins, 62 loses.

I thought about our final game of the '82 season when Joe Morgan came up in the clutch and drove in the winning run against the Dodgers. Afterward Dodger outfielder Dusty Baker said, "You look over in the Giants' dugout and you see winners: Frank Robinson and two of his coaches—Don Buford, who was with Frank on the Orioles, and Jim LeFebvre, who was with the Dodgers a few years ago—along with Joe Morgan and Reggie Smith. They all know how to win. They're all helping the other guys who are learning how to win."

And the first chance he had, Tom Haller got rid of Morgan, Smith, and LeFebvre. I could accept losing the latter, but not the two players. The Giants were back to square one.

Dan McGrath of the *Chronicle* saw the ramifications of Haller's decisions. "In shaping the team to his specifications," McGrath wrote, "Tom Haller has taken the club out of a race it might have won, and might be maneuvering toward a change in managers."

Not surprisingly, Steve Garvey rejected the Giants' offer and signed to play with the San Diego Padres.

On the day he was traded, Joe Morgan said, "I hope Tom Haller doesn't try to blame Frank if they finish more than two games out next year." But that appeared to be what Haller was setting up if the ballclub did slip downward, as seemed almost inevitable.

Chronicle columnist Glenn Dickey wrote that Haller had completely misread the reasons for the Giants' success last year. "The Giants did well because Joe Morgan had an exceptional year; because Reggie Smith carried the club for stretches when he was healthy; because Jack Clark played to his potential down the stretch; because the bullpen was the best in baseball overall.

"And because Frank Robinson did a superb job of managing, juggling players to get the maximum out of them, changing starters constantly to get the most effective ones in a rotation which was never set, working with his younger players to build their confidence, and making the most of his deep bullpen."

Dickey went on to say that my being undercut by Haller may have even more serious implications for the club. "Frank Robinson is their most visible asset, both because of his playing and managing success," Dickey wrote. "He is an articulate, honest man, respected by all who deal with him. He should be the symbol of the Giants. Instead he is being treated shabbily, his recommendations ignored."

○   ○   ○

Tom Haller also failed the Giants by signing only two of the top ten selections in the 1982 draft of high school and college players. When I saw the list of names, Steve Stanicek of the University of Nebraska was number 1 and Barry Bonds, Bobby's son, of Arizona State was number 2. I had heard a lot about Barry Bonds, and I asked Haller why he had not been our first pick.

"I'm not sure we can sign him," Haller said.

Why did he draft Bonds if he wasn't going to make certain that he signed the youngster? It turned out Bonds was asking $75,000 to sign. Haller offered him $40,000. Bonds said no, he wanted $75,000 or he would stay at Arizona State and go back in the draft in 1983. Haller offered $45,000. Bonds said no, etc. Haller went all the way up to $70,000 in his offer to Bonds. Bonds said no, etc. So Haller dropped out. To him Barry Bonds was worth $70,000, but he was willing to lose him for a piddling $5000 more. Barry Bonds is now hitting over 20 home runs a year and stealing over 20 bases a year for the Pirates, and he will only get better. Tom Haller was one very shrewd GM.

I asked Haller what position Steve Stanicek played. "He plays a little third, a little first, but we don't know exactly where he'll play for sure," Haller said. "Stanicek was a DH in college."

"That's great," I thought, "our number 1 draft choice is a DH—and we don't even have a designated hitter in the National League." I later found out that Stanicek had a bad knee. He was a great hitter in college, but your top draft choice has to be a definite can't-miss player. Stanicek was not one. Yet Haller approved the signing of Stanicek for $90,000, and he and our seventh-round pick were the only players the Giants signed among our top ten selections. Neither player had made it to the major leagues five years later.

In the high school draft that year, the Giants made another great pick, Pete Incaviglia, who now stars for the Texas Rangers. Incaviglia wanted $15,000 to sign, and the Giants refused to give him more than $8000. So he went to college and led the country in hitting home runs as a freshman. The Rangers later signed Incaviglia to a big bonus contract. You can imagine what the 1987 Giants would have done with the addition of Barry Bonds and Pete Incaviglia to their lineup.

But the point is that not only did the prospects for the 1983 Giants seem a little bleak to me, thanks to Tom Haller's player moves, but the farm system didn't get much help from him either.

17

☉ DRUG PROBLEMS

THE worst mistake I made as manager of the Giants was hiring Danny Ozark as third base coach. He had been fired by the Dodgers after 27 years with the organization. In between he had managed the Phillies from 1973 to 1979, and apparently he had hopes of managing in the major leagues one more time, at my expense.

Although I got on well with Ozark initially, it wasn't far into the '83 season that I realized that Tom Haller was using him as a pipeline from the clubhouse to the front office. Haller had used Jim Davenport in a similar fashion the previous year and a half. But they had been friends for many years, so it didn't seem out of place for me to see Haller talking to Davenport in the clubhouse quite a bit. It bothered me that Haller talked to Jim much more often than he talked to me. But I adjusted to the situation. I never adjusted to seeing Haller taking Davenport out to dinner when he could not find time for me.

But the situation with Danny Ozark was even worse. He asked me if he could locker in a room that had been built for coaches as he was older than everyone else. I gave my okay, even though I preferred that my coaches be spread around among the players. But soon I began finding, when I arrived at the ballpark around 3 P.M., that Tom Haller would be in the coaches' room talking to Ozark. At first, the moment I walked into the clubhouse, Haller would jump up and walk out of the coaches' room. He would say hello to me and keep going. As the months wore on, Haller appeared to be embarrassed when I caught him talking to Ozark. Tom would break off his conversation and silently hurry out of the clubhouse with his head down.

This situation made my relationship with Danny Ozark rather awkward. Ozark had been very loyal to Walter Alston the year I played for the Dodgers, but I had to wonder just how loyal he was being to me. If Tom Haller was thrusting himself on Ozark—Haller had known him as a Dodger player for several years—there wasn't much a coach could do. But I felt Danny should have come to me and offered some explanation for Haller's persistent attentions. But Ozark never brought up the subject, and I was not the kind to raise it.

The players who came into the clubhouse early began to notice the Tom and Danny act, and they began giving me funny looks. Like: "What's going on here? The general manager's always talking to Ozark, and he never talks to you?" It made for a difficult, divisive situation as the players who respected me lost respect for Haller and Ozark. Some of those who had gripes about me began taking them to the front office, rather than expressing them in my office.

Haller never told me that a player had brought a complaint to him. He should have told the player to come see me. Instead he encouraged the malcontents to bring their grievances against me to him. I think he liked to pick heads for ammunition to use against me in the plot he was brewing to have me fired.

There was plenty for Haller to talk about after we got off to a terrible start, winning only 7 of our first 22 games. Naturally Jack Clark, who was hitting .190, asked to be traded. But he also spoke some truths when he said, "For the seven years I've been here, it's always been a rebuilding thing with us. Then we surprised the front office with our success last year, but they went ahead and made changes anyway, and now we're another two, three years away. I don't see any other team making as many changes as we do every year. I look around, and I can't help thinking it's going to be hard for us unless I hit 50 home runs and drive in 150 runs. They let Joe Morgan and Reggie Smith go, so it's all on me."

The only problem I had with Clark's statement was when he suggested that I was playing "guys Haller wants played." I told the press, "When I get a phone call telling me who to play, that's when *I* ask to be traded."

Clark wasn't the only Giant with a hitting problem. Chili Davis, who had batted .261 with 19 home runs and 76 RBIs in 1982, would hit .233 with 11 home runs and only 59 RBIs in 1983. All of a sudden Chili just couldn't get his bat around on pitches. He had no bat speed at all. He was even fouling off change-ups over the opposite dugout while hitting from either side of the plate. This was very unusual for any player, but particularly for a 23-year-old.

We worked with Chili in batting practice, where the pitcher was just tossing balls up to the plate. When the pitcher was coming around to throw, I'd say, "Get it started, get the bat started, be out in front." And Chili would swing and foul the ball over the opposite dugout. It reached a point where Chili had only 9 hits in 94 at-bats, and I finally had to send him down to Phoenix for a week. He was slightly better when he returned, but for some reason Chili Davis didn't really get his stroke back until the following season.

We had to struggle all season just to hover around the .500 mark, and in late May we went over it for a day with a 7-6 victory against the Mets in New York. During that game there occurred one of those bizarre incidents that a manager hates to go through, but it was probably a good lesson for the ballclub because it showed all the players that I was in charge. I had to fine veteran pitcher Jim Barr for breaking the rules while out on the mound, where everyone in Shea Stadium and those watching the game on TV in San Francisco could see the show.

I liked Jim Barr, a tough guy who had pitched well for me in 1982, beat the Giants in arbitration, and won a $280,000 salary. On learning that, Haller had wanted to release Barr, rather than pay him that much money. But I fought to keep Barr, because he never gave in to a hitter, could start or relieve, and was always ready.

In the game at Shea, Barr was my third pitcher of the day and had pitched good ball for 3⅓ innings. Then he gave up a single, walked a man, and had a ball on the next hitter when I decided to bring in Greg Minton. From the day I took over the Giants, I had told my pitchers that when I or my pitching coach comes to the mound, we don't want to be shown up in any way. "Just give us the ball, and either wait for the reliever or leave—it's up to you," I said. "But don't try to talk me out of removing you or argue, because it could lead to a bad scene. If you want to discuss the situation later in my office, fine."

As I crossed the baseline heading for the mound, I looked toward left field to see how far Minton had come from the bullpen. Just as I looked back toward Barr, all I glimpsed was a body moving past me and a blurry ball in the air. Reflexively, I caught the ball in one hand and grabbed Jim Barr's arm with my other hand.

"Get back on the mound," I said, angry that he had flipped the ball to me in annoyance. We exchanged heated words; Barr said he could get the hitter and I told him he couldn't very well do that from the clubhouse because that was where he would be. Johnnie LeMaster stepped between us as Barr continued to argue and I came right back at him.

After the game I talked with Barr in my office for five minutes and fined him $500, and the incident was closed. Jim Barr continued to be an aggressive pitcher for me after I had made my point that I would not allow a player to show up me or anyone else on the ballclub.

In successive nights at the end of June we blew late-inning leads to the last-place Cincinnati Reds by playing sloppy baseball. In the second loss, errors were made by Jack Clark, Darrell Evans, Mike Krukow, and Brad Wellman, a nonhitting rookie who was playing because Duane Kuiper was on the disabled list. In addition, Jeff Leonard threw to the wrong base, and third baseman Tom O'Malley failed to tag a runner going past him. Instead, O'Malley threw to second for a force play, and the runner at third scored moments later.

Afterward I chewed out the players for five minutes, saying we weren't even playing as well as a good minor league club and we just couldn't continue to play like that. I was so angry I mixed in a lot of curse words, which I don't like to use, but I wanted to impress on them how bad they were. Our pitching, defense, hitting, and concentration were all horsespit, I said, and the criticism went for everyone on the ballclub.

"And nobody says anything after someone makes a mistake," I said. "You all come into the dugout, sit down, and go back out without anybody saying a word. If Joe Morgan or Reggie Smith were still with us, you would have heard a mouthful and we wouldn't be losing two games in a row to a team below us in the standings. To be a contender, you have to beat the teams below you and play good ball against the teams in front of you—and we seem to be doing just the opposite."

We began to be a little more alert mentally in games after that, but we kept making far too many physical errors. Many of them were made on routine plays where the ball was hit right at somebody. One of my major problems was that neither Brad Wellman at second nor Tom O'Malley at third, who could field well, was a productive hitter. So I was forced to play Joel Youngblood at third in 28 games and at second in 64 games because I needed his bat in the lineup. Youngblood couldn't make the pivot at second base, but he hit for average (.292) and with power (17 home runs)

But in our first 83 games we had 94 errors. In all my years in baseball

I had never seen any team except the Dodgers make as many errors as the 1983 Giants. But the old Dodgers had ways of overcoming their errors, usually featuring a pretty fair offense and outstanding pitching. Good pitchers who have an error made behind them tend to bear down and make the pitches to get some outs.

We did not have that kind of pitching staff. Two of our starters, Atlee Hammaker and Bill Lasky, were plagued by arm trouble much of the season, as was our top young prospect, Scott Garrelts. Mike Krukow couldn't get his winning percentage over .500 with us, going 11-11. The pitcher we gave up in the deal for Krukow, Al Holland, won 8 games for the Phillies in 1983 and saved 25. Holland's loss put more pressure on my stoppers. While Greg Minton was credited with 22 saves, he lost 11 games and was very inconsistent for the first time in my experience.

Gary Lavelle was my most consistent pitcher, winning 7 games and saving 20 with a 2.59 ERA. I suspect that one of Lavelle's losses was due to the fact that he came back too soon from a knee problem. Floyd Rayford of the Cardinals pinch-hit a two-run homer off Gary in the ninth inning. Afterward one of the writers, wondering if Lavelle had his normal stuff, asked, "Did his pitches have much movement on them?"

"You bet they did," I said. "One of them moved right out of the park."

Another problem we had was catching depth after Milt May was traded to Pittsburgh. May had been a fairly good hitter, but I don't think he could have thrown me out stealing. Of the last 280 attempted steals on him, 185 had been successful. Bob Brenly was on his way to becoming a regular, but there was no one behind him, which I couldn't believe.

When I joined the Giants, I was told we had four outstanding catchers in the organization. "Wow," I said, "that's something. Most organizations only have two real catching prospects." Our four catchers were Randy Gomez, Bob Cummings, Jeff Grantham, and Johnny Rabb. Something was seriously wrong with the Giants' system of evaluating or developing players, because not one of those four catchers made it in the major leagues.

I had Johnny Rabb in 1983 and found that he couldn't throw anyone out at second base. I mean, little old ladies would have had a shot at beating Rabb's throws, because the ball often sailed into center field. The amazing thing was there wasn't a word about Rabb's throwing problems in the scouting reports on him. Yet when he was brought up and I called his former managers in the minors, they told me Rabb had always had problems throwing. "We have to go quite a ways to turn this into a solid organization," I thought.

But without a complement of players that I could just write into the lineup every day, I was forced to try a lot of players in search of a winning combination. I used 16 different pitchers and 25 other players during this season. That kind of roster juggling is the sure sign of a scrambling ballclub.

We were making some improvements in the way we did other things. Although the Dodgers later took credit for having the first so-called NL Eye in the Sky, the Giants this season had a man in the press box, Ben Moore, communicating with the dugout about our defense. Moore, who had coached baseball at the University of San Francisco and also scouted for the Phillies, would meet with us before games when we discussed how we wanted to defense an opponent. Moore would oversee our defense during games and communicate via a walkie-talkie with coach Don Buford, who was wearing a headset in the dugout.

Bob Lurie was good about spending money on improvements. Every time I recommended that we upgrade a hotel we stayed at or add a charter flight, Lurie approved. I also convinced him to spend the money to make videotapes of every player in our system. As a player moved up, his tapes would move with him, and we'd have a record of when he was performing well so that we could more easily correct a flaw or cure a slump. In addition, if we were considering promoting a player from AA or AAA ball, we could have a look at him on tape before we brought him up.

I also kept pushing Haller and Lurie to expand our single video camera at home to a four-camera setup like the Dodgers had, and they finally did so toward the end of the season. By having not only a camera behind the plate, but one in center field and another down each baseline, we could have a complete record of every play in a game. Though we focused on our players, we also got the opposition pitcher throwing to our people and the opposition hitters facing our pitchers. The new system improved our evaluation of players throughout the league.

I sometimes thought of aiming our right-side video camera at the opposing third base coach so that we could analyze and steal his signs, but I never did. Somehow it didn't seem right for an old-school baseball man to engage in such thievery. I remember when Bill Veeck put a camera in the Cleveland scoreboard in an attempt to steal the opposing catcher's signs.

One innovation that I was not at all for was the hiring of Dr. Joel Kirsch as team psychologist. Kirsch convinced Bob Lurie that he could provide considerable help for the players and front office personnel of the

Giants. He said he would demonstrate his abilities for one year without a fee, and on that basis Lurie figured he had nothing to lose.

Initially Kirsch was supposed to bridge the gap between me and the front office, which meant Tom Haller. Nothing happened in that area, I suspect, because Haller was not interested in that gap being bridged. So Kirsch began spending a lot of time in the clubhouse talking to players. The next thing I knew Kirsch was on the road with us, and finally he was out on the field with us. I found out about that after the psychologist had taken Johnny Rabb out one day without my knowledge to work on his throws to second base. I told Kirsch that he was not to be involved in any area of a player's performance.

Over the next week or so, Rabb threw out 5 of the 11 base runners who attempted to steal on him. Kirsch immediately said that his work with Johnny Rabb had improved the youngster's erratic throwing.

"If you take credit for his success," I told him, "you'd better be prepared to take credit for his throwing failures too."

I could see that Rabb's mechanics continued to be off. He still cocked his arm behind his ear the way catchers did in the old days before releasing the ball. Now catchers just brought their arms around from the side.

Following that brief period of being on target, Johnny Rabb reverted to his usual trajectory and threw ball after ball into center field. I didn't hear a word about that from Dr. Kirsch, psychologist.

His basic work with the players was psychological counseling. Kirsch had those who were interested go through what he called "quiet time" prior to games; sitting quietly for ten minutes before taking the field and concentrating on and visualizing how they wanted to perform that night. Some players felt the exercise helped them, though I didn't see any dramatic improvement in individual performances, other than those of Darrell Evans after he moved up on the plate and Jeff Leonard, who, having beaten narcotics, beat on baseballs all season.

In August Kirsch did something that proved very enlightening to me personally. He surveyed the players on their feelings about me, and at first it annoyed me that this had been done without my knowledge. But Kirsch suggested that we have an open meeting with all the players, which he would mediate, so they could express their feelings about me. He said I would learn a lot, so I called a meeting before a game in Atlanta, on Wednesday, August 10.

Kirsch and I were seated at the head of the dressing room, with the players spread around in front of their lockers. "If you have something to say to Frank, this is the time to say it," Kirsch began. Four or five players expressed themselves, and the rest sat back. But Kirsch knew which players had complaints about me and what they were. If players didn't speak out or ask a question of me, Kirsch would say to an individual: "Didn't you say that you sometimes had a difficult time communicating with Frank?" Or: "Didn't you tell me that you felt Frank was at times too hard on you?" Or: "Don't you feel that Frank is often an intimidating presence?"

And the individual he asked would express himself, and that would encourage others who felt the same way to speak out to me. The meeting was conducted very well, and it was very constructive. In fact, overall it was the best meeting I had ever been associated with. Seeing myself through the players' eyes allowed me to see myself differently, through a cold, clear light. We were not dealing here with just baseball—we were dealing with players as individual people.

And I realized that I did not always communicate as well as I should, that I was sometimes too hard on people, and that I could be intimidating to some.

Earlier in the season and in other seasons I had heard that some players found me intimidating. When writers asked me about it, I had said, "I can be tough when I want to be, when I feel I have to be. Some people don't realize that I can be soft and easygoing when the occasion calls for it. But I know I intimidate a lot of people because they just see me one way. And when they see me the other way, they don't think it's for real. Those are the people who don't take time to know me. There are people on the club who are intimidated by me, but there isn't a heck of a lot I can do about it. I'm going to be me, period.

"But if people would take the time to get to know me, they would know I'm not really trying to intimidate. That's just the way I am, my manner."

But I feel you learn and grow all the time, and the meeting with Kirsch gave me a whole mass of player perspectives on myself for the first time. The meeting lasted an hour and 20 minutes, and the only reason we stopped was because we had to play a game, which we won. And I decided it was time for me to try lightening up a bit and being more open, not as heavy-handed with the players. Those who weren't really trying were one thing, but with the others I vowed to show more patience and to try boosting some egos that seemed to need it.

○   ○   ○

Tom Haller struck again when he signed pitcher Randy Lerch, who was released by Montreal, without asking me if I wanted him or even telling me that Lerch would join us. He just showed up.

Later we were short of starters, and I requested that Haller call up Scott Garrelts from Phoenix because I wanted to start him right away. Garrelts came in a few days later, but he had started a Phoenix game two days earlier. "Frank should have told Phoenix manager Jack Mull not to pitch Garrelts," Haller told the writers, though that is the general manager's responsibility.

"How was I to tell Mull anything when Haller was the one communicating with Phoenix about bringing Garrelts up?" I told the writers.

At the batting cage later that night Haller apologized to me for the first and only time.

In one August game against the Dodgers, we were behind 2-1 in the ninth when Steve Howe was brought in to relieve. Only days before, Howe had returned from a rehabilitation center where he had undergone treatment for cocaine addiction for the second time in eight months. But after Howe threw his warmup pitches, I asked the umpire to check his glove for a foreign substance. I suspected that Howe used pine tar to give him a better grip on his curveball. Howe was always going to the back of his glove, as if he kept the goo there. But the umpire found nothing.

My nose sweats on warm days, and I'm always wiping it off. I was standing outside the dugout rubbing at my nose when Howe suddenly yelled something at me, opened his uniform shirt, and wiped his hands on it as third baseman Pedro Guerrero started for me. I didn't know what was going on until after the game, when several Dodgers came heading toward me yelling insults. I realized that the Dodgers thought I had been rubbing my nose to unnerve Howe, who had admitted using cocaine. I yelled some curses back at the Dodgers, as did several of my players, and went into the clubhouse.

I had to laugh to myself. In the old days the bench jockeying in the majors was unremitting. If you had anything from a big nose or skinny legs to an ugly girlfriend or a drinking problem, you heard about it from the other team. It was expected. Now if you said or did anything that reflected on a player's configuration or personal life, he wanted to kill you. Players used to say that it was awful tough to hit the 3-2 pitch when guys in the other dugout were yelling, "Your girlfriend's an ugly bleep," and your wife was seated right behind your dugout.

The problems that drugs were causing baseball were no laughing matter. One of the writers asked me for my thoughts on drug use in the major leagues. "Well, nobody wants to talk about this," I said, "but I guarantee you that drugs are affecting the caliber of play. People say, 'Yeah, but alcohol was just as bad in your day.' I don't think so. When I played, one or two guys on a team might show up hung over or drunk. But I know for a fact that today a higher percentage of players are out there high on drugs."

I knew this simply from observing the sudden change in attitude and performance by any number of players. I'm talking about players who had performed at a high level and then plummeted, players like Vida Blue and Jeff Leonard. There were many others, whose names I won't mention because their involvement with drugs hasn't been publicly acknowledged. Some are out of baseball, some are still in the game, and therefore I would guess that they have gotten off drugs, because I really don't think you can sustain an athletic career for a number of years while abusing drugs.

But I'd see players who would play very well for a couple of weeks or for a month and then abruptly play very poorly for a couple of weeks or for a month. These were players who were just too good to again and again have such drastic swings in their performance. Something was affecting their play, and that something had to be drugs.

Their whole personalities would change. They became different people. Outgoing guys might become surly and withdrawn. Introverted guys might suddenly become extremely animated. Everyone reacts to drugs in a different way. Cocaine might totally relax one guy and make another so intense that he wants to kill.

There was a pitcher who had been mediocre for several years, consistently below average because of his tentativeness on the mound. He was so tense that he was afraid to really go after hitters. All of a sudden he was relaxed on the mound and no longer afraid to challenge hitters. He had some success for a time pitching under the influence, just as Steve Howe did. But eventually the drugs caught up with him, just as they did with Howe, and the pitcher was gone. He didn't have as much ability as

Steve Howe, who kept going in and out of drug rehab facilities for years. Howe finally seemed to have overcome his problems in 1987, and he made it back to the majors with the Texas Rangers. He still had a good arm and knew how to pitch. (Unfortunately, a post-season test revealed alcohol in his system, and his future in baseball was in doubt as we went to press.)

Howe contends that baseball continues to be as drug-ridden as ever, despite commissioner Peter Ueberroth's announcement to all the world in 1985 that "baseball is now free of drugs." I don't believe that for an instant, and that kind of naïveté does not help. Ignoring a problem never makes it go away—any more than decreeing that a problem is over actually puts an end to it.

After Howe signed with the Rangers, he told a writer, "I could come out publicly and ruin baseball. I've seen a lot of people do a lot of things. The things that went on in the San Francisco clubhouse you wouldn't believe. Guys would come in with coke every day."

Looking back now, I have no doubt that Howe was right, although I certainly wasn't aware of the habits of drug users then. But we've come to learn that people who use drugs know everyone on the other ballclubs who are drug users. They form a network and supply drugs to one another. So coke use may very well have gone on in the San Francisco clubhouse. I can recall seeing players who admitted having been cocaine users, and other players that I suspected of being users, gathering on the field before ballgames. They would talk around the batting cage and on the sidelines. They all knew where to find one another.

I had suspicions about a number of my players, but there was no way I could come up with evidence that they were actually using drugs. I suspected Vida Blue, but I couldn't run into the clubhouse after him every time he went into the bathroom during a game. Other players also went to the clubhouse regularly during games. A couple of players came to me after they had used the bathroom one day and told me there was some white dust on the floor that might be cocaine.

There was no point in my confronting the player who had been in the bathroom before. He'd simply deny any knowledge of the white dust on the floor. But any time I was suspicious of a player, I let the front office know about it. Then it was up to Tom Haller to conduct an investigation or hire someone to check out the individuals I suspected. Haller always said he would look into the matter; then he did nothing.

We had one pitcher whose wild mood swings and appearance changes had to be drug-induced. On the day he was to pitch, he was real hyper, couldn't wait to get out on the mound, and his eyes would be about the size of a half-dollar. He was so uptight he looked like he wanted to scream. Yet when I'd go out to talk to him on the mound, he would stare right through me, facing me but not focusing.

The next day he would be back to his normal mild-mannered self, without the Orphan Annie eyes or the hyperactive behavior.

But his standard pitching-day behavior was to go out and throw a no-hitter for three or four innings. Then all of a sudden he couldn't get anyone out, and I'd have to worry about the health of my infielders who had families. I'd pull him from the game, and he'd storm into the clubhouse and tear it up. The next day he wouldn't harm a fly.

This pitcher is still making a living in the major leagues. When I observed him elsewhere, he no longer was exhibiting that hyperactive behavior, so I presume he got off drugs.

Steve Howe was not so fortunate, according to what he told a reporter. "I've never been a social partygoer," Howe said. "I don't drink, not even beer. But I found a drug that's me, and now I have to be real careful, because I can't handle it.

"There have been so many times where I'd tell myself after three, six months of treatment, 'Hey, man, I got it licked. No problem.' Then you go to a party. You do one line [of cocaine] and it's all over. You've spent another $10,000. You crash your car. Your old lady leaves you. Once I started doing drugs, there were only two things I cared about: me and drugs. And, baby, that was it. I haven't been the same since."

From 1983 to 1987, Steve Howe's baseball career was interrupted seven times by cocaine addiction. Why? "Who knows why I kept going back?" he said. "I don't know why. If I knew that, I'd be the best drug counselor in the world."

I don't know if baseball needs drug counselors, but I do know that managers and coaches at every level in the game need to be educated about drug use and how to detect players who might be sniffing coke or whatever. I am much more aware of what to look for in a player's behavior today than I was when I joined the Giants. But I am no expert. And the managers and coaches who deal with players every day should be given some expertise in the area of spotting drug users and getting them help for the problem immediately.

I feel that drugs continue to be a blight on baseball today. We do not get the absolute best performances from some players and some teams because of drug use. And everyone—player, management, owner, and fan—suffers. So it's up to commissioner Ueberroth to take some action on drugs in baseball.

The 1983 Giants were not nearly as good as the 1982 team and finished with a 79-83 record. Without the presence of Joe Morgan and Reggie Smith in the clubhouse, the Giants went right back to their old ways of complaining about every little thing and pointing fingers at each other. No strong figure came forward to get them out of that attitude. Reggie would have said, "Knock off the damn bitching, and go out and do your job."

Now Jack Clark was the only strong figure in the clubhouse. And Jack had enough problems concentrating on his own game at that time. Reggie and Joe had seen to it that Jack hadn't had to carry the entire offensive load in 1982, which was why he'd had an outstanding season. They got some big clutch hits. In 1983 if Clark or Evans didn't come through for us, we usually lost.

Tom Haller tried to shift the blame from him to me for our disappointing season by telling writers that the ballclub lacked leadership and that it must come from the manager. *Chronicle* columnists Glenn Dickey and Lowell Cohn continually criticized Haller for the rift he had created with me.

"Working with Robinson, who has sound organizational ideas from his experiences in Baltimore, Haller could build the kind of organization the Giants need," Dickey wrote. "But he continually undermines his own efforts by treating Robinson as an adversary, rather than a colleague. Why? I suspect it's jealousy. Robinson has a stature dating back to his playing career that Haller has never had. Before the rift got to this point, owner Bob Lurie should have brought the two men in and reminded them that they should be working together."

Lurie did that more than once, but no matter what he said, it didn't change the way Haller felt about me or change his refusal to communicate with me. His plan was to get rid of me, and he kept working at it. For some reason, Lurie loved Tom Haller, which ended up setting back the Giants' progress toward contention by several years.

Still, I got on well with Lurie, who took me out late in the season when a rumor arose that I might be fired. He told me he didn't blame me for the type of season we were having. "I'd like to extend your contract for an additional year," Lurie said.

"Why not two years?" I said. "You gave me a two-year extension in 1982, so why not tack on two more years through the '86 season? That'll tell the players and everyone else that I'm the manager you want here."

Bob Lurie agreed to the extension; the details were to be worked out with my agent Ed Keating. I was very pleased and hoped the two extra years might change Tom Haller's attitude toward me.

Through it all at least I kept my sense of humor. Before one late-season game a writer had walked into my office and asked me, very seriously, if I thought that having sex before a ballgame had any negative effect on performance. "It doesn't hurt me," I said, "in making out the lineup."

Another writer asked me in September how I viewed the pennant race. "By looking up," I said.

Every manager needs a sense of humor to retain his sanity.

18

"IT'S TIME TO MAKE A CHANGE, FRANK"

THE details in my contract extension—which would pay me $155,000 in 1985 and $165,000 in 1986—weren't completed until just a few days before spring training. When Lurie announced it, he said once again, "There is no friction between Frank and Tom Haller. They have differences of opinion, but I don't want yes-men around. I hope the extension ends those rumors of friction."

But our differences continued even before spring training after Haller and I agreed that we should make every effort to sign Dusty Baker as a free agent. Haller started negotiations with Baker and then held him off for weeks. I asked Tom how things were progressing, and he said he was working on Baker. A week later I phoned Dusty, and he said, "Haller said he'd call me back three weeks ago, and I haven't heard from him."

Another week went by and I still had no word on Baker, so I called him again. "Haller called five days ago and said he'd get back to me," Dusty said. "I'm waiting."

"Well, I'd like to have you on the ballclub," I said. "I'll talk to Mr. Lurie and see if I can't get some movement going in the negotiations."

Lurie said he'd see what he could do, but Haller didn't sign Baker until April 1. He not only missed spring training but the first ten days of the season.

Haller did another dumb thing with one of our top young pitching prospects, Scott Garrelts, who normally threw the ball at 94 mph. In the spring he was barely braking 84 mph, and I kept telling pitching coach Herm Starrett, "This kid must have a bad arm. You don't go from throwing 94 to 84 if you're healthy."

But every time Herm questioned him, Garrelts insisted that his arm was all right, that he just didn't have his full strength yet. With some pitchers, even young ones, it takes them a little while to get their arms strong enough to throw at full velocity. But Scott Garrelts never did, even into the season, because he was hiding an injury to his shoulder, while battling to make the team. Later Garrelts told a writer, "Tom Haller knows what's wrong with me."

Haller had somehow known that Scott Garrelts had a bad arm but let him pitch anyway, jeopardizing the career of an outstanding prospect. Fortunately for the Giants, Garrelts's arm came back the following year, and he became the team's best relief pitcher, winning 9 games, saving 13, and striking out 106 batters in 106 innings.

I was much looser with the players in the spring, and they seemed to be enjoying themselves. I liked the overall attitude. There was a lot of joking around, until the work began, and then everyone got serious. Johnnie LeMaster said I was more conversational, more into the off-field doings. I had to laugh when Duane Kuiper told the writers, "You still don't know what Frank's thinking, but he's talking to us."

When we got to San Francisco just before the season started, there were more laughs at my expense. I was roasted by my players, as was A's manager Steve Boros by his, at a benefit to raise money for the Joe Morgan Youth Foundation in Oakland. Joe was the first to get me. "The Giants hired a psychiatrist last year," Joe said. "After he'd talked to Frank for a while, he said, 'You're crazy.' Frank said, 'I want a second opinion.' The psychiatrist said, 'Okay, you're ugly too.'"

Among the Giants' players, Duane Kuiper took the best shot at me. "This is my sixth year with the Ayatollah," Duane said, nodding at me. "I can sympathize with the American hostages in Iran, but at least they got out. When I tore up my knee in Cleveland, Frank rushed out and told me, 'Good, now I can activate myself.'"

When I got up to the mike, I said, "When you roast Frank Robinson, you're not roasting a turkey."

Then I went after Kuiper by saying, "I brought Duane Kuiper up to the major leagues in Cleveland, and I'll be the one to end his career here."

Next I hit Jack Clark; I said, "Jack wouldn't speak tonight. But when he goes 0-for-50 he'll tell everybody how it's my fault again."

Then I jabbed at my old basketball teammate at McClymonds High School, Bill Russell, who laughed the loudest when I said, "I was the 'thinking' guard on the team and Bill was our dumb center. I'd bring the ball down the court and hold up one finger, but Bill couldn't remember the play. And in those days we only had one play. Bill also had a little trouble counting in school. But he did learn to count to four because that was the number of hubcaps on a car."

When I finished, I looked down at MC Al Michaels, who had a new permanent in his hair, and I said, "In all my life, Al—and I'm 48 years old—I've never had to spend money to get kinky hair."

It wasn't easy keeping my sense of humor once the season started. We had the worst ballclub I had to work with in San Francisco. Darrell Evans, who had learned to hit consistently, had signed with the Tigers as a free agent. Tom Haller had signed veteran Al Oliver, a .304 lifetime hitter, to replace him at first base. I was for his acquisition and thought he would provide leadership on the field and in the clubhouse. Oliver did neither. He was such a terrible fielder that I couldn't play him every day, and whenever he sat, he bitched. Oliver was also more concerned with his own stats than with the team.

Before one April game I saw in the statistics that Oliver had never hit left-hander Dave LaPoint, whom we were facing that day. So I told Al I would give him a day off, as he was 37 and the rest might make him stronger late in the season. I didn't want to tell him that he couldn't hit LaPoint.

But Al went right to a writer and said, "Geez, it's April. Am I tired already? Why's he resting me now?"

During a game in May we were losing to the Padres 3-0. With no one out Manny Trillo, another free agent we had signed to play second, was on first base. Oliver stepped in and decided to try and bunt Trillo over to second, as if one run would really help us. Oliver popped up, and I said, "Even when they think on their own, they think wrong."

In late April and early May we lost nine games in succession, and I got so depressed I even talked publicly about resigning. "I'm not a quitter, but I'm serious about resigning if we don't turn things around in two weeks," I said. "I love baseball, and it would be tough to leave it. But each loss eats at you a little deeper and a little harder. You can only take so much. I've got to get the most out of this ballclub, and I haven't done that.

"I keep waiting for this to end, but I watch the players, and I wonder whether it affects them as much as it does me. I keep wondering what we should do next, what direction we should go in. I've tried different lineups, but the results are the same. We're just not putting any pressure on the other club."

The Giants had batted only .205 during the losing streak and had left 60 runners on base. Jack Clark was the only player who was hitting.

"I've never seen the game played as bad as we're playing," Clark said. "We're hitting bad, we're fielding bad, we're pitching bad, and we're looking bad. We make the other team seem like it's playing a bunch of little kids. I'd like to find an excuse, but I can't. We come out of spring training with the best record, but we go flat. We're just sitting back, letting the other team take it to us."

I was impressed with Jack Clark's new attitude and consistent hustle. I named him team captain, and Jack immediately took a leadership role on the field, but not in the clubhouse. He never communicated with me about problems among the players. But Jack got off to a great start, and by late May he was hitting .326 with 7 home runs and 29 RBIs.

"He's leading by example," I told the press. "The team needs something to give it some spark. Jack has not only turned over a new leaf, but he's reading from a new book."

Throughout the losing streak, Tom Haller's conversations with Danny Ozark increased, and that situation did not change once we broke the streak. But the players' griping and whining remained steady, as they tend to on losing ballclubs.

Shortstop Johnnie LeMaster had a career year in 1983, batting .240 and stealing 39 bases. Part of the season I had him batting leadoff, which was where he started again in 1984 until late April. With his average barely at .200, I dropped him to eighth in the batting order, and LeMaster immediately sulked.

"If I can't hit leadoff, then I can't play for you," he said.

"You did a heck of a job at the top the first half of last season," I said, "but that was last season. You'll bat eighth until you start hitting the ball with some consistency. You'll go back to leadoff when you get your stroke back."

Instead of working hard to improve, LeMaster showed total lack of aggressiveness on the field and just went through the motions. "You'll have to play better than that if you want to stay in the lineup at all," I told him.

I began pinch-hitting for LeMaster late in games in which we trailed.

After I sent up a batter for him in one game, LeMaster angrily threw his helmet. I called him into my office at game's end, and he said, "If you keep pinch-hitting for me, I can't build up any confidence at the plate."

"You've got to be kidding if you think I'm not gonna pinch-hit for a .203 hitter," I said. "Your attitude is a detriment to you and to the ballclub. You've got to be able to put the team before your personal feelings. I'm taking you out of the starting lineup until you come and tell me that you're ready to play the way Johnnie LeMaster is capable of playing."

I hated to lose LeMaster's defense. My backup shortstop, Joe Pittman, was really a second baseman. But I had to bench LeMaster for a game if I was going to maintain discipline on the ballclub. I also felt his lackadaisical attitude was beginning to spread to other players.

After LeMaster returned to the lineup for a few games, he came to me and said, "You lied to me."

"I what?"

"You told me I'd be put back at leadoff when I got my stroke back," he said.

"Do you have your stroke back?"

"No," he said.

Now I knew why sea captains say, "It's a lonely life on the bridge."

Bob Lurie had asked me to be easier on the players, and as I had already decided to be more accessible to them and more encouraging, I had no problem with the request. I tried to be kinder and more understanding.

But early in June we went on another losing streak. The seventh loss in a row was by a 14-5 score, a game in which we committed four errors. Afterward, Jack Clark said to me, "Nice guys finish last, Frank. We need you to be the guy you were and should be."

I had already decided it was time to toughen up. I closed the clubhouse door for 15 minutes and chewed out the players without mentioning any individuals. Then I said there would be no more music in the clubhouse, the TV set would remain off, and there would be a series of fines for missing signs, for base-running blunders, for failure to hit the cutoff man, and for various mental mistakes. Pitchers would be fined for letting up on the number 7, 8, and 9 hitters and for giving up hits to anyone with an 0-and-2 count on him.

"And as a number of you guys have been complaining about the postgame food, and a couple of you recently threw it around the clubhouse," I said, "we won't have food in the clubhouse anymore."

A writer later asked me how I had been able to get two months of frustration off my chest in 15 minutes, and I said, "I talk fast."

Catcher Bob Brenly told the press, "It's not like we didn't deserve everything that Frank said and did. We're a sorry bunch. The 14-5 loss was embarrassing. Our pitchers let a bunch of weak hitters tear into them, and none of them had the courage to knock anybody down. Then they wonder why hitters dig in and hit line drives all over the place."

The next day I had the players report five hours before game time and put them through a complete workout of running, hitting, bunting, and fielding drills. Nobody griped.

The headline on Glenn Dickey's column in the *Chronicle* read, "The Sad Truth Is, the Giants Simply Stink." And he wrote: "If the Giants continue to lose, pressure will build to fire Robinson; it is always easier to fire a manager than to fire 25 players. There will be much talk about 'changing the chemistry,' and of bringing in somebody like Billy Martin. Better owner Bob Lurie should bring in an animal trainer. If I've ever seen a bunch of dogs, the Giants team is it."

My efforts to try to get the guys to play up to their capabilities worked for a time, as we won five out of our next seven games and then put together a six-game winning streak. But then the ballclub reverted to losing again, and it seemed like I saw Haller with Ozark every day.

As if things weren't bad enough, in late June Jack Clark tore cartilage in his knee. The doctors said that he could continue to play, that Jack could not do further damage to the knee, and that the arthroscopic surgery could wait until season's end. Jack was told if he had the surgery immediately, he should be able to play again in August. Jack chose to have the surgery in June, and he never returned to the active roster that season.

"Times change and attitudes are different than they were in my day," I thought. I remembered when I tore knee cartilage in June with the Orioles. I had the knee taped daily and continued to play. The knee hurt, but I performed reasonably well, and the ballclub needed me. I had arthroscopic surgery in the fall and was ready to go again in spring training.

Jack Clark missed 105 games and in 1985 was traded to the Cardinals, where he went on to become the consistently outstanding player that he had finally been for me early in 1984. A few years later I had to smile when I read Jack Clark's comments on his Giants' experience. "It took me longer to mature as a player," Jack said. "I didn't always run out balls to first base. I was a little moody. The Giants kept saying we were three years away. I ended up waiting seven or eight years, and still never asked to be traded." I read that last line over several times. "In 1984, though," Jack continued, "I was ready to take charge, and did. Frank Robinson was the manager, and he even made me the captain. I got off to my best start ever. Then I tore the cartilage in my knee in June and didn't play again."

At the All-Star break the Giants were 17 games under .500 and Bob Lurie was asked when—not if—he would fire me. "Frank Robinson is the manager, and I'm not going to go much further than that," Lurie said. "I think he's doing a good job. If I thought he were doing a terrible job, then I would have made a change before this."

I certainly couldn't play the game for my guys, who were third in the league in hitting but who seldom produced the big hit with men in scoring position. The infield defense had been bad, with the exception of Manny Trillo, who was sidelined for several weeks with a broken bone in his hand. But Joel Youngblood had already committed 22 errors at third, and shortstop Johnnie LeMaster simply wasn't making an effort anymore. And we lacked a leader in the clubhouse who wouldn't accept losing and wouldn't let his teammates do so either.

Having tried everything I could think of to turn things around, I decided to see if maybe my coaches could do a little more with the players. I spoke to Joel Kirsch and put together a survey for the players to fill out, voluntarily, on their feelings about the coaches, how they were performing, and how they might improve. If there were any areas where a coach might improve, it was up to me to make him aware of them. I knew that a player's hitting did not depend on the hitting coach, for example. But a coach is a teacher who must be able to communicate with a player who's out of line and help him play up to his capabilities. Of course, some players resist instruction and can't follow advice, but usually those players end up being released.

Tom Haller instantly got word of the questionnaires I had circulated and put a stop to my survey before it began. "What is wrong with surveying the players on the competence of the coaches?" I asked him. "You had no objection when the players filled out a questionnaire on their feelings about me last season."

"That was baseball business," Haller said.

"What are my coaches teaching, handball?" I asked.

When Johnnie LeMaster's hitless streak had reached 33 at-bats, I sat him down for a week, then started him against Cincinnati, and hoped that at least he would play with his old fire in the field. He didn't. LeMaster also extended his hitting slump to 0-for-36.

The first weekend in August we went to Atlanta and won two games in a row on Friday and Saturday. I was feeling pretty good afterward, just lying around my hotel room watching the Olympics that night. At 12:30 A.M. Bob Lurie called and said, "Frank, I'm in town."

I said to myself, "That's it; I'm fired." Why else would Lurie be in Atlanta in the middle of the night?

He asked me to come down to his room in the hotel. I dressed and went right down to his suite. Lurie opened the door, and he looked like he'd been through a battle. His hair was all disheveled, his shoulders were slumped, and there were lines around his mouth. Bob ushered me into the suite. I noticed that the bedroom door was closed, as if he had someone in there.

"The team is not responding to you, Frank," Lurie said, "and I think it's time to make a change. I just feel we need someone else to run the team. Danny Ozark is going to take over for the rest of the season."

I nodded, and Lurie asked, "Do you have anything to say?"

"No. What do you want me to say?"

"I'm just kind of concerned about what Duffy Jennings [the Giants' public relations director] is going to say to the press."

"Well, Bob, no matter what Duffy puts out or what you or anyone else says, it's not gonna make this situation any better," I said.

"I just want to make sure this is handled right," Lurie said.

"It doesn't make any difference to me how you handle it," I said. "I'm gone." I opened the door and left.

"Good old loyal Danny Ozark's now the manager," I thought, heading back to my room. I wasn't surprised. In fact, four or five weeks earlier I had wanted to see Ozark about something, and when I walked into the room where he dressed, Tom Haller was right there talking. Haller immediately left, and I stared at Ozark for a long moment.

"I don't want your job, Frank," Ozark blurted. "I don't want to manage."

That told me he definitely wanted my job and suggested that Haller had already planted in his mind the possibility that Ozark might manage the Giants if Haller could get rid of me. Tom Haller did a better job of getting rid of me than he did as general manager of the Giants. Haller even admitted to the press later that he had not altered his long-time ambition to manage the Giants himself. He would have if Lurie had not turned him down. Ozark was not offered the job for 1985. He retired to his Florida home to collect his baseball pension and also be paid by the Giants as a part-time scout and consultant.

Of course, Bob Lurie was the loser, because by keeping Tom Haller, he set back the Giants' development by another year and a half. Under me the Giants had an abysmal 42-64 record in 1984, but they didn't improve a whole lot the last two months, turning in a 24-32 record. In 1985 Haller hired his friend Jimmy Davenport as manager, and the Giants lost 100 games. It wasn't until Lurie fired Tom Haller and replaced him with Al Rosen, a good baseball man who put together a solid organization and wasn't afraid to make trades, that the Giants became contenders. With a roster of good players, manager Roger Craig did an excellent job leading the ballclub to a division championship in 1987.

After I was fired, it came out in the papers that Bob Lurie had summoned three players to his office earlier in the season to discuss the attitude on the club. I had to smile when I learned who Lurie had called on: Jack Clark, Johnnie LeMaster, and Gary Lavelle. Clark had been the team's biggest pop-off until he finally saw the light in 1984 and I named him captain. LeMaster had whined and sulked for a year because I wouldn't bat him leadoff when he barely hit .200. Gary Lavelle was the God Squad leader who, it was reported by Glenn Dickey, "took exception to Robinson's lifestyle." I couldn't understand that one unless Lavelle objected to seeing me having a drink in hotel bars. I never drank on airplanes as many managers do.

But the point was that if Lurie wanted an objective report from players on me, he might have sought a different trio, although I didn't seem to be wildly popular with the players, judging from several comments I read after being fired. The only player who wholeheartedly came out in support of me was Jeff Leonard, who said, "I think it's a crying shame to let anyone of Frank's ability go." Then he went out and hit a grand-slam home run to beat the Braves in the Sunday game of our series in Atlanta. "A few of the guys quit on Frank," Jeff said afterward. "I dedicated the slam to Frank Robinson."

The only regret I had was that I had been a little too easy on the players, as Bob Lurie had asked me to be, though he denied that he had made that request. I had planned to be more open and understanding, but I should have combined that with being myself. I should not have been as accepting of poor play, mental mistakes, and excuses. By the time

I resumed being more demanding, it was too late. But as a manager you live and learn every day you're on the job.

But the way the Giants handled my dismissal and the aftermath really irked me. Number 1, firing me in the middle of the night was upsetting. Lurie could have waited until the next morning to tell me before I went to the ballpark or even after the road trip, which would end in Houston in four days.

Obviously Bob Lurie didn't want to fire me in San Francisco. The press there had been consistently behind me and critical of Tom Haller's refusal to work with me, which Lurie approved by not demanding a change in the situation. So he fired me in the middle of the night in Atlanta, when the San Francisco columnists were not present. They were mostly covering the Olympic Games in Los Angeles. Lurie tried his best to avoid receiving a bad press, though it would later follow anyway as the writers knew that Tom Haller was undercutting me with Lurie's okay. With so much attention focused on the Olympics, Lurie also hoped that Giants' fans—of which there were already far too few—would pay little attention to my being fired. Several days later the *Chronicle* ran a telephone poll of fans that asked the question: "Should the Giants have fired Frank Robinson?" Of the 14,299 people who called the newspaper, 10,542, or 74 percent, said I should not have been fired.

When I left Lurie that night in Atlanta, I went back to my hotel room and called my coaches with the news. Ozark was out, and I suspected he had been behind the closed door in Lurie's suite. Herm Starrette was staying in a motel with his family, who were visiting him. Don Buford, Tommy McCraw, and bullpen coach John Van Ornum came to my room, and I ordered up two bottles of Stolichnaya vodka, which we sipped until the sun came up. The only phone call to me was placed by Giants' traveling secretary Derk Smith, who asked if he could make any arrangements for me. I told him to book a flight for after 3 P.M. the next afternoon as I wanted to talk to the players and meet with the press before I departed. Even Duffy Jennings didn't call to ask if I would see the press.

Tom Haller didn't call that night, the next day, or even when I returned to my home. He was a man with a lot of class, although to describe him accurately you might have to drop the first two letters of class. I didn't see Haller until a couple of years later when we were playing in an old-timers' game in Washington, D.C. I was in uniform leaning down in a chair tying my shoes when I felt a tap on my shoulder.

I looked up, and it was Tom Haller, who said, "Look, I've never said anything to you since you were let go, Frank...."

I don't know what else he said, if anything, after he saw the disdain on my face. But I was so angry, I just turned back to tying my shoes without uttering a word to Haller. Here was a guy who had been my general manager and had screwed me royally, yet he hadn't even had the decency to pick up a phone and wish me good luck, or whatever. He hadn't had the guts to talk to me, but he thought at this late date that I would converse with him.

I went to the Atlanta ballpark early Sunday to make sure my bag had been packed. I walked around and shook hands with the coaches, and Danny Ozark said, "Sorry this happened, Frank." I gave him a look that said, "I bet you are," but I shook his hand anyway.

When I was talking to the press, Duffy Jennings came over and offered his hand to me. I just glanced at his hand and kept talking, and Duffy moved away.

When I spoke to the players, I told the younger guys to work hard to improve themselves and prove they could play in the major leagues. Then I told the older players to work hard and try to stay in the majors as long as they could. "Because there's going to come a day like today was for me," I said, "when they tell you you can't be here anymore."

Then I went home. The only one who called me there from the entire Giants' organization was vice president Corey Busch, Lurie's assistant. Our families had been close, and we remain friends. But I had to think that Tom Haller wasn't the lone member of the Giants' organization who was without class or any sense of professionalism.

19

PITCHERS ARE
JUST DIFFERENT

O_N the flight to California, I thought, "The great irony in all of this is that I'm a much better manager than I ever was before, and I'm out of a job. And the odds—which might read 'the posture of baseball's powers that be'—are against my ever being hired to manage another major league ballclub." But I sincerely felt that if I had a team with just 80 percent of the talent that is normally associated with a winning ballclub—as was the case with the 1982 Giants—I could make it into a contender. If you don't have a basic minimum of talent to work with, no manager can mold 25 players into a contending ballclub.

Pitching is at least 75 percent of baseball, and the most difficult task a manager faces is learning how to fine-tune his staff. I did a better job of that with the Giants than I did with the Indians. Yet I never had a truly outstanding starter in San Francisco. I never had a starter who won over 13 games in a season. If he had taken care of himself, Vida Blue could have been the staff leader. He could have given the younger pitchers a tremendous boost because, when he was together, Vida Blue knew how to pitch as well as anyone in the league.

But pitchers are a strange breed. Maybe that's because they don't play every day. Most have four days off between trips to the mound. As a kid I pitched some and had some success because my arm was strong then, but I gave it up because I *had* to play baseball every day. When I wasn't pitching, I played the outfield. I just couldn't see sitting around for several days when there were balls to be hit and caught, not just thrown to a catcher 60 feet 6 inches away.

For some reason, pitchers are just different. One of my favorites was Giants reliever Greg Minton, who was a tough competitor with a sense of humor. But you never knew what Minton might say. I remember a pre-season game in 1983 against the Brewers when Minton really got shelled. He gave up ten hits in less than two innings. His sinker just wasn't sinking, but I left him in to get the work while hoping he'd come around.

Afterward when Minton was asked about his outing, he explained, "I had a 61-mile-an-hour fastball that didn't sink, so what would you expect against a lineup like the Brewers'? I don't know why the sinker works when it does work. So I sure as hell don't know why it doesn't work when it doesn't work."

But Minton could also be feisty. In 1984 I threatened to fine pitchers $100 for every hit they gave up after they had two strikes and no balls on a batter. This followed a week in which Giants' pitchers had given up 15 hits to batters who had 0-and-2 counts on them. Naturally some pitchers hated the rule.

"Look," I told the staff, "I'm taking the pressure off you and the burden off you. You don't have to throw a strike. You're allowed to throw a ball, which is the easiest thing a pitcher does. You can waste a pitch just out of the strike zone and get a lot of batters with a bad pitch. It's not asking too much when you're way ahead in the count *not* to come in with a fat pitch."

Greg Minton said, "If I get two quick strikes on a batter, I'll just throw the next pitch to the backstop."

"If you throw the ball to the backstop and a run scores, it's gonna cost you $500," I said.

I tried this experiment for several games, but I heard so much negative feedback from veteran pitchers that I dropped the fines for giving up hits on 0-and-2 counts. Their main complaint was that the new deal was making them defensive with hitters.

"How much more defensive can you get if you give up hits on 0-and-2 counts?" I asked.

But I gave in to the pitchers, who were having enough troubles. I didn't want them saying I was making them feel bad. This was probably one of the biggest issues that I relented on in San Francisco. I felt very strongly that pitchers should not give up hits on 0-and-2 counts, because they'd have three more pitches to work with before having to come in with a strike. In most cases, with three free pitches, the pitcher should be able to make a batter hit *his* pitch, and not groove one. A pitcher works very hard to get two strikes on a batter, and I couldn't understand why he would then come in with a pitch the batter could hit.

The whole idea of pitching is to get ahead in the count so that you are in control out on the mound. The batter is then on the defensive. So you can waste a pitch and still make the batter swing at your pitch. Everyone agreed with my theory in principle: A pitcher should be able to work on a hitter easier when the count was 0-and-2 and take the batter out without throwing a good strike.

But I canceled the fines because I'm still not absolutely sure of my position. I've been around a number of managers who said to their pitchers: "We want you to finish off a hitter as quick as you can. If you can get him with three pitches, do it."

Cal Ripken of the Orioles believes in that, and even says, "I don't care if we give up a hit on 0-and-2."

I can understand that philosophy if you have the right pitcher on the mound, one you know is not going to throw a fat pitch when he's ahead of a hitter by two strikes. But I don't think you can give every pitcher, especially the young ones, that kind of leeway, particularly when there are men on base.

In an 0-and-2-count situation, you often see a manager, rather than the pitching coach, go out to the mound. I did that regularly to remind the pitcher of the situation. "I don't want you to come in with a pitch this guy can hit now," I'd say. "Work on him." I would also go out, with men on base, when the count was 2-and-2 on a dangerous hitter. "I don't want you to walk this guy intentionally," I'd say, "but don't give him a fat pitch, either."

Several times in 1987 when I was bench coach for the Orioles, we had situations where there was a man on second or men on second and third and a good hitter up. With first base open and a veteran pitcher on the mound, you'd figure he would work the hitter carefully. If the pitcher couldn't get the batter to swing at a bad pitch, he could always put him on the open base and set up a possible double play. But on a number of occasions our pitcher in that situation gave up a hit that cost us a run or two.

"I took it for granted the guy would not throw a good pitch to hit," Ripken said after one such hit, "not with a base open. But you can't take it for granted."

"You're right, Cal," I said, seated beside him in the dugout.

"I should have gone out to the mound and told him," Cal said, and he started doing that.

The pitcher still might give up a big hit after you reminded him, but at least he would have been aware of what you expected. If you have a catcher or infielders who deliver reminders to pitchers, it saves the manager some trips to the mound. But sometimes it doesn't matter how many people go out and remind a pitcher of what he should not do in a situation; he does it anyway and later makes an excuse or tries to lay the blame on somebody else for his foul-up.

With the Orioles in 1987, we had two veterans who regularly talked to the pitcher in threatening situations, third baseman Ray Knight and catcher Terry Kennedy, who were often joined by shortstop Cal Ripken Jr. Sometimes their visits to the mound helped, and other times they didn't.

Late in one game the Orioles were leading by a run with Doug Corbett pitching in relief. There was a man on second with two outs, and Corbett, an eight-year veteran, got two quick strikes on the batter. Knight and Kennedy both went to the mound and told Corbett the same thing: "Don't give this guy a good pitch to hit."

Corbett nodded as he rubbed up the ball. Then he threw a pitch right down the middle of the plate and—whack!—it sailed out of the ballpark.

After getting the next batter out, Corbett came into the dugout and tossed his glove on the bench. "You know, as a veteran pitcher," he said, "I knew what I had to do. I knew what Ray and Terry said when they came to the mound was the right thing: 'Don't give this guy anything to hit.' But that put a negative thought in my mind, and I just laid the ball in there."

In other words, if Knight and Kennedy hadn't said anything to him about what he should *not* do, he would have done the right thing. I said to myself, "That negative thought didn't throw the pitch."

Later that inning, Ray Knight came over to me and said, "Can you believe what Doug said, a veteran pitcher making a statement like that?"

"It's hard to believe, Ray, if you haven't heard that kind of comment a number of times before," I said. "But I have."

I didn't tell him that it wasn't just pitchers who made excuses. But in the bottom of that inning, Ray Knight went up to bat. The pitcher got two strikes on him, no balls. The pitcher threw a sinker below the strike zone, and Ray laid off it, 1-and-2. First base coach Terry Crowley motioned to Knight to wait for a higher pitch before swinging. The next pitch was as low as the last one, but Knight swung and missed it for strike 3.

Looking disgusted, he came into the dugout. "You know, I was doing all right," Ray said. "I took the 0-2 pitch so he'd have to come in with a pitch. Then I looked at Terry, who motioned me to make the pitcher come up in the strike zone—and he put a negative thought in my mind and I swung."

"Oh no, Ray!" I said. "You're the guy who just told me you couldn't believe a veteran pitcher would say something like that. What about a veteran third baseman?"

Players in general are funny, because if a coach or manager doesn't talk to them or suggest things to them the way Terry Crowley had to Ray Knight, a player is likely to say, "He's not helping me. He never says anything to me. I don't know where I stand."

Some players seem to think a manager should talk to them on a daily basis, but I don't see how it's possible for any manager to talk to each of his 25 players every day. As a manager you say, "Hello, how're you doing?" to most players in the clubhouse before games. Usually you don't have to say a lot to your regulars, because they know you have enough confidence in them to play them every day. Certain guys, like Buddy Bell in Cleveland, seem to need more reassurance from a manager. It's the guys who aren't playing a whole lot, the role players who spend a lot of time sitting on the bench, that I tried to talk to more. I also felt I had to talk to my relief pitchers to keep them up between appearances.

With the Giants I tried to rotate my stoppers, Minton and Lavelle, to keep them fresh. But every once in a while one of them, feeling I had slighted him, would show up in my office, and we'd have to talk it out. I'd have to explain why I used the other guy rather than him. When you don't talk enough to some players, they feel unloved.

Probably the most dramatic change in pitching that I've observed in my years in baseball has been the disappearance of the knockdown or brushback pitch. When I came into the National League as a player, most pitchers would brush you back off the plate with an inside pitch if you dug in and many would knock you on your butt. That was all part of the game, and that's why I was hit by pitches 198 times. There were some pitchers who intentionally threw at batters to put fear in their hearts, but not all that many. Most just threw inside, and if the ball hit you, it didn't matter to them.

With the Reds we had a pitcher named Bob Purkey who was not a hard thrower, but he made sure that the inside part of the plate belonged to him. Every time Willie Mays of the Giants or Roberto Clemente of the Pirates batted against Purkey, he knocked them down. Mays and Clemente were two of the best hitters in the league, but Bob Purkey never had trouble with either of them.

By the early 1970s the older pitchers were moving on and the younger pitchers stopped throwing inside. A pitcher has the right to take part of the plate away from the hitter, but most of the younger ones did not view it that way. They didn't want to create any ill feelings. The result was that hitters began digging in at the plate without fear of having to bail away from a pitch. Without that worry on their minds, hitters began having field days.

All of a sudden any pitcher who continued to throw the ball inside, to keep the hitter loose up there, began hearing all kinds of protests from batters. The next thing you knew was that if a pitch came inside, the hitter would drop his bat and charge the mound. I remember a game when I was managing the Indians in which my pitcher, Jim Bibby, was throwing fastballs inside to Willie Horton of the Tigers. Horton was a slugger, and if you didn't move him off the plate, he'd kill you. But after a pitch came close to him, Horton, a big man, yelled to Bibby: "One more of those and I'm coming out after you."

I called time and went to the mound to talk to Bibby. "Don't pay any attention to him, Jim," I said. "Pitch your game, you know what you're doing."

I glanced in at Horton, who was out of the batter's box, staring daggers at Bibby, and snapping his bat at my pitcher. "What the hell do you think we're gonna do," I hollered at Horton, "throw the ball out over the plate and let you kill us?"

I turned to Bibby and said, "Stay inside on him, don't change." And Horton popped up an inside fastball.

Compared to the National League, the American League was always known as the place where country-club baseball was played. In fact, when I brought my hard-sliding style to the AL, I heard a lot of noise about it, as did Hal McRae some ten years later when he went from the Reds to the Royals. But there were never as many brushback and knockdown pitchers in the AL as in the NL, and by 1987 I couldn't think of a single one.

With the Giants I had several pitchers who would work inside—including Jim Barr, Al Holland, and Bill Lasky—but no one who would really knock a hitter back off the plate. I remember a four-game series against the Phillies in 1982 when Bob Dernier got eight hits off my staff, including two home runs, in 14 at-bats. Dernier not only remained upright but wasn't even backed off the plate once. He just wore us out, and our pitchers kept throwing the ball up there to him, as if to say, "Go ahead, Bob, do whatever you want to do."

I kept telling my pitchers to throw the ball inside, to lay claim to their portion of the plate. I know a lot of minor league pitching instructors tell their players, "You have to learn to pitch inside if you want to make it in the major leagues." You can advise a player, you can instruct a player, you can even demand that a player throw the ball inside—but there is no way you can force anyone to actually do so. A pitcher may throw everything inside in the bullpen, but stand a batter up in front of him, and his pitches are all from the middle of the plate to the outside.

We had a young pitcher with the Giants named Alan Fowlkes, who'd had a good college career and a pretty successful minor league career. We brought him up from Class AA. Fowlkes had a decent fastball and a good slider, and he had some success for us with his first couple of times on the mound. But the word spread quickly—as it does in the major leagues—that Fowlkes was a breaking ball pitcher who wouldn't throw inside. And his pitching pattern was beyond basic. His first pitch would be a slider on the outside corner. His second pitch would be a slider on the outside corner. His third pitch would be a slider that never reached the outside corner, because the batter would lean out over the plate and drive the pitch.

"Alan, you have to throw the fastball inside for a strike," I said, "and establish in the batter's mind that you can get ahead on the count. That'll also make your breaking ball more effective because the batter won't be able to lean out for it. You jam him inside, then catch the outside corner with the slider."

But Fowlkes was so reluctant to throw the ball on the inside corner of the plate for a strike that he'd throw inside for a ball. Then, as he was behind in the count, he'd revert to his slider-on-the-outside pattern and get creamed. He knicked around the big leagues for a few years and then, inevitably, faded away.

In my opinion it is not only the reluctance of young pitchers to hit a batter accidentally that keeps them from throwing inside. I believe the use of aluminum bats in Little League, in high school, and in college base-ball is a major factor. An inside pitch hit by a wooden bat usually breaks at the handle, and the batter is out. A batter swinging an aluminum bat hits one off his thumbs, and the ball dinks over the infield for a base hit. Once a pitcher gives up a bunch of those cheap thumb hits, he stops pitching inside.

Another factor in this equation is that new rules have started to protect the hitters a little too much. If an umpire thinks a pitcher is throwing at a batter, the pitcher is given a warning and fined $50. If the pitcher is warned by the umpire a second time, he is automatically expelled from the game.

The result of all this is that most pitchers work only on the outside part of the plate, which gives the hitters carte blanche. They know exactly where the ball's going to be, and it's "So long—it's been good to know you." This is why record numbers of home runs are flying out of ballparks, why earned-run averages are soaring, and why there are so few 20-game winners in the majors over a 162-game schedule anymore. The American League had two 20-game winners in 1987; the 1971 Orioles alone had four on the staff—Mike Cuellar, Dave McNally, Jim Palmer, and Pat Dobson. They all pitched inside.

A favorite refrain of pitchers today is, "I had to throw a strike. I didn't want to walk the hitter." The refrain usually occurs after the pitcher has gone to 3-and-2 on a batter, thrown the ball down the heart of the plate, and watched it carry over the fence for a home run.

In earlier years pitchers went to 3-and-2 counts on batters without grooving the next pitch. They would throw to the inside corner and the outside corner, but they wouldn't give in to the hitter. Hitters used to say, "Warren Spahn doesn't even know what the middle of the plate looks like. He's never thrown a ball anywhere near it." With a 3-and-0 count, Spahn wouldn't even come near the middle of the plate. I really don't think anyone ever formally introduced Warren Spahn to the middle of the plate. That's one reason why he won more major league games, 363, than any other pitcher over the last 45 years.

No matter what some pitchers are told, they will throw the pitch they want to even if they know there is every likelihood they will get hammered. I had a pitcher in Cleveland who was like that. Jackie Brown was a sub-.500 pitcher because he wouldn't listen. I remember a game in Anaheim when we were going over the Angel hitters.

"Jackie," I said, "I don't want you to throw Bobby Bonds a fastball any time when he can hurt you. If you go to 3-and-2 on Bonds with the game on the line and there's a base open—even if it's third base—don't throw him a fastball."

"I gotcha," Brown said.

Then we came to Bill Melton of the Angels, and I told Brown not to throw him anything inside, because he yanked inside pitches over the fence. "Pitch Melton outside, and he'll hit the ball to right center, where we'll be playing him," I said.

So we were leading 3-2 when the Angels got two men on base in the fifth inning and Bobby Bonds came to bat. Jackie Brown threw him two curveballs that missed. His next pitch was a fastball that wound up over the right-center field fence.

While I was stomping around the dugout, Bill Melton stepped in. Brown threw him a fastball inside, and Melton hit it for a home run.

When Brown came into the dugout, I said, "Why did I tell you not to throw Bonds a fastball no matter what?"

"I didn't want to walk him," Brown said.

"Okay, you didn't walk him, and he trotted around the bases behind the two men he drove in."

Jackie Brown hung his head.

"What about Melton?" I asked.

"I just got the ball in on him, a mistake," he said.

Even on a 3-and-2 count pitchers do not have to come in with a good pitch. They have the corners to work on, and giving up a walk is less costly than giving up a home run. But a problem that gets worse every year is that pitchers are rushed up to the major leagues. They haven't refined their pitching to the point where they can work to the corners, and when they get behind in the count, they come in with a pitch down the pipe. I never hit more than 49 home runs in a season, but I guarantee that if I had been swinging against the caliber of pitching in the major leagues today, I would have reached 50 more than once.

Many pitchers come up to the big leagues these days not knowing how to pitch around hitters. I've heard numerous pitchers ask, "What do you mean by pitching around a hitter?"

"That means I don't mind if you walk the batter," I've told them. "I want you to pitch to him, but if he hits the ball—I want it to be *your* pitch. In trying to make your pitch, if you miss, don't worry about it. I'm not gonna be all over your case. But the idea is not to give in to the hitter. Just because the count goes to 3-and-2, don't say you don't want to walk him and then come in with less than your best pitch. I still want that pitch to be *yours*. No problem if he walks."

Some young pitchers get it, others make excuses. I don't know how many pitchers have said to me, after giving up a big hit on a 3-and-2 count: "I was trying to hit the corner."

"But the ball went right down the middle of the plate."

Home plate is 17 inches wide. If a pitcher says he's throwing to a corner and the ball bisects the plate, he is missing his mark by 6 or more inches. I don't believe most major league pitchers can regularly miss delivering the ball where they aim to by a margin of 6 or more inches. So I just don't buy it when a pitcher says he was trying to hit a corner after the ball has rocketed out of the stadium.

When I first started managing, I was a little soft with my pitchers. Several times I went out to the mound to relieve a pitcher only to let him talk me into leaving him in. Then I watched the pitcher get bombed. I soon learned not to listen to a pitcher who says he's still got his stuff and wants to stay in. "I can get this next batter," a pitcher will say. Or: "Just let me finish this inning."

Another problem a manager can have in going out to change his pitcher is changing his mind en route. I discovered this late in the '82 season. We were playing the Dodgers, battling for the pennant. Fred Breining had pitched a great game, and the score was 0-0 going into the ninth. Breining's out pitch was a fork ball, which is now called a "split-fingered fastball," but he started missing with it and walked the leadoff batter. The following two men up got hits, but no run scored.

Rick Monday, a left-handed hitter, was coming up next against the right-handed Breining, so I went out to get him. I had Al Holland and Greg Minton both warming up, but they were not as warm as I would have liked, and I thought about that as I went to the mound. Meanwhile the Giant fans at Candlestick were booing me loudly. Home fans always boo a manager when it looks like he's about to relieve a pitcher who has been pitching an outstanding game. You try not to ever let the crowd influence you, but I think maybe I did let it that day.

Breining didn't try to talk me into leaving him in the game. He didn't have to. "Take it easy and concentrate on Monday," I said. "Take a deep breath, and let's get this guy."

I went back to the dugout, and Rick Monday hit a grand-slam home run. We lost the game 4-0.

As a manager, it makes no sense to second-guess yourself. When you make a decision, you have to know in your heart you're right. If you make a move and it doesn't turn out right, you still should not second-guess yourself. Otherwise, the next time you feel you should make that move, you'll be hesitant. That does not mean you don't replay your decisions that backfired over and over in your mind later.

Over five years later I am still thinking about my decision to leave in Fred Breining in that game. If I had brought in the left-hander Al Holland, Dodger manager Tom Lasorda would have sent up Pedro Guerrero to pinch-hit for Monday. Guerrero was on the bench because he had a pulled hamstring. I still kick myself for not forcing Lasorda to use Guerrero. A player with a pulled hamstring is not as good a hitter as he is normally, because he can't pivot hard on his injured leg. And if Guerrero hit a ground ball, he couldn't outrun a double play.

Other reasons why I should have brought in Holland were that I had a lot of confidence in his ability to get a hitter out with the bases loaded, as he had done on a number of occasions, and Fred Breining had to be a little tired in the ninth inning. It will probably always stay with me that I should have made the move I had set out to make—but didn't.

Several times before, I had gone out to pull a pitcher and had changed my mind and then watched as a base hit followed. Each time I said to myself, "It'll never happen again." But since that home run off Breining, every time I left a dugout to change pitchers, I called for the reliever *before* I crossed the baseline. That way a pitcher couldn't change my mind and I couldn't change my mind, because the relief pitcher was already officially in the game.

20
⑥ BACK TO BALTIMORE

W<small>*HEN*</small> I got home from Atlanta, Barbara was in the kitchen cooking. I kissed her and said, "It's good to be home."

"What's really nice is that we have two months of the summer left," Barbara said. "We can have some fun in the warm weather for a change. And you get paid for the next two years, so you don't have to worry about looking for a job for some time."

I went to unpack and the phone rang. It was Harry Dalton, general manager of the Milwaukee Brewers, who said, "Do you want to go to work?"

"When?" I asked.

"Now. We need a hitting instructor."

"Where's the ballclub?"

"In Kansas City, then we go to Chicago."

"I'll need a few days, Harry. But I'll meet the club in Chicago."

After I hung up, I said to myself, "Geez, I didn't even talk to Barbara before taking the job." So I walked into the kitchen and told her I was going back to work.

"Whaaaaat?" she exclaimed.

"Now don't get excited," I said. "Not tomorrow, not right away."

"Well, I'm glad to hear that," she said.

"I won't be leaving for three days."

Barbara was not thrilled, but Barbara Robinson has always stood behind me in my nomadic baseball career. This time was no different. She
knew I wanted to stay in the game and that I felt, should another managing job open up, I was better off being employed.

But then I opened the sports section and saw that the Brewers were
over 20 games out of first place, and I thought of the club's manager,
Rene Lachemann. I called Dalton back and said, "I want you to make it
clear to the press that I am not joining you to take Lachemann's job. I
know there will be speculation, the way the ballclub's playing. But I was
just undercut as a manager, and I won't be a party to that kind of thing."

Dalton assured me that Lachemann was secure till the end of the season, and Harry kept his word. Lach was a nice guy to work for, and I
enjoyed coaching again.

At the end of the season Dalton called me into his office and said he
was not rehiring Lachemann. He was bringing back George Bamberger
as manager, and George would be hiring his own coaching staff. Earlier
Dalton had asked me what else I wanted to do in baseball, and I had told
him I was thinking about trying to get into the front office with some
club. Now Harry said he wanted to hire me as his assistant. He told me
I could learn the business at his elbow when the ballclub was at home.

"I also want you to be our minor league hitting instructor and to work
for me on special assignments," Dalton said.

I got the impression that I would be learning the general manager
and farm director's duties at the break-in level, which seemed to be a
real opportunity. But the minor league duties were not very appealing. I
liked working with youngsters, as I had found with Rochester in 1978,
but I sure didn't like riding on buses or the fact that I would be traveling
throughout the Milwaukee farm system. I told Dalton I would take the
job but asked him not to announce it until the winter meetings in the
event a better position became available to me. Harry said he understood,
and we left it at that.

I was thinking about going to the winter meetings in Houston, which
would open in December. Showing my face around couldn't hurt, but then
I recalled how boring those affairs could be and decided to stay home.
Bowie Kuhn, of all people, was the only person who ever even gave me
a laugh at the winter meetings.

That was in 1981 in Orlando, Florida, following my first season as manager of the Giants. I ran into commissioner Kuhn, and he said, "Hello,
Frank, I heard you got yourself a couple of good pitchers."

That was something I hadn't heard, but I wondered if Tom Haller had made a trade and not told me, even though he was at the meetings. "What do you mean?" I asked the commissioner.

"You know," Kuhn said, "Larry Sorensen and Silvio Martinez."

Then I got it. Sorensen and Martinez had recently been traded by the Cardinals to the Indians. "Commissioner," I said, "I haven't been manager of the Cleveland Indians since 1977. As you're the commissioner of baseball, I thought you might have heard that I now manage the Giants."

Embarrassed, Kuhn cleared his throat and excused himself, probably the first time in his life that he was at a loss for words. As Kuhn walked away, I said, "But it was nice seeing you again, Mr. Rozelle." Then I had to laugh.

Harry Dalton phoned me to say he wanted to announce my hiring in late November. I asked him again to hold off until the winter meetings began, and he said he would.

But when the meetings started, I received a call from Edward Bennett Williams, the owner of the Orioles. He asked about my situation with the Brewers and wondered if I would be interested in returning to the Orioles as a coach. I said I would like to get back with the Baltimore organization as I had always felt appreciated there, by the ballclub and the populace at large. Williams said he wanted me to be bench coach and assist manager Joe Altobelli during games, and also to coach the outfielders as I had before. Neither Altobelli nor GM Hank Peters knew that Williams was hiring me, he said. I told him I wanted to explain my decision to Harry Dalton before the Orioles announced that I was back.

"I'm disappointed," Dalton said, and I said I was too. "I would love to work with you, Harry, except for the minor league aspect. But the bench coach job pays more, and I've decided I want to manage again someday, and I think it's best for me to be in the major leagues."

My hiring was a little rough on Joe Altobelli and on the Oriole coaches, as speculation in the press had it that if the ballclub faltered, I would be named manager. That just showed how rapidly a manager's fortunes could change. Only a little over a year ago Altobelli had been a hero in Baltimore when he led the Orioles to a 1983 World Series victory over the Phillies in five games. But in 1984 the Orioles had finished fifth, 19 games out of first place, and writers were reporting player complaints about "a lack of communication" with Altobelli, whom they were calling "Foggy."

If Joe Altobelli was uncomfortable with me, he certainly never treated me as if he was. I wasn't uncomfortable with him because I knew what my job was and I did everything I could to help the ballclub. I got along well with Joe, who was a quiet, pleasant man, and I knew all the other Oriole coaches except for Jimmy Williams.

The Orioles were 29 and 26 when Altobelli was fired in June 1985. Edward Bennett Williams made Earl Weaver an offer he couldn't refuse: Weaver returned as manager and received a reported $500,000 for the remainder of the season. But the ballclub fared little better under Earl, winning 53 games and losing 52.

We all thought the team would turn around in 1986, and for four months the Orioles played well. On August 5 we were only 2½ games out of first place; then the bottom dropped out, and we won exactly 14 of our last 56 games. Earl Weaver tried everything he could, including 141 different lineups, but we went from bad to worse. And you could see the old fire dwindle in Earl. He put as much effort into managing as he ever had, but the spark was gone by early September. Earl even asked if he could leave before the season ended. He was told that if he left, he wouldn't be paid, so he stayed. For the first time in his 17 years as manager of the Orioles, Earl Weaver suffered a losing season. We finished with a 73-89 record, as 12 regulars spent time on the disabled list and the fabled Orioles' defense and solid pitching were no longer evident.

In September 1986 general manager Hank Peters told me that his counterpart with the Oakland A's, Sandy Alderman, had asked for permission from the Orioles to interview me for the manager's job. I said, fine, as Oakland was my hometown and the A's had a good young ballclub.

A week or so later Hank asked me, "Have you heard from the A's?"

"No," I said.

"That's kind of strange," he said. "They called to get my okay to talk to you."

"It is strange."

Then I read in the papers that Sandy Alderman and Roy Eisenhardt, the president of the A's, had flown to Chicago to try and convince former White Sox manager Tony LaRussa to manage the Oakland ballclub. Tony was reportedly resistant to the offer, apparently not wanting to leave Chicago.

The day after this meeting Hank Peters came to me again. "Oakland called again and said they still want to interview you," Hank said. "So be patient."

I was nothing but patient, as my phone was not ringing off the hook with managing offers. But a few days later the A's hired Tony LaRussa as manager, and I was happy for Tony but annoyed with the Oakland front office. It seemed to me that out of respect for me, someone should have called and said the A's were sorry they didn't get to interview me, but that they had decided to go with LaRussa.

Earl Weaver resigned in 1986 and I was interviewed for the job of Oriole manager, along with Cal Ripken. We talked beforehand, and both of us said we would hire the other if either got the job. Cal was hired and kept me on as his bench coach, a position that has supplanted the third base coach on many teams as the number 2 man in command of the club.

Cal and I are good friends, and we worked very well together. I would stand next to him in the dugout and move the outfielders and infielders on defense when necessary. I would mark down any lineup changes for the Orioles or the opposition on Cal's cards and on mine. But my primary duty was to act as a sounding board for Cal, because a manager has no one to talk to during a game but himself. He has to make all the decisions, often in an instant. With me there, Cal could think out loud.

I wouldn't even answer Cal when he was thinking aloud. When he would say, "I can't let this pitcher pitch to this guy," I knew he wasn't asking for my opinion. If he asked me a direct question about a move he was considering, as he did occasionally, then I would express my view.

If Cal commented when a player made a mistake—say, an outfielder threw to the wrong base or a runner didn't go from first to third on a hit—Cal wouldn't go down to the dugout to talk to the player, I would. Cal could keep his mind on the game and know that the message had been delivered.

And then I would notice things a player did and go talk to him on my own to get his thinking. If an outfielder tried to make a diving catch on a line drive with a man on and the ball went through, I might say, "I think you should have played that ball on a hop in that situation." I would give the player my thoughts so he wouldn't make the same mistake again. If I had tried to move a fielder who hadn't seen me motioning him, I would remind him to keep an eye on the dugout between plays.

Players would come to me and talk about hitting during ballgames. Our hitting instructor in 1987 was first base coach Terry Crowley, and as he was out on the line when we were hitting, he would pass along things for me to tell players when they came in from the field. So I did a little bit of everything during games, which got very hectic at times.

Despite my close relationship with Cal Ripken, though, there was one strange aspect to it. I was number 2 in command, but Cal never spelled out to the players that I was to take over if he was ejected by an umpire or was otherwise unable to be present in the dugout. I kept thinking Cal would announce, "If I get run by an umpire, Frank runs the ballclub. Jimmy [Williams, the third base coach], you take the signs from him just as if I was here."

When Cal was thrown out of a game in Baltimore, he didn't actually leave. He stayed on the runway steps out of the umpires' view, I gave him the count on each hitter, and he ran the ballclub from there. Other times when Cal was ejected, he handed me the lineup cards and I took charge, so I was the second in command. I guess Cal assumed that everyone knew that, so why make an announcement.

It was enjoyable being bench coach for Earl Weaver and for Cal Ripken, because I love baseball. But the pleasure often turns to anguish when you're working with a losing ballclub. It was particularly saddening to see a great organization like the Orioles, which had done so much for me, go through such a sharp decline.

Why? Well, start with the Oriole pitching, which had been a strength of the club going all the way back to the Baby Birds of over 25 years ago. But in 1987 the Oriole pitching was the worst in the league, next to Cleveland's, giving up over five earned runs per game. Out of pure desperation and with no one else to turn to, Cal Ripken started rookie pitchers in 62 games in 1987. And the rookie pitchers were by no means outstanding. There wasn't a power pitcher among the six we tried. Baltimore scouts had always signed a lot of hard-throwing youngsters until a few years ago, so either they could no longer find them or they weren't looking hard enough.

We shuttled players all season in a vain search for a winning combination and used 17 pitchers and 23 other players, a typical losing ballclub's revolving door.

On the surface the Oriole hitting did not seem that bad, as we set a club record with 211 home runs. But all too often the home runs came with no runners on base. We scored only 729 runs all season (with 715 runs, the Royals were the only American League team to score fewer), an average of 4.81 runs per game. As our pitchers gave up 5.01 runs per game, we were in big trouble.

It was not unusual for the Orioles to collect 13 hits in a game and get 4 walks, yet score only 4 runs. In one such game we had the bases loaded in an inning with nobody out and the heart of our batting order coming up—Cal Ripken Jr., Eddie Murray, and Fred Lynn—but we didn't score.

In game after game it seemed to me we took a lead and then our hitters appeared to relax.

I think that was due to the makeup and character of the players on the ballclub. They didn't seem to bear down hard enough to get that extra hit or to take that extra base or to knock somebody on their butt at a base to help us score another run. You have to put away opponents, and we were not doing it.

We just did not hit consistently in clutch situations. Too often we got a couple of hits with two men out and then didn't score. RBIs are the most important stat on offense, and that's where the hitter must bear down hardest because that's when the pitcher comes at you hardest. This is why you see guys who hit over .300 but still don't drive in many runs. Other guys can hit .250 and drive in 100 runs because they are tough with men on base, when a hit is most important, and they know the pitcher is trying his utmost to get them out. Brooks Robinson was like that. He didn't hit for average, but he battled pitchers with men on base and brought them home.

Eddie Murray and Cal Ripken Jr. are the big run producers for the Orioles, and they have to come through if the team is to do well. As soon as Eddie and Cal go on a tear at the plate, the team follows. That's what happened when we won nine games in a row after the 1987 All-Star Game. Eddie and Cal picked up the other players. But when Eddie and Cal do poorly, the other players do too, because they feel like they *have* to drive in runs and they press.

The only Orioles who were consistent at the plate in 1987 were second baseman Billy Ripken, who batted .308 in 58 games before he was injured, and outfielder Larry Sheets, who came a long way. Sheets batted .316 and had 31 home runs and 94 RBIs in his third season in the major leagues.

But for two years I was told that the talent in the Orioles' organization was at the lower levels. So I was led to believe that our Rochester club would have a lot of good young talent. I looked at the Red Wings' lineup and second baseman Pete Stanicek looked like a prospect, as did third baseman Craig Worthington. But there was no other standout, and also on the club were four veterans who had been around for years without sticking in the majors—shortstop Jackie Guiterrez and pitchers Mike Griffin, Mike Kinnunen, and Jose DeLeon. Each of them was taking up a spot on the roster that a younger player should be filling to develop his skills for the Oriole roster.

All three of the Orioles' top minor league clubs had winning records in 1987, and I feel there was more emphasis placed on winning than on developing future major league players. At Charlotte, our AA club, we had a 31-year-old first baseman, which told me the emphasis was all wrong. It was obvious that the Orioles had to start signing better young talent.

In addition, the famous Oriole system of teaching all our players the same fundamentals had broken down in recent years. Apparently more and/or better coaches and instructors were needed throughout the system, as we were having far too many players come up to the major leagues unversed in the fundamentals. Unversed in the Oriole way of playing baseball.

Al Bumbry was very familiar with the system after playing 13 years with Baltimore. When he retired in 1985, he wanted to become a roving outfield and base-running instructor in our organization. Bumbry was told he would be hired for a salary of $12,500 a year—if he would also be willing to work in the Oriole publicity department in the off-season. Al Bumbry loves the Orioles, but he had other offers that would pay him more. He went to work for the Red Sox for $30,000. Meanwhile, the quality of our organization continued to decline.

Strange things were happening throughout the system. The major league club made two player errors that were not like the team's normal judgments. In May 1986 a hard-throwing veteran pitcher named Dave Stewart called me looking for a tryout. Stewart was a free agent that nobody had signed. I was told the organization was not interested in Stewart, but the A's were in town that day and gave him a tryout. He had a fine season for Oakland and won 20 games for the ballclub in 1987.

The other mistake was even worse. Bullpen coach Elrod Hendricks had caught Dennis Martinez after the pitcher returned from winter ball. Hendricks reported that Martinez had a great new fork ball, and recommended that this 11-year Oriole veteran be signed. The Orioles had gotten rid of Martinez in 1986 because he could no longer win ballgames. He also had a bad drinking problem, but Dennis Martinez had had that problem for years. Everyone on the ballclub knew about it, but nothing was done to help Martinez. His problem was swept under the rug because Martinez was a talent. As long as he could pitch 230 innings a year and win 15 ballgames—even though he should have won 20—Dennis Martinez was useful.

I think baseball tends to take advantage of its players in that no one cares much what an individual does as long as he performs well. Then when he can no longer perform, baseball gets rid of the player. Sometimes that decision is hurried by what baseball knows about the player, even though it had that negative information for years. The negatives weren't all that bad as long as the player won ballgames.

But Dennis Martinez fooled a lot of people. He got sober and won 11 games (losing only 4) for the Montreal Expos in 1987. If the Orioles had tried to help him with his drinking problem, Dennis Martinez might not have been let go in the first place.

Alcohol was the drug of choice in baseball when I played. In my early years some old-timers would sit around the clubhouse after games and drink half a dozen beers, then go out together to a bar and drink some more. There were always a few players who did this into the 1970s. It was accepted. But the players seem to have gotten away from drinking these days. You seldom see a player have more than a beer or two after a game. That's one of the good changes that has occurred in baseball.

The drug of choice today, of course, is cocaine. While I don't believe its use by players is as widespread as booze was in the past, I do believe that drugs have more seriously damaged players' careers than alcohol ever did. And then some players do both.

I suspect that we had a player on the Orioles who used drugs in 1987, Alan Wiggins, and I feel a little sad that I didn't broach the subject with Alan after he exhibited some bizarre behavior. While with the Padres, Wiggins twice had been suspended from baseball by commissioner Ueberroth for drug-related incidents. He had undergone rehabilitation and was certified to be drug-free when the Orioles acquired him in a 1985 trade. Wiggins, along with some other Oriole players, was to be regularly tested for drugs by the ballclub. As I understood that Wiggins was being tested, I didn't ascribe his strange behavior to drugs. But in August the commissioner suspended Wiggins from baseball, so he must have failed to pass a drug test, and in October he was released by the Orioles. In a subsequent settlement, the Orioles agreed to pay two-thirds of Wiggins's guaranteed $800,000 contract for 1988.

I liked Alan Wiggins and thought I had a good rapport with him because I was always honest with him. In a spring training game, Wiggins bunted a ball that bounced straight up off home plate, but he didn't run and was thrown out while standing in the batter's box. He said he thought the ball was foul, which was why he didn't run it out. Wiggins had been playing baseball professionally for ten years, but he didn't know that home plate was in fair territory?

After that game, as part of his continuing drug therapy, Wiggins went to give an antidrug talk to our minor league kids. When he returned, he said nobody recognized him when he walked into the meeting room. Alan told me, "A guy was standing there saying, 'That Wiggins made a horse-spit play.' And another said, 'If I was manager of the Orioles, he wouldn't play for me.' Frank, tell me, am I really that bad?"

"No," I said, "you're worse than that."

"Am I really horsespit?"

"Yes you are."

Alan Wiggins was not a bad individual, but he was in a bad situation in 1987 after the Orioles signed Rick Burleson to play second base, Alan's position. He thought the job was just given to Burleson and got upset. Alan opened the season as our DH. When Burleson didn't hit, Alan went to second. He hit pretty well and was okay in the field for a while. But when he stopped hitting, his fielding got bad. We went back to Burleson until it was clear he could no longer hit, so he was released. Billy Ripken was brought up, and he was not only exceptional in the field, but he hit better than he had in the minors.

When Mike Young, who had been injured in the spring, returned to the active roster as the designated hitter, Alan Wiggins became strictly a spot player. He became frustrated. In late July we went on a ten-day road trip, and Alan began taking out his frustrations on everyone on the ballclub.

The trip began with an exhibition game in Rochester. Rick Vaughn, our media information director, had arranged a pregame autograph session for the fans in the stands. Rick took groups of three players at a time over to the stands during batting and infield practice. Wiggins got angry because he wasn't called on. "Why didn't you ask me to sign autographs?" Alan asked Rick Vaughn.

Rick thought he was kidding and said, "Alan, when we call you during the winter and say we've got a $1000 appearance for you to make, you always say, 'I don't need it.' You always refuse us, so this time I didn't ask you."

"Well bleep you then," Alan said and walked away.

When we got to Texas, Cal Ripken was standing by the cage and watching batting practice while Wiggins complained to him about lack of playing time. "You weren't hitting, so I had to get you out of the lineup," Ripken explained.

"Well why is Billy [Ripken] playing?" Alan asked.

"Billy's making the plays in the field," Cal said.

"I was doing the same thing," Alan said.

"Alan, I just try to put the best players on the field."

"Well why'd you take me out for Billy?"

"I guess I must be a dumb manager," Cal said.

"Shake my hand," Alan said. "That's the first true thing you've ever said to me."

During the '86 season hitting instructor Terry Crowley had started a little contest in the dugout, which I had taken over in 1987 because Terry had moved out on the line at first base. The contest is known as "call it." Any time a player wanted to predict that someone was going to hit a home run, he'd say to me: "I got a call." He'd make his prediction, and I would record whether he was correct or not in a little book I kept. There was no money or prize involved, everyone competed for recognition as "Leader of the Calls." It was fun, and it helped keep guys in the ballgame, which is not easy to do on a losing club.

The only rules were that I had to acknowledge the player's call and once there were five calls on an individual, the book was supposed to close. A player would holler, "Frank, I got a call," and I'd say, "Okay, you got a call. Make it." I had been very lenient about accepting calls, letting six or seven come in on one player at times. And there had been several occasions when Wiggins came up to me and claimed he'd made a call when he hadn't.

"You didn't have him," I said.

"Yes, I had the guy, Frank."

"All right, if you insist you had him, Alan, I'll put you down," I replied.

The first night in Texas on this July road trip, we were getting beat. Then Eddie Murray hit a home run, and Wiggins jumped up and said, "I had him."

"No you didn't," I said. "I didn't acknowledge you."

"I tried to get your attention three times," he said.

"Well you know the rules. If I don't recognize you, you're not in," I said.

"Damn it, I had him," Wiggins said, and he went on and on, taking my mind off the game and also intruding on Cal Ripken, standing next to me.

"If you want the call that bad, I'll give it to you," I finally said. "Now go sit down."

"You don't have to *give* it to me, because I had it."

"Wiggins, didn't I just tell you I gave it to you? You got the call; now go sit down."

"I don't want it," he said.

Exasperated, I said, "Get out of my face, Wiggins. Get away from me, and sit down at the other end of the bench."

Wiggins moped down to the far end of the bench and sat in silence with his arms crossed over his chest. He didn't make another call in Texas. But the next day he said to me, "You snapped at me real quick."

"No I didn't," I said. "You continued to try to argue with me, and during a game is not the time to argue."

"Another time this year you were down on me, in New York," he said. "You told me I was playing second base that night. Then in the pitchers' meeting you kept saying, 'Burleson, you play this guy here.'"

"Yeah, I remember that. I was also corrected by Rip, who said, 'Wiggy is playing,' and I apologized to you. Don't you think I forgot you were playing that night?"

"No."

"What do you think?"

"Never mind, I know what you were trying to tell me."

"What was I trying to tell you?"

"You were trying to tell me, 'Wiggy, you're playing tonight, buddy, but Rick Burleson is the second baseman.'"

"Is that really what you think I was trying to tell you?" I asked incredulously.

"Yeah."

Refusing to let him get me into an argument, I just shook my head and walked away from Wiggins. But I guess he was trying to get Terry Crowley into an argument when we got to Milwaukee. We arrived on Tuesday, an off day. Cal Ripken Jr. asked to take extra batting practice before the regular session, along with Jim Dwyer and Ron Washington. We insisted that anyone who wished to take extra batting practice make the request in advance so that it could be set up. The field time had to be scheduled, pitchers lined up. We told everyone that we didn't want any walk-ons, because if one player just walked on, others were sure to follow.

On this day Alan Wiggins was in the clubhouse at least 45 minutes before we went out on the field, and he didn't say a word about wanting extra batting practice. Then we sat in the dugout—me, Wiggins, and some other players—for about 15 minutes, and Alan didn't mention wanting to hit.

Ripken, Dwyer, and Washington started hitting, while Terry Crowley and I stood behind the cage watching. Wiggins walked over to Crowley. "When am I hitting?" Wiggins asked nastily.

"I didn't set this up, Alan," Crowley said. "I'll have to check. I don't know if we have enough pitching. I'll let you know."

"Are you refusing to let me hit?" Wiggins asked.

"No, I'm not," Crowley answered. "I just told you I don't know how much pitching we've got. Why don't you shag around, and I'll get back to you."

"You're not gonna let me hit?"

"No, Alan, I told you—"

While walking by, Cal Ripken heard this exchange, and he said, "Wiggy, you are hitting third." The manager kept walking out toward the protective screen by second base.

Wiggins followed him and said, "You're making a real big deal out of this."

"I told you that you could hit third," Ripken said. "That's it. End of it."

I had walked past them into the outfield. I couldn't make out the words they exchanged but when I looked back, Cal's arms were going, so I knew he was getting upset. They went at it for almost ten minutes, until it was time for Alan to hit. He took his swings.

After the early workout, the writers came in and Wiggins called them over and said, "I was refused extra batting practice. The only reason I got to hit was because I insisted on it."

Cal Ripken had to set the record straight with the writers.

The following day, during batting practice, Wiggins started in on Jim Dwyer, which was stupid because the two of them didn't get along anyway. In fact, Alan Wiggins had alienated most of the guys on the ballclub. But Dwyer was taking his swings, and Alan called out to the pitcher, "Hit him in the head, stick one in his ear."

Dwyer turned in the cage and said, "If he hits me, Wiggins, I'm gonna stick the ball up your bleep."

When Dwyer finished hitting, he whirled out of the cage and grabbed Wiggins by the shirtfront. If Ellie Hendricks hadn't jumped in and separated Dwyer and Wiggins, there might have been a fight.

In the clubhouse later, Cal Ripken and Wiggins had a loud argument. It continued in Cal's office. Afterward he said that Wiggins had cursed him and grabbed the front of his shirt, which was very stupid because Cal could break Wiggins in half. Ripken suspended Wiggins for three games.

I had seen many players react badly to not playing, but never one who went around attacking everyone on the ballclub the way Wiggins did. I initially thought maybe Alan was issuing a cry for help, but then maybe his anger and animosity were intensified by the use of drugs.

I know that recovering drug abusers are counseled not to ingest alcohol. However, it was no secret that Alan Wiggins was drinking beer in the clubhouse after games and on airplanes. If he was doing that out in the open, I wonder what was he doing in private? And if he was using drugs, why wasn't that fact detected in the regular tests he was supposedly being given?

Once again I submit that baseball has a long way to go in the war on drugs. And it is up to commissioner Peter Ueberroth to take the initiative in this war, not to say it has been won when clearly it hasn't been.

21

CORKED BATS AND SCUFFED BALLS

YOU never know what kind of position the commissioner or league presidents are going to take on an issue in baseball. All of a sudden there was a big to-do about players cheating in 1987. Pitchers were charged with scuffing or cutting balls to make them dance at the plate, and hitters were charged with using corked bats to make more balls arc over the fences.

In fact, three players were given ten-day suspensions for getting caught cheating. Billy Hatcher of the Houston Astros received his suspension from National League president A. Bartlett Giamatti after Hatcher's bat broke on contacting a ball during a game and several inches of cork flew out. "I had no idea the bat was corked," Hatcher said. He was the first player ejected from a game for altering his bat since 1974, when Graig Nettles of the Indians broke his and a hail of Superballs flew out of it.

Pitcher Joe Niekro of the Minnesota Twins was also suspended for ten days. American League president Bobby Brown sat him down after Niekro, pitching to Brian Downing of the Angels, threw a slider that took an unusual dive. The plate umpire went to the mound and asked Niekro to empty his pockets. An emery board flipped out of his back pocket, and a small piece of sandpaper—that he had slipped out of his glove and into another pocket—was also found. The last pitcher to be suspended for cheating was Gaylord Perry in 1982. Like Niekro, Perry had become blatant in his ball doctoring, barely bothering to hide the fact that he was applying K-Y jelly to the horsehide.

But I still can't understand why Niekro emptied his pockets for the umpires. Pitchers have been cheating for decades because they know that umpires are not allowed to physically search them for substances they could be using to doctor baseballs. One of the silliest rules in baseball is that an umpire cannot physically touch a player he wants to check. How can you examine someone without touching him? The players know the rule, and they cannot be forced to empty their pockets. Why did Niekro do so? I suspect that he was so shocked by the request—one no umpire had ever made before to my knowledge—that he just responded automatically.

The only thing an umpire can physically inspect is a player's equipment. Thus when an umpire said to Joe Niekro, "Let me see your glove," Niekro was required to hand it over. But pitchers have been cheating for many years and only periodically have the umpires made a serious effort to catch the offenders. I feel that was because they so rarely received backing from the league offices to really go after the rule breakers. In my view the league offices simply relaxed the rules and allowed pitchers to get away with cheating.

Granted spitball and K-Y jelly ball pitchers are hard to detect because the evidence on the cover dries up by the time the pitch arrives at home plate. Preacher Roe of the Dodgers and Gaylord Perry both wrote about how they doctored pitches. Don Drysdale didn't have to tell anyone that he occasionally loaded up a pitch. Anyone—including umpires—who saw the way a Drysdale fastball suddenly and precipitously dropped knew that a foreign substance had contributed to that action. No other pitch acts anything like a spitball or grease ball.

As a player, I always thought the rule makers ought to end the hypocrisy and legalize the spitball. We knew the guys who threw the pitch and when they were likely to throw it. The spitball can be hit, and just as not every curveball breaks sharply, not every spitball reaches the plate and spits.

In the 1960s a number of pitchers threw a Vaseline ball for their out pitch. Vaseline left a grease smudge on the ball, which would be pointed out to an umpire, who would shrug. On a number of occasions I heard an umpire say, "What can I do about it? We don't get any backing from the league office."

A pitcher named Phil Regan was accused many times of throwing a

Vaseline ball, which he vehemently denied. In 1968 Regan, playing for the Cubs, got on base in a game and donned his warmup jacket. When the ball was hit, Regan ran hard and slid into second. When he got up, a tube of Vaseline was found lying in the base path. The umpires gathered around Regan, one holding up the tube of Vaseline.

"I don't know where that Vaseline came from," Regan said. "I never saw it before in my life."

Phil Regan was not ejected from the game, not suspended, not even reprimanded. He continued to throw his Vaseline ball, but he did stop dropping tubes of petroleum jelly on the ballfield.

When nothing is done about rule breaking, it fosters more cheating. I first noticed that some pitchers were scuffing or actually cutting baseballs in the 1980s. I've since heard that Whitey Ford admitted throwing cut pitches for the Yankees in the 1960s. He cut the balls with a ring on his finger or his belt buckle.

When I was managing the Giants, Rick Rhoden of the Pirates was scuffing balls in the same place in every ballgame. It was so obvious he was cheating that everyone was calling on umpires to eject Rhoden and report him to the league office. With the Giants I had the umpires go out to check Rhoden after I showed them six baseballs that were scuffed in the same exact spot. But the umpires didn't even check Rhoden's glove to see if he had hidden an abrasive in it.

I collected 24 scuffed balls from Rhoden that day, put them in a plastic bag, and brought them to the league office the first chance I had. "Look, I have two dozen balls, each of them scuffed in the same place," I said. "There is no denying that Rick Rhoden is scuffing baseballs now."

"That's not proof," I was told. "If a new ball is put in a game and hit on a fly and you find it's scuffed, that is proof."

The National League was trying to tell me that 24 balls had been hit on the ground and been scuffed in the exact same spot. Obviously the league office was not interested in ending the cheating by pitchers.

Rick Rhoden was pitching for the Yankees in the American League in 1987, and we had the umpires check him in Baltimore, but they found nothing. If they had gotten Rhoden to empty his pockets, they would certainly have found something. The umpires didn't bother to ask for the glove of the veteran Rhoden. Pitchers who have something in their glove which they cheat with have worked out ways to get the evidence out of their gloves before turning them over to the authorities. Even Joe Niekro had, undetected, moved the sandpaper from his glove to his pocket before the umpires reached him.

The only pitcher I can recall who could not remove the evidence from his glove was Seattle pitcher Rick Hunnicutt during the '80 season. That was because when plate umpire Bill Kunkle, after seeing scratches on the ball, went out to examine Hunnicutt's glove, he found a thumbtack taped in it. When the evidence is irrefutably there, the league is moved to suspend a player.

For at least two seasons Mike Scott of the Houston Astros had been suspected of scuffing balls, along with his teammates Nolan Ryan and Dave Smith. And during the '87 season Giants' manager Roger Craig, who had taught Scott how to throw the split-fingered fastball that Mike credited with his success, had sworn he would prove that Scott scuffed baseballs. In 1987 Peter Gammons of *Sports Illustrated* reported, "Cubs' players claim to have seen sandpaper fluttering near Scott and collected balls scuffed by the Phillies' Kevin Gross. Gross, in fact, acknowledges using a scuffed ball, on July 5, in a game against Scott.

"'In a couple of innings, the ball that Scott was throwing was still on the mound when I started my inning, so I used it,' says Gross. 'And I threw some of my best pitches using that ball he left.'"

Not long thereafter, Kevin Gross was found to have sandpaper on the mound and to have scuffed baseballs that he had thrown. The National League suspended him for ten days. That gave each of the major leagues at least one pitcher suspended for altered equipment in a season, apparently a major league record.

As for the controversy in the National League that had managers charging a number of players with corking bats, particularly Met third baseman Howard Johnson, the league's answer was to X-ray suspect bats. Johnson had never hit over 12 home runs in a season prior to 1987, when he stroked 36, but his X-rayed bats revealed no cork or anything other than wood innards. Nor did the X-rayed bats of any other players reveal any cork.

At the height of the controversy, commissioner Peter Ueberroth acted in his decisive fashion, announcing, "The time has come to inspect the bats in addition to the balls," and he allowed managers to call for one bat check each game.

I had to laugh when I read the reaction of Cardinal manager Whitey Herzog, who said, "Now as soon as one bat is checked, everyone on the bench can go get their corked bats because the umps can't check any more."

Some people questioned whether the X-rays that the leagues were using to examine bats were the most accurate means of checking. An

Austin, Texas, firm, Scientific Management Systems, Inc. (SMS), offered to use the computerized industrial tomography it employs to check space shuttle parts and other equipment. The process was guaranteed not to damage bats, but both leagues rejected the SMS offer even though the price was right. The bats were to be examined free.

I never hit with a corked bat, but the practice of illegally altering bats to help players drive the balls farther has been going on for over a quarter of a century, if not longer. The late Norm Cash admitted after he retired that he had used corked bats throughout his career. Earl Weaver told me that he played on a ballclub in the minors in which the entire lineup used corked bats. Even Earl hit a bunch of home runs that season.

But pitchers and hitters will continue to cheat as long as the league presidents and the commissioner of baseball permit it. As pitching gets worse every season in the major leagues, I expect there will be more ball doctoring by pitchers who will have to do something to improve their performance if they are to stay in the major leagues. I don't think this is the way baseball should be played.

I also don't feel that baseball should be played in the friendly atmosphere that prevails today in which players on every ballclub are buddy-buddy. Opposing players stand around on the field before ballgames and chat like long-lost brothers; they even go out to dinner with one another after the game. The free agency that has seen so many players move from team to team since the late 1970s has contributed to this attitude.

But how can you be friendly with an opponent and then go out and knock him on his butt while sliding into a base? I upset a lot of people when I came into the major leagues because I slid hard on every play. If I slid into second and accidentally spiked a guy and he got upset, so what? I was taught by George Powles all the way back on the sandlots of Oakland that it was my job to break up the double play. I was not to let anyone keep me from doing my job. Although I wasn't playing baseball for money then, I was playing to win. The possibility of my hurting other guys and their hurting me was just part of the consequences of playing to win.

But very, very few base runners slide hard enough these days to hurt an opponent, much less themselves. I have seen players slide into second and accidentally knock down an infielder. Then the runner has jumped up and said, "Are you okay? I'm sorry, I didn't mean that."

The lack of aggressiveness by players on the base paths is not solely the players' fault. I have heard of managers who encourage players not to slide hard for fear they will get hurt and be lost from the lineup for a time. That is why you occasionally see a player go into second base on a double-play ball and not even bother to slide. I have seen players actually move out of the way of the infielder touching second and starting his throw to first. I wonder: Could Ty Cobb sit through plays like that and hold his lunch?

Hard-nosed baseball is virtually a thing of the past. History. The fires with which the game was once played are now banked and barely glimmering. And those of us who loved the sharp-edged competitiveness of baseball have lost a good deal.

22

JOINING THE FRONT OFFICE

ON October 5, 1987, Edward Bennett Williams took the first steps in his decision to revamp the Orioles' front office and rebuild the entire organization. He fired general manager Hank Peters and the director of player development, Tom Giordano, and said the farm system had deteriorated under their leadership. Within a month, headlines in newspapers across the land predicted that I was to be named the new general manager. At that time I had not heard from Williams and refused to get my hopes up. The only fact I knew for certain was that I had not been offered a contract to return as bench coach of the Orioles.

Not long thereafter I met privately with Williams and outlined all the areas that I felt needed to be improved in the Oriole system to begin getting the ballclub back into contention. The number 1 priority was to get Eddie Murray back into a proper frame of mind. Eddie had been angry with the Oriole owner since Williams had remarked to a writer late in the '86 season that the first baseman "was not having an Eddie Murray-type year," that he was doing "nothing." Eddie Murray had had an off year that season but not a bad season. One of the reasons was that he went on the disabled list for the first time in his ten years with the team, missing 24 games. Forgetting what he had contributed not only to the ballclub but to the community, many Oriole fans began booing Murray. Eddie had given $500,000 to the Outward Bound Camp for kids in Baltimore, annually purchased 50 tickets to all home games for underprivileged kids, and devoted numerous hours of his time to charities in the area.

"Eddie Murray is the kind of ballplayer and citizen the Orioles cannot afford to lose," I told Williams. "But we can't afford to keep him unless you sit down with Eddie and clear up your differences. You're gonna have to make the first move, and you're probably gonna have to be very humble about it. You're gonna have to apologize to him privately and also publicly."

"Whatever has to be done, Frank, I'm willing to do," he said. "I shouldn't have made that remark to a reporter, and I'll apologize to Eddie."

"Well that's the only chance we have to save Eddie for this ballclub," I said. "If we can get Eddie Murray back with his head clear, he's gonna be a terrific player for us. If we can't, obviously we're gonna have to trade him. Because if Eddie Murray doesn't want to play here, he's not gonna be the real Eddie Murray. I would like to have him here, and I think we can if you two clear up your differences. One of Eddie's other problems is gone now. As you know, he became very bitter toward Hank Peters. I don't know what the problem was there, but Eddie didn't talk to Hank all last season."

When I returned to Los Angeles, I talked to Eddie Murray and told him what I had proposed to Williams, and Eddie agreed to meet with him. I was relieved, feeling the situation would be resolved.

In November, Williams hired Roland Hemond as the Orioles' new general manager. Prior to becoming an assistant to the commissioner, Hemond had been general manager of the Chicago White Sox for 16 years, and I had never heard a bad word said about him.

I was also hired and given the title of special assistant to the president, and I began working very closely with Roland Hemond to learn the entire baseball operation. From the start I became involved in every baseball decision made in the organization.

"I'm going to teach you everything I can about my position," Hemond said, "because any time I can't be reached, you are in charge."

I also work closely with Doug Melvin, our new farm director, and I work with Edward Bennett Williams on special assignments. My first assignment took me to Puerto Rico to look at some players in winter ball. I have always enjoyed judging talent. I also began the hunt for a full-time scout in Puerto Rico. Although this trip took me away from my family on Thanksgiving for the first time, I couldn't have been happier with my new job. It's a great opportunity for me to help turn around an organization I love and to work with good people.

The first black manager in baseball just may, in the years to come, become the first black general manager in the game. Of course, if I'm ever offered the chance to return to the field as manager of a contending ballclub, I can't say at this time that I wouldn't accept the job.

I like living in Baltimore. It's a working man's town and I'm a working man, and people are always friendly. Barbara told me she had a problem when we initially returned to the city in 1985. I came home one day and Barbara was upset. She said the doorman of our apartment building had received a complaint from another tenant who objected to the fact that Barbara walked our dog in the plaza across the street.

"I asked the doorman to tell me who complained, and I went to confront the man," Barbara said. "I asked him, 'Are you complaining about where I walk my dog because I'm black?' 'Oh, no, Mrs. Robinson, I didn't complain,' he said. Then I asked him if he was a bigot and he denied it. I was so mad. Everybody else walks their dog in the plaza."

"Yeah but look at our dog," I said. "He's black."

Barbara laughed, and we heard no more complaints.